Office Administration

for CSEC®

T0355243

Carol Carysforth • Charon Maxime
Yvonne Metz • Mike Neild

A Caribbean Examinations Council® *Study Guide*

OXFORD
UNIVERSITY PRESS

Great Clarendon Street, Oxford, OX2 6DP, United Kingdom

Oxford University Press is a department of the University of Oxford.
It furthers the University's objective of excellence in research, scholarship,
and education by publishing worldwide. Oxford is a registered trade mark of
Oxford University Press in the UK and in certain other countries

Text © Carol Carysforth, Mike Neild, Charon Maxime and Yvonne Metz 2012
Original illustrations © Oxford University Press 2015

The moral rights of the authors have been asserted

First published by Nelson Thornes Ltd in 2012
This edition published by Oxford University Press in 2015

All rights reserved. No part of this publication may be reproduced,
stored in a retrieval system, or transmitted, in any form or by any
means, without the prior permission in writing of Oxford University
Press, or as expressly permitted by law, by licence or under terms
agreed with the appropriate reprographics rights organization.
Enquiries concerning reproduction outside the scope of the above
should be sent to the Rights Department, Oxford University Press, at
the address above.

You must not circulate this work in any other form and you must
impose this same condition on any acquirer

British Library Cataloguing in Publication Data
Data available

978-1-4085-1665-2

11

Printed and bound by CPI Group (UK) Ltd, Croydon, CR0 4YY

Acknowledgements

Cover photograph: Mark Lyndersay, Lyndersay Digital, Trinidad
www.lyndersaydigital.com
Illustrations: Harry Venning (cartoons) and The OKS Group
Page make-up: The OKS Group

The authors and the publisher would like to thank the following for permission to
reproduce material:

p3 CXC; p6 iStockphoto; p8 iStockphoto; p9 iStockphoto; p13 Alamy/Toby Allen;
p17 iStockphoto; p19 Alamy/Vadym Drobot; p20 WireImage/Getty; p21 Alamy/
moodboard; p22 Alamy/Blend Images; p31 iStockphoto; p32 iStockphoto; p34
iStockphoto; p40 iStockphoto; p42 Fotolia; p43 iStockphoto; p44 iStockphoto;
p45 iStockphoto; p48 iStockphoto; p56 iStockphoto; p62 Alamy/Huntstock, Inc;
p64 ILO; p68 iStockphoto; p76 iStockphoto; p81 iStockphoto; p84 Alamy/Richard
G. Bingham II; p86 Getty/Stockbyte (top); iStockphoto (bottom); p91 iStockphoto;
p92 iStockphoto; p96 iStockphoto; p100 Getty/Stockbyte; p111 iStockphoto; p117
iStockphoto; p119 Alamy/Alex Segre; p122 Getty/Image Source; p129 iStockphoto;
p131 iStockphoto; p132 iStockphoto; p137 iStockphoto; p138 iStockphoto; p145
Nelson Thornes/Oliver Thornton; p147 iStockphoto; p157 iStockphoto; p161
iStockphoto; p166 coastcaribbeanimages; p168 Digicel Group; p171 Alamy/
PhotoAlto; p176 iStockphoto; p178 iStockphoto.

Although we have made every effort to trace and contact all copyright holders
before publication this has not been possible in all cases. If notified, the publisher
will rectify any errors or omissions at the earliest opportunity.

Links to third party websites are provided by Oxford in good faith and for
information only. Oxford disclaims any responsibility for the materials contained
in any third party website referenced in this work.

Contents

Contents

This Study Guide has been developed exclusively with the Caribbean Examinations Council (CXC®) to be used as an additional resource by candidates, both in and out of school, following the Caribbean Secondary Education Certificate (CSEC®) programme.

It has been prepared by a team with expertise in the CSEC® syllabus, teaching and examination. The contents are designed to support learning by providing tools to help you achieve your best in Office Administration, and the features included make it easier for you to master the key concepts and requirements of the syllabus. *Do remember to refer to your syllabus for full guidance on the course requirements and examination format!*

Inside this Study Guide is an interactive CD which includes electronic activities to assist you in developing good examination techniques:

- **On Your Marks** activities provide sample examination-style short answer and essay type questions, with example candidate answers and feedback from an examiner to show where answers could be improved. These activities will build your understanding, skill level and confidence in answering examination questions.

- **Test Yourself** activities are specifically designed to provide experience of multiple-choice examination questions, and helpful feedback will refer you to sections inside this Study Guide so that you can revise problem areas.

- **A Case Study** has been included for each unit in the book to increase your understanding of the unit content. Although you will only have a case study in your exam If you are taking the alternative paper to the SBA, reading each case study and answering the questions will help you to revise and consolidate your knowledge.

- **Answers** are included for each of the Test Yourself and Practice exam questions in the book and Case Studies on the CD so that you can check your own work as you proceed.

This unique combination of focused syllabus content and interactive examination practice will provide you with invaluable support to help you reach your full potential in CSEC® Office Administration.

1 Office orientation

1.1 The role and functions of the office

LEARNING OUTCOMES

By the time you have completed this section you should be able to:

- describe the role and functions of the office in business activities.

DID YOU KNOW?

The 'role' of an office is its purpose and why it exists. The 'functions' of an office are the tasks and activities carried out there.

FIND OUT MORE

Visit an office either at your school or college, or in a business that you or your parents know. Talk to some of the people who work there and ask them politely about the jobs that they do and the work they carry out.

KEY TERMS

The **mission statement** of a business states its main purpose.

The **vision statement** focuses on what the business aims to do in the future.

The **goals** of the business are the aims that it wants to achieve. These are often stated in the strategic plan of the organisation.

Introduction to office orientation

All businesses have some type of office. The owner of a local store may perform office work at home on a table at night whereas the manager of a small garment factory may set aside one or two small rooms for this purpose. A large business, such as a bank, may have a large suite of offices and employ specialist staff to work there.

What do these people do all day? What is 'office work' and why is it necessary? Unit 1 answers these questions. It describes how offices are organised, the work carried out there and the equipment that is used to do these tasks. You also find out about the skills, attitudes and attributes needed by people who work in offices.

What do offices do?

All offices carry out certain activities. These support the business and enable it to operate more efficiently. Some activities are common to all offices, such as answering the telephone, preparing documents and filing important papers in order to keep them safe.

Functions of an office

Many functions are carried out in an office. These often vary depending upon the type of business and what it does. The functions are linked to the **mission statement**, **vision statement** and **goals** of the business. These are sometimes listed on the company website.

Table 1.1.1	The role and functions of an office
Role and functions	**Examples**
Production	A factory office will prepare documents for goods that are being despatched. A retailer will produce receipts for customers who buy goods
Distribution and exchange of goods and services	A factory buys raw materials and sells the items that it makes to customers. Retailers buy stock to sell to customers. Some businesses provide services, such as telecommunications businesses, schools and hospitals. Office staff will keep records relating to all of these activities
Collection, processing and preservation of data (manual and/or electronic)	In a hotel, office staff will record and confirm guest bookings. A hospital office will ensure patient records are stored securely. Data on patients may be recorded manually or using a computerised system

Dissemination of information	A school or college office will keep records of student attendance and performance for disseminating (passing on) to parents
Organisational management and legal control	Accounts offices keep financial records that record sales and predict **profit** (or loss). This is vital information for managers who run the business. It is also required in order to comply with tax laws in most countries

EXAM TIP

Make sure you can list and describe at least four functions of an office.

Examples of business aims

Most firms need to make a profit in order to survive, so this is an aim for businesses such as hotels, banks and factories. They will also want to provide excellent customer service. A hospital would have other goals, such as providing speedy and effective treatment to patients.

The mission of CXC (the Caribbean Examinations Council) focuses on the needs of students and the services it provides to educational institutions.

KEY TERMS

Profit is the amount of money remaining from sales and other revenues when all goods and expenses have been paid for.

MISSION STATEMENT

Our mission is to provide the region with:

- syllabuses of the highest quality; valid and reliable examinations and certificates of international repute for students of all ages, abilities and interests;

- services to educational institutions in the development of syllabuses, examinations and examinations administration in the most cost-effective way.

Figure 1.1.1 How will CXC's mission statement affect the functions undertaken in its offices?

THINK ABOUT IT!

All staff are expected to provide excellent customer service. Why is this important for every business?

FIND OUT MORE

Talk to your tutor about the mission, vision and goals of your school or an organisation with which you are familiar. Find out if these are stated in a strategic plan. Then decide how these relate to the work carried out in the office. You can also check out www.samples-help.org.uk/mission-statements/famous-mission-statements.htm to read the mission statements of some famous companies such as Coca-Cola, Disney and Adidas.

TEST YOURSELF

1 Identify FOUR functions that are carried out regularly in a modern administrative office.

Now check your answers against those on the accompanying CD.

How offices are structured and organised

LEARNING OUTCOMES

By the time you have completed this section you should be able to:

- describe how office structure and activity may be organised according to the size and nature of a business.

KEY TERMS

Staff deployment relates to the way that people are allocated various duties and responsibilities. These duties should be appropriate to their job title/level of job and contribute to the efficient, cost-effective running of the business.

What is office organisation?

All office staff should know what tasks they are responsible for. That is why each person has a job title and specific duties to perform that contribute to the smooth running of the office as a whole. This ensures that:

- all important tasks are done promptly and efficiently
- there are no confusing overlaps between staff
- staff can be trained in the skills they need to do their job correctly
- each person knows what their colleagues are doing and who to communicate with about different tasks
- everyone knows who is in charge.

FIND OUT MORE

Investigate the usual duties that a clerk/typist, a secretary and a word-processing clerk would carry out in an admin office.

Then make sure you can describe these clearly.

What is office structure?

In a small office there may be one person doing the accounts and another person answering customer enquiries. In a large business several employees will do accounts work and they may be in a separate department. Other departments may include administration, human resources, IT, customer services, sales and marketing, purchasing, operations and despatch.

These departments will be shown on the company's organisation chart, which identifies different staff roles and their relationships to each other.

EXAM TIP

Remember that senior staff who run the business are always at the top of the chart. The lines down the chart show authority. So, the Human resources (HR) manager is responsible for the HR supervisor who is responsible for the HR clerk.

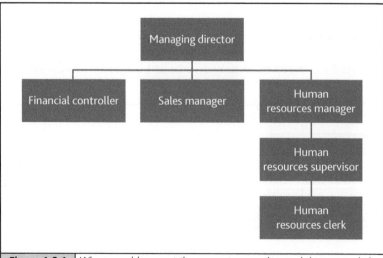

| Figure 1.2.1 | Where would you put the accounts supervisor and the wages clerk on this organisation chart? |

Table 1.2.1	Advantages and disadvantages of organisation charts
Advantages of organisation charts	**Disadvantages of organisation charts**
Everyone can see their place in the organisation. They can see who is in charge and who is responsible for whom. They show the different areas or departments and job titles, so people know who to communicate with about certain matters. They can sometimes indicate where there may be problems (see below).	They quickly become out of date. They do not show informal relationships or friendships between employees that may affect how decisions are made. The charts do not show the working conditions, whether the business is a good place to work, or whether there are prospects for promotion.

Differences in office structures and activities

No two businesses are identical. For example, a small family hotel would have a very different structure to a large hospital or bank. This is because the size and nature of the business will affect:

- the number of staff positions needed
- the number of staff levels in the organisation and the relationships between staff
- the duties and responsibilities of each person. For example, a business that produces goods will have production staff whereas a retail business will not
- the deployment of employees. In a small firm you may be expected to do many different tasks. In a large firm the work may be more specialist, for example, accounts staff work in the accounts department
- whether certain activities are **centralised** or **decentralised**
- the extent of computer hardware and software.

DID YOU KNOW?

Titles vary for the most senior person, for example, president, chief executive, managing director and principal. At CXC the most senior person is the registrar.

KEY TERMS

A **subordinate** is someone below you on the organisation chart and for whom you are responsible.

Your **line manager** is the manager directly above you on the organisation chart and is connected to you by a vertical line.

Span of control means the number of subordinates a manager has to control. If there are too many subordinates, the manager may struggle to cope.

KEY TERMS

Centralisation is when a specialist section carries out a specific task for the whole company, such as reprographics, word processing or records management, for example.

Decentralisation is when each department carries out certain activities itself. For example, the finance and HR departments might do their own photocopying and file their own documents.

TEST YOURSELF

1 Delroy has worked for the owner of a small hotel since leaving school. He has now been offered a job in the marketing department of a large pan-Caribbean insurance company. Identify THREE differences he is likely to find in terms of the office structure and activities.

Now check your answers against those on the accompanying CD.

FIND OUT MORE

Research centralisation and make sure you know the main advantages and disadvantages. Then read the case study about CXC on the CD.

Office layouts and ergonomics

LEARNING OUTCOMES

By the time you have completed this section you should be able to:

• compare different types of office layouts

• examine the ergonomics of the office.

Figure 1.3.1 Which type of office would you like to work in and why?

KEY TERMS

Team spirit is a positive feature of effective teams. They share the blame if there is a problem and pull together to get things done.

EXAM TIP

Know at least two advantages and disadvantages for each type of office.

Types of office layout

There are several ways in which an office may be laid out. They may be traditional, open-plan or virtual.

• **Traditional offices** are a feature of many older buildings. In this case you may share an office with someone or work alone. Some people like the privacy but others feel lonely and isolated. Remember that enclosed, cellular or conventional offices are exactly the same as a traditional office.

• **An open-plan office** is a large area in which several people work together, often in cubicles made of soundproof screens. These give each worker privacy while reducing the noise.

• **A virtual office** is one that exists only in cyberspace because the people who use it communicate with each other by computer. They may be working from home or travelling at home or abroad.

Some businesses have a mix of different types of offices. For example, senior managers may have their own offices so that they can talk to their staff and visitors in private, but other staff may work in an open-plan environment. Sales people who travel frequently may communicate in a virtual office.

Table 1.3.1	Advantages and disadvantages of different types of offices		
	Traditional	**Open-plan**	**Virtual**
Advantages	More private Quieter and fewer distractions or disturbances Better for confidential papers or discussions	Better for team working/**team spirit** Easier to communicate Can share equipment Easier supervision Space saving so cheaper	Low cost No premises required No commuting or travel costs Team members can work at any time of day from anywhere in the world
Disadvantages	Expensive Supervision of staff more difficult Fixed layout Some staff may feel isolated or lonely	Less privacy Less security Can be hard to concentrate Individual spaces may be limited/ cramped	Can be lonely Relationships can be impersonal Success depends on good communications Supervision is more difficult

FIND OUT MORE

Some workplaces have large communal spaces where staff can meet and some have sporting facilities too. If you have ever wondered what the offices are like at Google, Facebook or Pixar, go onto YouTube and have a look!

What is ergonomics?

Even the best office in the world can be a nightmare if it is not designed ergonomically. So what is **ergonomics** and why is it important? Check Table 1.3.2 to find out.

KEY TERMS

Ergonomics relates to the layout of a room, or the design of an item (such as furniture or equipment) to maximise user comfort and safety.

Table 1.3.2	Ergonomics in the office
Issue to consider	**Key points**
Layout and size	Furniture should be situated away from doors or fire exits Staff must have sufficient space to work safely Aisles and walkways must be clear and uncluttered
Furniture and equipment	Staff must have easy access to filing cabinets and equipment that they use regularly Desk areas must be large enough to hold working papers and small items of equipment, for example, a stapler and telephone Noisy equipment should be kept in a separate area Equipment should be plugged in to a nearby power socket to avoid trailing wires
Seating, lighting, ventilation and temperature	Computer users must have a comfortable chair with an adjustable back and seat and a swivel action Each worker should have good 'natural' light – windows must be clean and have adjustable blinds to minimise glare or shadows. Good artificial light is also essential There must be an adequate supply of fresh or purified air Air conditioning must be adjustable and enable people to work in the right temperature
Related injuries	Cuts and bruises from bumping into poorly sited furniture and equipment Electric shocks from incorrect use of electrical equipment Musculoskeletal disorders such as repetitive strain injury (RSI) and upper limb disorders (ULDs) to hands, wrists, arms, neck, shoulders or back – caused by repetitive movements and continual poor posture Tired eyes or migraine if the computer screen is flickering

DID YOU KNOW?

The office layout should take into account the way that team members communicate and the flow of work from one person to another.

Even if the workplace is ergonomically designed, you have a responsibility to use equipment carefully and obey all health and safety regulations. This includes checking on the way you are sitting at a computer so that you minimise strain on your back and your neck. You should also take regular breaks.

TEST YOURSELF

1 Briefly explain how a knowledge of ergonomic issues in the office can contribute to the safety of employees and overall office efficiency.

Now check your answer against the one on the accompanying CD.

EXAM TIP

This question needs you to apply your knowledge, not just remember what you have read. The key words to consider are safety and efficiency.

Office equipment

LEARNING OUTCOMES

LEARNING OUTCOMES

By the time you have completed this section you should be able to:

• describe the contribution of various types of equipment to office efficiency.

Figure 1.4.1 Where would you find photocopiers of this size?

DID YOU KNOW?

Many organisations use document scanners to scan the mail that they receive into an electronic filing system. This reduces the amount of paper they need to keep. You can read more about this on pages 70–71.

KEY TERMS

Multimedia means that a variety of different media is being used, such as sound, graphics, photos and film.

Introduction to office equipment

A wide range of equipment is used in offices to undertake tasks quickly and effectively. Many items of equipment relate to document production – from computer printers and document scanners to photocopiers. The type of equipment used in an office will depend upon the work carried out and, more importantly, the volume of work undertaken. A small inkjet printer is fine for light-to-medium use, but it would not be suitable for high levels of production. In this case you would be more likely to find a laser printer installed and shared by several users.

Similarly, if you work in a small office where photocopying requirements are relatively light, you will use a very different machine from that found in a company where thousands of copies are required every day.

DID YOU KNOW?

Most types of office equipment are made in several different models and sold at a range of prices depending upon their size and features. Businesses will select the model that will be the most cost-effective and suitable for their individual needs.

Types of office equipment

Every piece of office equipment has a particular purpose. The type of business you work for and the documents you handle will determine the equipment you need to use.

Office equipment can be divided into several broad areas of use or functions. Understanding these will help you to remember what types of equipment are available and why they are used.

Table 1.4.1 Types of office equipment

Area of use/function	Equipment
Document creation	Voice recorder, computer
Communicating documents	Scanner, facsimile machine (fax)
Making multiple copies of documents	Printer, photocopier, risograph
Preparing professional documents/booklets	Guillotine/paper trimmer, laminator, binding machine
Destroying sensitive papers	Shredder
Making a **multimedia** presentation	Digital camera, computer, projector and screen

Document creation equipment

- **Voice recorders** are slim, portable gadgets that are used to create audio files that can later be downloaded onto a computer. They can be used to record discussions at meetings as well as notes, ideas and dictated letters and memos. Many students use them to record lectures so that they can write up proper notes later.
- **Computers** enable office staff to create, edit and save many types of documents quickly and easily. These can then be printed and/or shared with colleagues or sent to contacts outside the organisation by email. Documents can be multi-page and contain charts, diagrams, illustrations and photographs.

THINK ABOUT IT!

Computers have made life easier for students and office workers alike and have contributed to the overall efficiency of every office. Think about the work that you do on a computer and then list FOUR ways in which using a computer – and having internet access – has made you more efficient.

Equipment for communicating documents

- **Document scanners** make an electronic copy of a document or photograph that can be saved in a computer file or transmitted as an email attachment. You simply feed the document into the machine, or place it on the flatbed of the scanner (depending upon the model), select scan on your computer and save the digital image that the scanner produces.
- **Facsimile machines (faxes)** also scan documents and simultaneously transmit the digital images to another fax machine. This enables photographs and documents to be sent around the world quickly and easily.

Equipment for making multiple copies of documents

- **Computer printers.** These are used to produce hard (paper) copies of documents created or stored on a computer. There are two main types:
  - **Inkjet printers** are smaller, cheaper and usually slower. There is often one per workstation. They work by shooting very fine jets of ink onto the surface of the paper. Most take two ink cartridges – one containing coloured ink and the other containing black ink.
  - **Laser printers** are generally larger and more expensive. They operate more quickly and the print quality is crisper. Each printer may be used by several workstations. Laser printers use toner cartridges and work by shining a laser beam onto a special drum and using the toner to create an image on the paper.

For more specialised use you may also see impact printers and plotters.

- **Impact printers** (such as the dot matrix printer) work by hitting the page with a force. They are mainly used for printing multi-part forms, such as those used in some car-rental agencies. They are slow and cannot print in colour.

DID YOU KNOW?

Additional equipment may be used in parts of the business that carry out specific tasks. Sales staff may use calculators, cash registers and bar-code readers, and staff handling mail may use letter-opening machines, franking machines and sealing/inserting equipment.

FIND OUT MORE

Check out the features of different voice recorders at www.amazon.com and decide which model you would choose to buy.

Figure 1.4.2 When would you use this equipment?

DID YOU KNOW?

Today many small businesses buy inkjet or laser printers that are all-in-one, multifunctional devices. They enable the user to scan and copy documents as well as print them. Some also operate as fax machines.

FIND OUT MORE

Plotters are available in a variety of sizes – very wide ones are used to produce billboard posters. To see one in operation go to YouTube and watch some of the Plotterpro videos at www.youtube.com/user/plotterpro.

- **Plotters** are mainly used to print posters or technical drawings that have been prepared on computer using special software such as Photoshop or CAD (computer-aided design). They use a pen to draw continuous lines, which is something that is impossible on any other type of printer.

- **Photocopiers** are standard items in all offices. They are used to make copies of many types of document, such as those received in the mail or stored in the files. They are also useful for making multiple copies of computer printouts that would take too long to produce on a small inkjet printer.

  Photocopiers vary tremendously in terms of their size, speed and features – from small desktop models to large sophisticated machines that link to the computer network. Many will provide two-sided copies, they will enable copies to be reduced or enlarged, and they will collate and automatically staple multiple pages, if required. Some print in colour, but these are more expensive.

Figure 1.4.3

DID YOU KNOW?

Linking a photocopier or risograph to the computer network means that users can create a document and send it electronically to the machine to be printed.

- **Risographs** are often used for large-volume copying because they are quicker (they can produce up to 130 pages a minute). They are easy to use and the cost per copy is much less than using a photocopier or laser printer. They need less maintenance than many photocopiers and produce multiple copies in colour as cheaply as in black and white. For that reason they are popular in many schools and colleges. They can be linked to the computer network and they work by creating a digital 'master' from which the copies are produced.

Equipment to help prepare professional documents/booklets

A wide range of additional equipment is available to prepare special or multi-page documents so that they look professional. This can include the following.

- A **guillotine or paper trimmer**. These cut or trim documents to size. Guillotines have a curved blade and are intended for multiple pages. Paper trimmers are more precise and use a small circular blade.
- A **laminator** puts a thin protective plastic film over documents that are to be pinned up or handled frequently.
- **Binding machines** enable the pages to be fastened together as a booklet. There are various types: thermal binders use heat to seal the pages to the spine whereas comb and wire binders make holes in the paper and then insert the pages over a special spine. The cheapest are slide binders, which simply slide over the left-hand edge of the paper.

Equipment that destroys documents

A **shredder** is a device used to destroy sensitive or confidential documents so that they cannot be read. Cross-cut shredders are more effective than strip-cut shredders because they slice the document in two directions rather than one.

Equipment for making a multimedia presentation

- A **digital camera** enables the user to take digital images that can be uploaded to a computer. They can then be integrated into presentation software or put together to produce a slide show. They may also be printed. Some printers will print direct from the camera memory card, but for a professional presentation it would be more usual to upload the photographs and edit/correct them first.
- A **projector** is needed to put the image from the computer onto a large screen. The choice is vast but, for business use, the projector should enable high-resolution images to be shown on the screen from a distance. It is also necessary to consider whether films are to be shown. Some projectors are wireless enabled, which reduces the need for wires or cables.

> **DID YOU KNOW?**
>
> You can also punch multi-page documents using a special heavy-duty hole punch and staple them with heavy-duty electric staplers.

> **DID YOU KNOW?**
>
> Microsoft PowerPoint is a popular computer package for preparing business presentations.

> **EXAM TIP**
>
> Remember to link your answer to the functions of a sales and marketing department and the type of documents it would produce. (See Unit 11 for more about sales and marketing.)

> **FIND OUT MORE**
>
> You are starting work in a sales and marketing department. What type of equipment do you think would be needed there and why would it be used?

> **EXAM TIP**
>
> Equipment is meant to help people save time by enabling them to work more quickly. Think about this when you are answering any question about 'efficiency'.

> **TEST YOURSELF**
>
> 1 a   List THREE benefits for a school in buying a risograph.
>   b   Identify TWO other major items of equipment that you might find in a school office and explain how each one will contribute to the efficiency of the office staff.
>
> Now check your answers against those on the accompanying CD.

1.5 Skills, attitudes and attributes and their effect on office relationships

LEARNING OUTCOMES

By the time you have completed this section you should be able to:

- describe desirable skills, attitudes and attributes of office personnel
- assess the value that good human relationships have to office efficiency.

KEY TERMS

Your **skills** are the abilities you have learned. They usually require regular practice.

Your **attitude** is how you think and behave, which is shown in the way you respond to a situation.

Attributes are characteristics that you are born with, but they can also develop.

THINK ABOUT IT!

If you had to describe your skills, **attitudes** and **attributes** to someone at an interview, what would you stress and why? What aspects do you think you could improve?

DID YOU KNOW?

Planning aids to help you to establish priorities and complete tasks on time include a diary, a planner chart and a computerised follow-up system.

What desirable skills do office workers need?

All office workers need basic **skills** to do their job, such as literacy, numeracy and the ability to use a computer. However, additional skills enable them to do their jobs more efficiently. A list of desirable skills, and why these are so important, is shown in Table 1.5.1.

Table 1.5.1 Desirable skills

Desirable skill	What this means	Why you need it
Literacy	The ability to read and write	All office workers read and create documents
Numeracy	The ability to work with numbers (with or without a calculator!)	All office workers must be able to calculate accurately
Computer literacy and proficiency in using productivity tools	The ability to use a computer competently The ability to work productively by selecting and knowing appropriate software packages and search engines, saving and retrieving documents efficiently and backing up your work	Computers are a feature of all modern offices You will be expected to work professionally and understand the software that you use, for example a diary/email package such as Microsoft Outlook for scheduling meetings and flagging up important emails
Effective communication	Writing and talking clearly and using appropriate language, the ability to listen Using appropriate body language (see Unit 2)	You will deal with many people at work, from senior management and clients to colleagues. You must be able to communicate appropriately with all of them
Time management	Using time effectively, not wasting time (for example, by chatting or being distracted online), planning your work and prioritising important jobs	You must respond appropriately to urgent requests, concentrate so that you work efficiently all of the time, and meet important deadlines
Analytical problem-solving	Obtaining the information needed to solve a problem, considering all aspects, not jumping to conclusions	You must be able to solve minor difficulties to the best of your ability. You should know who to tell if you have a more major problem

FIND OUT MORE

You can find many hints and tips about time management online. Research the information yourself and look at Google Images to check out any office planning aids that you are not familiar with.

THINK ABOUT IT!

What qualities would your ideal work colleague have and why? Write them down. How well do you match up to this list?

EXAM TIP

Questions often focus on time management. Can you think how you would improve your time-management skills?

What attitudes do office workers need?

In most offices you will work with other people. This means you have to be sensitive to their needs as well as your own. You may sometimes have to compromise or conform to other people's expectations in order to fit in and learn to work productively with lots of different people.

Team work

Today most people work in teams. A team is a group of people who:

- have the same aim (for example, to finish a task by Friday)
- work together cooperatively to achieve that aim
- help and support each other – especially if there is a problem.

A team can be very beneficial because individuals all have different strengths and weaknesses, so between you there are more strengths than any one single person could have.

Tolerance and appreciation of diversity

At work you will meet a variety of people of different ages, genders, nationalities and ethnic groups. Their religions and beliefs may not be the same as yours. Some may be able-bodied but others may not be. They will also have different personalities and backgrounds.

Tolerance means accepting other people, even if they are completely different from you. Meeting other people enables you to broaden your own knowledge and it can be both educational and fascinating. In this situation you **appreciate diversity**, because it adds to your own experiences and helps you to become wiser as a result.

Being safety conscious, environmentally aware and socially responsible

Some people are very pleasant to work with but seem to live in a bubble. They seem focused on their own needs and rarely look any further. Having a broader outlook means that you are far more aware of the world around you and its potential effect.

- Being **safety conscious** means that you know that taking risks can cause problems, not just for you but also for others. So you work carefully, report hazards that you notice and obey all safety instructions without being told.

KEY TERMS

Group dynamics refers to the personalities in the group and how these people fit together. This can influence the way the group performs and how it thinks and responds to situations.

| Figure 1.5.1 | What team skills does a successful sporting team demonstrate? |

THINK ABOUT IT!

Think about two or three groups or teams that you belong to at school and in your personal life. How do they differ and why? What is your role in each one and how influenced are you by the other members?

DID YOU KNOW?

You can find out about the Caribbean Environment Programme at www.cep. unep.org/ and read its mission statement. Then click on its staff directory and think about the job roles of the office staff who work there.

- Being **environmentally aware** means that you think about the consequences of your actions on the planet, so you minimise waste when you are photocopying or printing your work. You recycle printer cartridges, turn lights off when you leave a room and follow any rules about recycling or disposing of waste materials.
- Being **socially responsible** means that you try to help other people, especially those less fortunate than yourself. This can include charitable giving, assisting the elderly, becoming involved in the community. Many workplaces pride themselves on being socially responsible and encourage their staff to do the same.

Desirable attributes

Some people find it easy to mix with others, to respond positively to a challenge, to be well organised and arrive on time for appointments. Others do not. If this includes you, then you need to work at developing appropriate types of behaviour for the workplace. These are summarised in Table 1.5.2.

Table 1.5.2 Desirable attributes

Attribute	What this means
Regularity/punctuality	Never being late for work and only being absent for a genuine reason, so people can rely on you
Positive work ethic	Being cheerful and enjoying work. You do not clock watch and do not need supervising all of the time. You are reliable, loyal and always do your best
Integrity, honesty, confidentiality	This means you have high standards of fairness and keep your promises. You would never take the credit for someone else's work or let them take the blame on your behalf. You tell the truth and can be trusted with secrets
Willingness	You respond positively to a request or a challenge. You do not deliberately act slowly or moan
Deportment	You dress appropriately, are fussy about personal freshness, your hair is always clean and tidy. You always respect other people
Self-esteem, confidence	You believe in your own worth and are honest about your abilities. You work to high standards and respond positively to new challenges

THINK ABOUT IT!

Marcia is very shy and likes to stay in the background. She has been offered the chance to work in a local store at the weekend, but you think the owner will mistake her shyness for unwillingness to get involved. How would you convince her of the importance of displaying an appropriate attitude at work and developing suitable attributes?

The importance of good relationships

Good relationships at work enable everyone to be more productive. You cannot work efficiently if you are unhappy or have just had an argument with someone because you will be concentrating on yourself and not your work.

To develop a positive working relationship you need the cooperation of all of the people involved. However, there are some golden rules that apply to the way you should behave, regardless of who you are dealing with.

- Always be courteous and tactful to everyone.
- Treat people who are senior to you, or older than you, with respect.
- Be helpful and pleasant.
- Make allowances for other people having 'a bad day' or personal problems that you do not know about, as these might affect their behaviour.
- Think about what you are going to say to people before you say it!

Additional points to bear in mind are shown in Table 1.5.3.

DID YOU KNOW?

Everyone who visits a business judges it on how the staff behave – and that includes you!

Table 1.5.3 Developing good relationships at work

Developing good relationships at work	
With your supervisor	Appreciate the pressure that they may be under and how this may affect them Make your priorities the same as theirs Do not bring them a problem that you could solve yourself Respect their seniority and status
With your colleagues	Treat everyone the same – do not be nice to some and not to others Repay favours when you can Be loyal Keep secrets that you are told and promises that you make Offer to help out if someone has a problem
With internal/ external clients	Remember that it is your job to help all of your clients Greet and address all clients promptly and courteously Be approachable and friendly, smile at people and really *listen* to what they want Never keep people waiting – if there is a delay, explain and get help If you do not know something, find out. Know who can help a client if you cannot

TEST YOURSELF

1 Suggest FOUR ways in which a new employee should behave to develop good working relationships with their new colleagues.

Now check your answers against those on the accompanying CD.

SECTION 1: Multiple-choice questions

1 Zara is creating a ten-page staff handbook and needs to make 100 copies. Which three items of equipment would she be most likely to use?

  a A shredder, a guillotine and a stapler

  b A printer, a fax and a laminator

  c A computer, a photocopier and a binding machine

  d A scanner, a printer and a laminator

EXAM TIP

Remember – you should only choose one right answer for each question here.

2 Being environmentally aware means that you prefer to:

  i   Save time.   iii Save water.

  ii Save paper.   iv   Save money.

  a i and iv only   c All of the above

  b ii and iii only   d None of the above

3 The person directly above you on an organisation chart is always:

  a The chief executive.   c Your colleague.

  b Your subordinate.   d Your boss.

4 The most appropriate way to greet a visiting client is to:

  a Ask them what they want.

  b Shake hands.

  c Smile and introduce yourself.

  d Ask them to sit and wait until you are ready to deal with them.

5 Activities carried out by an administration department are likely to include:

  i   Producing documents.

  ii   Storing data.

  iii Visiting customers.

  iv   Obtaining finance.

  a i and ii only   c All of the above

  b ii and iii only   d None of the above

6 A characteristic of an open-plan office is:

  a It does not exist – users communicate in cyberspace.

  b Many staff work in open areas separated by cubicles to give some privacy.

  c There are no walls or screens between managers and staff.

  d It is designed to have ergonomic benefits.

7 Two results of buying modern office equipment are likely to be:

  i   An increase in staff.

  ii   An increase in efficiency.

  iii An increase in clients.

  iv   An increase in quality.

  a i and iii only   c All of the above

  b ii and iv only   d None of the above

8 An advantage of working in an ergonomically designed office is that:

  a It has the latest equipment.

  b There is better team spirit.

  c It will be easier to work efficiently and safely.

  d It will be an open-plan area.

9 Your supervisor is very annoyed because you forgot to give a client an urgent message that you had promised to pass on. How would you react?

  i   Say you did not understand the instructions.

  ii   Keep out of the way.

  iii Blame someone else for distracting you.

  iv   Explain that you have been too busy.

  a i and iii only   c All of the above

  b ii and iv only   d None of the above

10 The main feature of a centralised records management system is:

    a Expensive equipment.

    b Having a computerised system.

    c It holds all of the records in one place.

    d Records are kept in different departments.

Further practice questions and examples can be found on the accompanying CD.

SECTION 2: Short answer questions

1 Identify THREE items of equipment that would help a manager to give a professional presentation.

2 List FOUR skills that would be required of a junior clerk.

3 Identify ONE major benefit that a business would gain if there were good working relationships in the workplace and ONE major benefit the staff would gain.

4 List TWO advantages and TWO disadvantages of working in a virtual office.

5 Draw an organisation chart and show the relationship between the sales and marketing director, the marketing manager, the sales manager, a sales representative and a sales coordinator.

6 State FOUR ways in which a member of staff could improve their time-management skills.

7 Identify the main benefit to a business of buying each of the following items of equipment.

    a A shredder

    b A binding machine

8 Identify THREE aspects of an office that an ergonomic specialist would review.

9 Identify FOUR ways in which you could contribute to a positive team spirit among your colleagues.

10 State THREE advantages of deciding to buy a combined printer/photocopier/scanner/fax machine for a small office and ONE disadvantage.

Further practice questions and examples can be found on the accompanying CD.

2 Communications

2.1 Channels of communication

LEARNING OUTCOMES

By the time you have completed this section you should be able to:

- describe the various channels of communication used in the office
- identify factors affecting communication.

KEY TERMS

Channels of communication are the routes the information takes to get from sender to recipient.

The grapevine is the name of the unofficial communication channel in an organisation.

DID YOU KNOW?

The grapevine can go in any direction at all!

DID YOU KNOW?

Some organisations are changing from a hierarchical to a matrix structure (see page 41) so that it is easier for staff to be involved in decision making.

Introduction to communication

People at work communicate constantly. They talk on the telephone, write letters and memos, send emails and meet to chat or exchange ideas. Wherever you work you are likely to be surrounded by documents and messages, and be expected to communicate regularly with colleagues, clients and contacts in other organisations. This unit focuses on how to do this effectively.

Formal and informal channels of communication

The different ways in which information can be sent and received are often called **channels of communication**. The channel used will normally depend upon the reason for the communication, who the sender is and who the recipient is. Some channels are more formal than others.

- **Formal channels** are used for official matters and to pass on important or serious information. This type of information flows up and down the organisation (see Figure 2.1.1), such as an official letter about new pay rates from the HR manager to staff.
- **Informal channels** are mainly used between people who are in frequent contact. An example would be a telephone call to a colleague to check a customer's address.
- **Unofficial channels** are informal and often unplanned. **The grapevine** is the name for the social network that exists between staff who may chat about work matters, such as a small group gossiping at break time.

Factors affecting communication

The flow of communications

The degree of formality is closely related to the way communications are flowing, as shown in Figure 2.1.1.

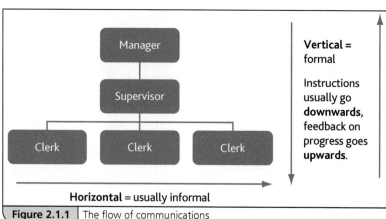

Vertical = formal

Instructions usually go **downwards**, feedback on progress goes **upwards**.

Horizontal = usually informal

Figure 2.1.1 The flow of communications

Communication climate

Most modern organisations prefer an **open** climate where staff are consulted about most issues. Many modern organisations encourage collaboration to foster good ideas. This is why their workplaces are designed to enable staff to meet informally throughout the day.

The opposite is a **closed** climate, where staff are discouraged from contributing to discussions. This may be deliberate or just because the organisation is very large and hierarchical, so that staff and senior managers rarely meet or have a chance to share their views.

THINK ABOUT IT!

There are advantages and disadvantages for a manager involving staff in all important decisions. Can you think what these might be?

Figure 2.1.2 Discussions are part of office life

Different channels of communication

The channel of communication can also relate to the method, as shown in Table 2.1.1. You will learn more about these methods as you progress through this unit.

Table 2.1.1	Communication channels
Channel	**Method**
Oral	Interviews; meetings and conferences; radio and television; telephone
Electronic	Teleconferencing and videoconferencing; telecommuting and telemarketing; using a computer to access the internet/World Wide Web/email; telephone and fax; scanning to email and scanning to save in a file; OCR and OMR (see page 25)
Written	Letters; memoranda; agendas, notices of meetings; reports, minutes, questionnaires, itineraries, notices, press releases, advertisements
Visual	Pictures, charts, graphs; signals; multimedia presentations; body language

DID YOU KNOW?

Social networking sites like Facebook operate like one big grapevine. They have increased the flow of unofficial communications all over the world.

EXAM TIP

You must be able to link information across different units. Here you need to think about the work carried out in a sales office (Unit 11) and communications.

TEST YOURSELF

1 Identify TWO examples of formal communications and TWO examples of informal communications that you might meet if you worked in a sales office.

Now check your answers against those on the accompanying CD.

Oral communications

LEARNING OUTCOMES

By the time you have completed this section you should be able to:

• describe oral channels of communication used in the office.

DID YOU KNOW?

Some oral methods are **one-way**, others are **two-way**. A radio broadcast is one-way (unless you can phone in to take part), whereas a telephone call is two-way because information is exchanged between people.

Figure 2.2.1 Even celebrities can be nervous when they are interviewed

EXAM TIP

If you are asked to prepare a checklist in the exam, you can put headings as in Table 2.2.1, and leave space to put ticks and crosses when an action has been carried out.

Oral communications are **spoken**. The information may be exchanged face to face (when you meet someone) or over the telephone. Radio is another example, whereas television is both oral and visual.

Types of oral communications

Interviews

An interview is a formal discussion when one person is providing information to other people. Celebrities and politicians are often interviewed by the media to find out their views. In business, one example is the **job interview**, when an applicant is questioned by one or more managers in an organisation.

Few people enjoy being interviewed because they worry they will be asked a question they do not understand or cannot answer. Some people are very shy, others have difficulty speaking fluently and clearly.

Ideally an interview should be a two-way process, when the applicant talks with the interviewer about their accomplishments and future aims. It helps if both interviewee and interviewer have prepared well in advance. The interviewer should start by checking basic facts from the application form or résumé, then ask questions to assess the applicant's interest in the work and their ability to cope with the job. The applicant should then be given the opportunity to ask questions before the interview is concluded (see Unit 3).

Table 2.2.1 Checklist for job interviews	
Do ✓	**Don't ✗**
✓ Allow plenty of time to get there	✗ Be late
✓ Wear appropriate clothes	✗ Be unprepared
✓ Research the business in advance	✗ Be unresponsive
✓ Think of questions you could ask	✗ Speak very quietly
✓ Think about questions you could be asked – and suitable answers you could give	✗ Boast
	✗ Ask questions about holidays and time off
✓ Focus on your good points	✗ Use slang expressions
✓ Smile and make eye contact with the interviewer(s)	✗ Be critical about your school or any of your teachers
✓ Look interested and enthusiastic	

Meetings and conferences

Most businesses hold meetings and other events on a regular basis. These enable people to come together to discuss specific issues of common interest.

Meetings can be informal, such as a team meeting or a departmental briefing from a manager to staff. Or they can be formal, such as the Annual General Meeting of a company. You will find out more about meetings in Unit 6.

A **conference** is usually a residential event to which **delegates** from different organisations are invited. There is a programme of activities and talks, which is organised in advance. These often involve professional speakers or experts on topics of interest.

FIND OUT MORE

Many conferences are held in the Caribbean every year. Look at www.caribbeanconference.com to find out more about those held on topics of interest to the region.

KEY TERMS

Delegates is the official name for participants at a conference.

Radio and television

The skills required to give a professional performance on radio are different to those required for television. Speakers on the radio are judged on what they say and their tone of voice, for example, whether they sound friendly or irritable. On television, appearance and body language also matter (see page 35). People who appear regularly usually receive training to ensure they look at the correct camera, speak clearly and do not fidget or wave their arms around. For a radio interview, they are told to focus on the presenter and to try to ignore the microphone.

THINK ABOUT IT!

Next time you are watching television, try assessing the speaker on how clearly they speak, whether they hold your attention, and what aspects of their performance are good or not so good.

DID YOU KNOW?

Business people being interviewed on radio or television can usually ask to see the questions in advance to help them prepare.

Telephone

Telephones are an essential item in all businesses. You will learn more about these on page 44.

Most business people have a cellphone (also called a mobile phone), so that they can keep in touch with the company while they are travelling. Smartphones can also be used to send emails and check information online.

Figure 2.2.2 Why is a cellphone useful away from the office?

TEST YOURSELF

1 Research a smartphone, such as the latest Blackberry, and find out its main features. Assume you are preparing for a meeting where you want to persuade your boss of the benefits of having one.

   a Identify THREE ways the business would benefit (rather than you!) and practise explaining these clearly and succinctly.

   b Identify THREE ways in which you could make a good impression at a face-to-face meeting with your boss.

Now check your answers against those on the accompanying CD.

EXAM TIP

This question requires you to apply your knowledge. Start by identifying a benefit of having a Blackberry. Then apply the benefit to a business situation.

Focus on electronic communication

LEARNING OUTCOMES

By the time you have completed this section you should be able to:

• describe electronic channels of communication used in the office.

EXAM TIP

You will find it useful to know this list of benefits.

Figure 2.3.1 | A videoconference

There are many benefits to businesses from using electronic communications.

• The basic equipment is inexpensive and easy to use.
• They enable communications to take place at any time and over any distance.
• Transmission costs are low.
• Information is sent and received instantly.
• Many types of documents or files can be transmitted, including text, graphics, photographs, audio and video.
• Discussions between several people can be held by telephone or video, saving time and travel costs for all concerned.

Types of electronic communication

Teleconferencing and videoconferencing

All conferences involve a group of people. These systems enable meetings to be held even when members of the group are in different locations because they can communicate with each other electronically.

• In a **teleconference** the group is connected by telephone, normally at two or more locations. Most switchboard systems enable several internal extensions to link together simultaneously with a number of external callers. Alternatively, specialist software can be downloaded or a teleconferencing service can be used.

• In a **videoconference** the group can see, as well as hear, one another. This may be because they are linked by computer/internet or because each group is in a special videoconferencing facility where there is operator assistance if something goes wrong.

Both methods have advantages and disadvantages as shown in Table 2.3.1.

Table 2.3.1 Advantages and disadvantages of teleconferencing and videoconferencing

Advantages	Disadvantages
• Travel and accommodation costs are reduced • Travel time is saved • People can participate who would be unable to travel far • The discussion can be recorded and replayed • Meetings are usually shorter and more focused, with less socialising between members	• Needs reliable equipment and good connections • Needs good control or one person may dominate the meeting • Needs good preparation in order to be successful • Hiring videoconference facilities for long meetings is expensive

Advantages	Disadvantages
• There is less chance of the meeting being cancelled owing to bad weather • can usually can take place on the business's own premises	• If the only contact is by voice, it is very difficult to identify how people are feeling or reacting • It is not possible to have any confidential discussions while participating

Telecommuting and telemarketing

Telecommuters work from home using a computer. They usually have a link to the office computer network or they communicate via a **virtual office** (see Unit 1, page 6).

Telemarketing means using the telephone to promote goods and services. This can be an effective way for a business to interest customers in new products or to respond to people who have made an enquiry. At its worst, it involves **cold-calling** people at home, which can be intrusive and annoying for householders.

Computers and the internet

Virtually all businesses use a computer to carry out administrative tasks. They will also want to have access to the internet so that they can send emails and access websites. Many businesses have their own website.

DID YOU KNOW?

Websites may be simple, informative sites or they can be interactive so that customers can make bookings or buy goods online.

Having a website is sometimes described as 'having an internet presence', which is not technically correct. The 'internet' describes the entire electronic structure over which computer networks can communicate. The **World Wide Web** is just one aspect of the internet. It was invented by Tim Berners Lee in 1989 when he developed a way for people to use the internet by creating pages of information using **HTML**, and to access those using **web browsers** and through **hypertext links**.

The web is one way of communicating over the internet. **Email** is another. This enables messages to be sent quickly and easily anywhere in the world to anyone with an email address.

DID YOU KNOW?

The abbreviation 'URL' stands for uniform (or universal) resource locator and is the full text for any webpage or file that you view on the web, including the domain name.

DID YOU KNOW?

Many people use Skype to make video calls to friends and family members overseas. This is free for two participants who both have Skype, but there is a charge if more than two people want to communicate simultaneously.

KEY TERMS

Cold-calling involves phoning people, who are not expecting any contact, in order to promote or sell products.

FIND OUT MORE

There are several videoconferencing facilities throughout the Caribbean. Check out www.eyenetwork.com to find out more about videoconferencing and to see if there is a studio in your territory.

KEY TERMS

HTML is the computer language in which webpages are created.

Web browsers are applications that enable you to access the internet, for example, Mozilla Firefox or Microsoft's Internet Explorer.

Hypertext links are the blue underlined items that you can click to move from one website to another.

Factors to consider before having a website

Most businesses can benefit from a website, but not all of them! A small local trader, such as a one-person taxi business, would be better simply advertising in Caribbean Online Yellow Pages.

Businesses that set up a website must consider several key factors beforehand to ensure they have an effective online presence. An out-of-date website, one with an obscure domain name, one that is not easy to navigate or takes a long time to load gives a bad impression of the business. So does an email enquiry service that no one answers. The main factors and the potential benefits are summarised in Table 2.3.2.

Table 2.3.2 Having a website – factors to consider and potential benefits

Factors to consider	Potential benefits
• The cost of creating and monitoring the website, especially if a specialist firm designs it • The cost of training a **webmaster** and/or other staff • The domain name – which should ideally be the same as the business name, short, easy to remember and spell • Whether the website will be accessed on computers *and* mobile phones, as screen size is different • Whether the website will simply give information, or whether customers will be able to place orders on it • If orders are being placed on the site, how payments should be received • Security issues to protect personal data and prevent hacking or viruses • Back-up systems to prevent data loss	• A global presence for the business and access to new customers/markets • 24/7 contact with potential customers • The potential for a small firm to compete with a large business – size is irrelevant online • Greatly increased customer interest and responses • Ability to carry out online market research, for example, by using pop-up questionnaires • Increased sales and rapid payments as goods are not usually sent unless payment has been made • Lower running costs for some businesses that can relocate out of town • Online marketing opportunities, for example, through website advertising, paying for search engine listings, etc.

KEY TERMS

Webmaster is the title given to a member of staff responsible for a business's website.

FIND OUT MORE

The suffix on Caribbean domain names differs depending upon where the website is hosted. For more information check out www.marcaria.com/domains/domain_registration_caribbean.asp to find out more about registering a website in your own territory.

DID YOU KNOW?

Most large businesses also have an **intranet**. This is like an internal website, but the information is only available to employees.

Telephones and fax

Business telephones are a major method of communicating in any office. To ensure calls can be received at any time, a small office may have an answering machine and a large business will have voicemail (see page 45 for more information.)

Fax machines work by scanning a document or picture and converting it to a digital image. This is then communicated to another fax machine using telephone lines. Text, graphics and photographs can be sent from one fax machine to another anywhere in the world.

Scanning

A scanner 'scans' a document or photo and converts it to a digital image. The user can choose whether to:

- **scan to email** – in which case the scanned image is automatically attached to an email message for transmission. This method is used when the main aim is to send a copy of the document to someone
- **scan to file** – in this case the user gives the file a unique name and saves it in a designated folder. This method is used when the image may be needed again in the future.

OCR and OMR

Optical character recognition (OCR) enables the user to electronically capture typed or written text, save it on their computer and then edit it. Some OCR software also includes spellcheckers.

Optical mark recognition (OMR) can recognise marks placed in (or omitted from) certain positions on a piece of paper. This software enables multiple-choice examination papers to be marked electronically. It is also used to quickly analyse the results of surveys and questionnaires.

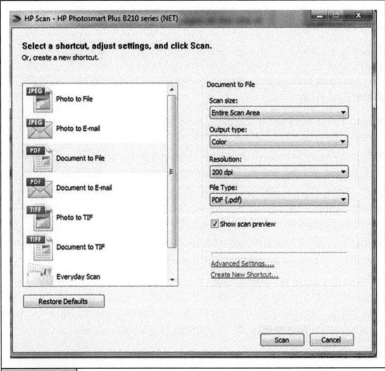

Figure 2.3.2 | Scanner options

EXAM TIP

Make sure you can quickly compare fax and email and state the main features of each.

FIND OUT MORE

You often make notes in class and would like to be able to save and amend these on your computer so you decide to use OCR software. Research the choices available to you at www.amazon.com and decide which OCR software you would like to buy.

EXAM TIP

Always check that you have the correct number of points in your answer. Here you need to think of TWO issues and FOUR factors.

TEST YOURSELF

1 Identify TWO issues with some websites that give a bad impression of the business and FOUR factors that a business must consider carefully to avoid these problems.

Now check your answers against those on the accompanying CD.

LEARNING OUTCOMES

By the time you have completed this section you should be able to:

• describe written channels of communication used in the office.

DID YOU KNOW?

Many businesses use **open punctuation**, where commas are inserted only in the body of the letter to help understanding but not at the end of addresses or date lines, etc.

DID YOU KNOW?

All business letters are dated, have a salutation (such as 'Dear Sir' or 'Dear Mrs Jordan') and a complimentary close (such as 'Yours faithfully' or 'Yours sincerely').

EXAM TIP

Put the current date in any letters or memos that you prepare in the exam unless you are told otherwise.

All businesses prepare a variety of written communications every day. Some, such as memos, are for **internal** use and are sent from one person to their supervisor or colleagues. Others, such as business letters, are for **external** use and are sent to clients, suppliers and other contacts.

You will learn about preparing memos and business letters in this section, as well as emails, reports and questionnaires. In Section 2.5 you will learn about press releases, notices and advertisements. In Unit 6 you will learn about notices of meetings, agendas and minutes. Travel itineraries are shown in Unit 7.

Types of written communication

Business letters

These are formal **external** communications. They are *always* sent on headed paper. This gives key information about the organisation, such as its name, address, telephone number, fax number and website address.

There is a standard business letter layout that is shown in Figure 2.4.1.

Points to note

• Slang and abbreviated words, such as 'don't' or 'can't', should never be used in business letters.

• The style and tone of the letter should suit its purpose. So, a sales letter should be upbeat, a letter responding to a complaint should be apologetic, a job application letter should be factual.

• Letters must be polite, but do not overuse the word 'please'. Think of alternatives such as 'we would be grateful if'.

• Never end with 'thank you' on its own. Use a standard phrase such as 'We appreciate your help in this matter.'

• There are usually three or four paragraphs. The first gives the reason for writing and introduces the main topic; the second (and possibly the third) go into more detail; the closing paragraph states what will happen next or the action expected.

Memos

Memos are internal documents that are sent between members of staff. Although many organisations now use email instead, they may sometimes be used for complex matters and to send information to staff who do not have email access. They are also used when a printed record is required for future reference. The most usual layout is shown in Figure 2.4.2 on page 28.

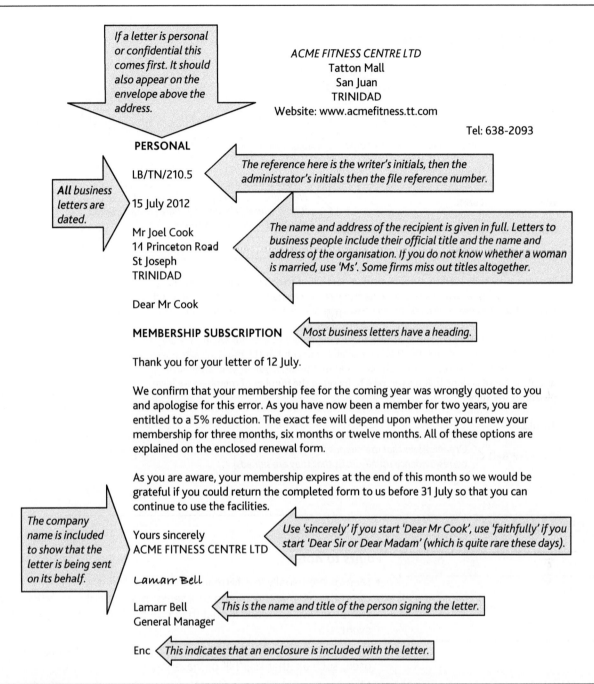

ACME FITNESS CENTRE LTD
Tatton Mall
San Juan
TRINIDAD
Website: www.acmefitness.tt.com

Tel: 638-2093

If a letter is personal or confidential this comes first. It should also appear on the envelope above the address.

PERSONAL

The reference here is the writer's initials, then the administrator's initials then the file reference number.

LB/TN/210.5

All business letters are dated.

15 July 2012

Mr Joel Cook
14 Princeton Road
St Joseph
TRINIDAD

The name and address of the recipient is given in full. Letters to business people include their official title and the name and address of the organisation. If you do not know whether a woman is married, use 'Ms'. Some firms miss out titles altogether.

Dear Mr Cook

MEMBERSHIP SUBSCRIPTION *Most business letters have a heading.*

Thank you for your letter of 12 July.

We confirm that your membership fee for the coming year was wrongly quoted to you and apologise for this error. As you have now been a member for two years, you are entitled to a 5% reduction. The exact fee will depend upon whether you renew your membership for three months, six months or twelve months. All of these options are explained on the enclosed renewal form.

As you are aware, your membership expires at the end of this month so we would be grateful if you could return the completed form to us before 31 July so that you can continue to use the facilities.

The company name is included to show that the letter is being sent on its behalf.

Yours sincerely
ACME FITNESS CENTRE LTD

Use 'sincerely' if you start 'Dear Mr Cook', use 'faithfully' if you start 'Dear Sir or Dear Madam' (which is quite rare these days).

Lamarr Bell

Lamarr Bell *This is the name and title of the person signing the letter.*
General Manager

Enc *This indicates that an enclosure is included with the letter.*

| **Figure 2.4.1** | A business letter |

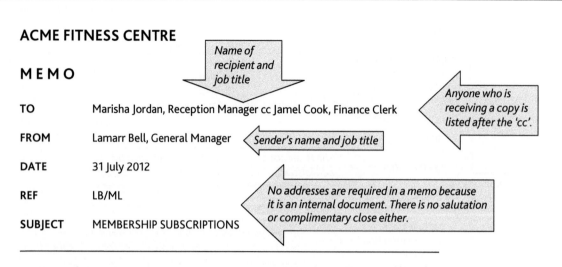

ACME FITNESS CENTRE

M E M O

TO	Marisha Jordan, Reception Manager cc Jamel Cook, Finance Clerk	
FROM	Lamarr Bell, General Manager	
DATE	31 July 2012	
REF	LB/ML	
SUBJECT	MEMBERSHIP SUBSCRIPTIONS	

Name of recipient and job title

Anyone who is receiving a copy is listed after the 'cc'.

Sender's name and job title

No addresses are required in a memo because it is an internal document. There is no salutation or complimentary close either.

We have now had several queries from members about their subscription renewal. Anyone who has been a member for over five years is entitled to a 10% reduction and those who have been members for over two years are awarded a 5% reduction.

Please can you ensure that all staff take these discounts into account when they are giving information to members. This is especially important at the moment, when we are trying to boost membership of the club. On that point, if you or your staff have any ideas about actions that we can take to increase the number of members we have, please let me know.

Thanks.

Lamarr Bell

Organisations that use memos for official internal correspondence usually insist that they are signed.

Figure 2.4.2 | A memo

DID YOU KNOW?

'Memo' is an abbreviation of 'memorandum' and the plural is 'memoranda'.

EXAM TIP

Never forget that memos do NOT have a salutation or a complimentary close.

Points to note

- Memos are usually less formal than a letter, but it will depend upon the recipient. A memo to a senior manager about a customer complaint will be more formal than one to all staff about a social event.
- Slang expressions should be avoided, but abbreviated words can be used, such as 'thanks', 'I'll' or 'haven't'.
- Memos are normally quite short and concentrate on one topic.

Emails

Emails can be sent internally or externally. If Lamarr had emailed Marisha with the information in the memo the wording would be the same but the format would be different. This is because the **header** is set up by the software and includes the following.

- **Sender's name** – inserted automatically on emails that you send.
- **Recipient's name** – inserted automatically when you reply to an email.
- **Date and time** – also inserted automatically.
- **Subject** – you must enter a brief title to summarise the content.

Points to note

- Emails are informal, but this does not mean that you can use the same phrases in a business email and an email to a friend!
- Sometimes external emails have a salutation, such as 'Dear Jamel', and a complimentary close, such as 'Best wishes'. This really depends upon who you are writing to and the style of emails where you eventually work.
- You can copy an email to other people and have two choices. If you click on **cc**, the names of the recipients are shown at the top of the message, so everyone can see who has received a copy. If you click on **bcc**, the names of recipients are not listed. Therefore no one knows that these persons have received a copy of the email.
- You can forward to other people an email that you have received.
- You can flag important emails as high priority, but only do this when it really is important.

Reports

Many reports are routine and regularly completed, such as your school report. In business, managers may report on activities in their department. There are also accident reports, safety reports, visit reports and financial reports. Some reports are written to give the result of an investigation. An example could be a report summarising the outcome of a questionnaire that was given to customers, or a report summarising current sales figures and trends.

Points to note

- In all reports the headings and spacing must be consistent and no slang or abbreviated words must be used.
- An appropriate title should be put at the top.
- A formal report will start with the **Terms of Reference**, then state the **Procedure** followed by the **Findings** (that is, the results of the investigation), the **Conclusion** and then any **Recommendations**.
- An informal report usually has three sections: an introduction, which states the reason for writing the report; **the body of the report**, which gives the information that has been obtained; **a conclusion**, which sums up the information and says whether any action is needed or not.
- The report ends with the writer's name, job title and date.

DID YOU KNOW?

Writing an email in CAPITALS is called 'shouting' and is considered impolite.

FIND OUT MORE

Ask your teacher about the style and layout of emails and memos used at your school or college. Also check the layout of any business letters that your family may receive and see what similarities and differences there are between different examples.

EXAM TIP

Check your spelling carefully in any documents that you prepare.

DID YOU KNOW?

Numbered points are often used in the body of the report to separate different items clearly.

An example of a formal report is shown below.

**REPORT ON THE PROPOSAL THAT RECEPTION STAFF
SHOULD WEAR A UNIFORM**

Terms of reference
At the request of Marisha Jordan, the Reception Manager, I investigated the advantages and disadvantages of introducing uniforms for staff working on reception at Acme Fitness.

Procedure
1   I talked to the staff who work in reception, both male and female.
2   I visited the reception areas of local organisations to check if their staff wore uniforms.
3   I talked to visitors in our reception area.
4   I contacted clothing suppliers and obtained their catalogues and price lists.

Findings
1   All reception staff were in favour of wearing a uniform providing it was washable. They also wanted to be involved in selecting the style.
2   Four out of six local firms require their reception staff to wear a uniform and staff also wore name badges. Supervisor's uniforms were usually slightly different.
3   Eight out of ten visitors approved of uniforms to enable them to distinguish reception staff quickly.
4   All clothing suppliers had suitable ranges.

Conclusion
1   The proposal to introduce uniforms appears to be popular and should be discussed further.

Recommendations
1   The proposal should be discussed further by the management team and a decision taken on whether a uniform policy should be introduced and, if so, the budget available.
2   If uniforms will be introduced, the reception staff should be involved in selecting the fabric, style and colours, linked to the corporate colours of Acme Fitness.

Kareena Williams
Office Administrator
25 July 2012

Questionnaires

Questionnaires are issued to obtain information. An example is the form given to hotel guests on their last day to check whether there were any problems with their stay. Although they often ask for people's opinions, questionnaires are structured to give people specific choices so that it is easy and quick to analyse the responses. There are various ways to do this, but ideally only one method should apply throughout the questionnaire. For example:

- put a tick or cross on a dotted line or in a box
- delete the option that does not apply
- write 'yes' or 'no' as appropriate
- make a judgement and give a score of 1 to 5 (but make it clear whether 1 is high or low!).

DID YOU KNOW?

Questionnaires should be kept short, otherwise people get tired of answering the questions.

Points to note

- Start by listing the information that you need to obtain. Then decide the best order for this.
- Put the name of the business and the title of the questionnaire at the top.
- Decide what instructions you need to include, such as writing in black ink or block capitals. Tell people what to do with the questionnaire once it is completed.
- Tell people how to correct any errors that they make.
- Decide whether you want people to include their name and the date on the form or whether contributions can be anonymous.
- Leave enough space so that the questionnaire is easy to read and people have sufficient room to enter their responses.

Figure 2.4.3 | Do you enjoy completing questionnaires?

Figure 2.4.4

EXAM TIP

If you are asked to draft a document, always start by writing DRAFT in capital letters at the top of your work.

TEST YOURSELF

1 You work for Marisha Jordan at Acme Fitness Centre. She has asked her staff for ideas to boost membership and awareness of the club and they have suggested the following: a 'bring-a-friend-for-free day' once a month; offering guest membership for up to a month for visitors to the island; sponsoring a team to run in a charity event; devising a questionnaire for members to check their satisfaction with existing facilities and asking whether they can suggest any improvements.

a DRAFT a memo to Lamarr, that Marisha could sign, telling him about these suggestions.

b Prepare TWO sample questions that you think could be included in the questionnaire for members.

Now check your answers against those on the accompanying CD.

2.5

Focus on visual communication

LEARNING OUTCOMES

By the time you have completed this section you should be able to:

- describe visual channels of communication used in the office
- prepare and interpret visual communications.

Visual communications attract attention. They can be used to simplify complex information, show comparisons, illustrate ideas and influence customers.

Pictures, charts and graphs

A **picture** is said to 'speak a thousand words'. This is why many adverts include pictures. It is also why Acme Fitness Centre will have posters in the gym showing smiling, healthy, fit people. This gives the message that going to Acme is fun and that being a member will help you to look like the person in the poster.

THINK ABOUT IT!

Pictures can sometimes give an unintentionally negative impression. For example, what message would Acme Fitness Centre send if all of the pictures were of men or young people? How could that affect membership?

Charts provide information in graphical form. Explaining the organisational structure of a business in words would take a long time, yet an organisation chart makes it quick and easy. Other types of charts include:

- **bar charts**, which usually illustrate a trend
- **multiple bar charts** (or histograms), which show comparisons (see Figure 2.5.2)
- **pie charts**, which show proportions as a percentage of the whole (see Figure 2.5.3)
- **flow charts**, which show a sequence of events or actions.

Figure 2.5.1 What would this picture tell you about Acme Fitness Centre?

DID YOU KNOW?

You can see all types of charts on Google Images. Click on the 'Image' option on Google then enter 'flow chart' to see some examples.

DID YOU KNOW?

Tables, diagrams and pictograms are other types of graphical images. Check these out on Google Images too.

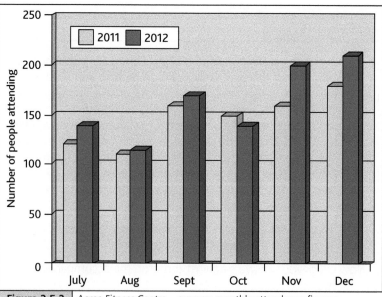

Figure 2.5.2 Acme Fitness Centre – average monthly attendance figures

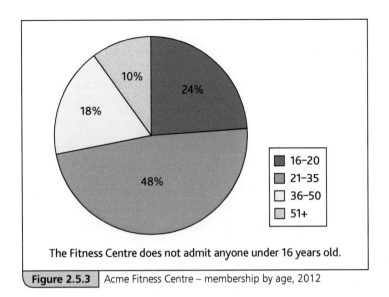

The Fitness Centre does not admit anyone under 16 years old.

Figure 2.5.3 | Acme Fitness Centre – membership by age, 2012

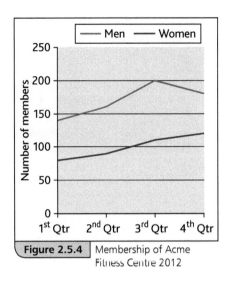

Figure 2.5.4 | Membership of Acme Fitness Centre 2012

Graphs may have one line or several (see Figure 2.5.4). Those that have more than one line are called multiline graphs. Because the lines go up and down, increases and decreases can be seen at a glance. Line graphs are used to show different types of statistical information such as sales figures, population growth or decline, crime rates, etc.

Creating charts and graphs

When you are creating a chart or graph it is better to draft it out in pencil first.

- Note that the x-axis goes across and the y-axis goes down. The x-axis usually represents the time period.
- Keep the spacing consistent.
- Decide on different colours (or patterns) for lines or bars.
- Wedges on a pie chart must be in proportion to the percentage they represent, and when the wedges are added together they must equal 100%.
- Include a legend on a pie chart, multiline graph or multiple bar chart to show what each item represents.

Interpreting charts and graphs

- Read the title, headings and legend first, so that you know what the chart or graph represents.
- Read any notes at the bottom.
- Study the data to spot any trends or comparisons. Check whether figures are increasing, decreasing or staying the same, and over what time period.
- Compare each data entry to find the highest and lowest. Think of factors that could affect this.
- Group the information that you have found logically so it is easier to understand.

EXAM TIP

Remember that a single-line graph or bar chart can show a trend, but in order to make a comparison you will need a multiline or multiple bar chart.

DID YOU KNOW?

Most types of charts and graphs can be prepared easily on a computer.

Figure 2.5.5 What do these signals on a package tell you?

Signals

Signals and signs give you a message without any need for words. Red traffic signals mean 'stop'. A chequered flag tells you a race is over. International shipping labels signal how to handle a package regardless of what language the workers speak.

Signals can also be used:

- on files and in filing systems, to denote confidential or priority files
- on wall planners and wall charts, to highlight key events
- to warn about hazards and to show safe working practices.

Both company logos and computer icons are types of signals. You know what is represented without needing to be told.

Promotions and visuals

Marketing clerks (see Unit 11) may have the task of creating notices, advertisements and press releases to promote an event. All of these documents must have an effective heading that attracts the reader immediately.

Preparing a press release

A press release needs an attention-grabbing headline. They must be easy to understand, and the vital information should come *first*. Subsequent paragraphs go into more detail so that if the article is cut to fit the space available, the important information is retained. Contact details enable the paper to obtain additional information if more space is available.

SUNWISE STORES LTD

FOR IMMEDIATE RELEASE

HOLLYWOOD STAR VISITS SUNWISE!
Jodi French is coming to town

Jodi French, the Hollywood star, will be opening the new Sunwise Store in Placeville on Saturday, 10 September. Jodie starred in the blockbuster movie *Together* and has been a friend of Sunwise's owner, Bob Pierce, since their school days.

The new store is in the town centre and facilities include a coffee shop, a play area for young children and free parking. All customers visiting on opening day will receive a free gift!

Sunwise was formed in 1992 and now owns stores throughout the Caribbean. *(Continue with basic company information)*

-ends-

For further information contact Celeste Bridges
Cellphone: 03892 283728
Email: celeste@sunwise.com

Figure 2.5.6 Example press release

Preparing an advertisement or notice

Advertisements for products or services are different from job advertisements (see example on page 67). Those in magazines contain photographs and other graphics. They aim to persuade the reader to buy the item through association with the image.

THINK ABOUT IT!

Any business which is promoting its activities will want to attract attention. It will do this by including visuals and signals as well as text. This is why you see advertisements, notices and press articles containing graphics.

Sunwise Stores are promoting their new store and have produced a press release to send to local papers. The aim is to obtain free publicity. Read the press release opposite and then decide TWO images that Sunwise could include to make it more instantly appealing to readers.

DID YOU KNOW?

The cost of advertisements is either by size, such as for display adverts, or by number of words, such as for classified adverts. In this case, every word counts!

Newspaper advertisements are likely to contain more text, particularly in your local paper. They aim to provide information to readers and follow the AIDA principle – attract **Attention**, raise **Interest**, create **Desire** and encourage **Action**.

Notices try to do both. They often include a graphic or image and then give essential information in order of importance. This must include: **What** event is being advertised, **When** it is happening, **Where** it will be and **Who** is organising it (see also page 169).

Multimedia presentations

These incorporate various types of visuals, including tables, charts, graphs, pictograms, diagrams, drawings, maps and photographs. Video footage can be used for greater impact.

Body language

This refers to the messages we send by our gestures, facial expressions, posture and where we position ourselves in relation to other people.

- **Gestures** help you to communicate at a distance, for example, when you wave to someone who is too far away to hear you. They also emphasise what you are saying. Shrugging your shoulders often means you do not care, looking around says you are bored. If a customer starts tapping a foot or drumming their fingers, it is a sign they are impatient.
- **Facial expressions** can signal surprise, disappointment, joy, boredom, annoyance, etc. Making eye contact is usually seen as a sign of honesty.
- **Your posture** displays your attitude. Positive people sit, stand and walk tall. If you feel negative you may slouch or sit in a hunched up position. Folding your arms and/or crossing your legs are defensive positions. Leaning forward shows keenness and interest. Leaning back shows you are relaxed or confident.
- **Your body position** tells others about you. The closer people stand to each other, the more they know and like each other. Turning your body towards someone shows interest. 'Reflecting' someone else's body language shows empathy.

FIND OUT MORE

Look through your local newspaper for advertisements and identify those that appeal to you. Think about why they attract you. Now look for notices about events and promotions in your area. Study the text and graphics. Try to decide the differences between those that are very good and those that are not.

DID YOU KNOW?

If you stand too close to strangers they will normally move away to keep their distance.

FIND OUT MORE

Find out more on YouTube. For example, watch the short film 'Office Etiquette & Advice: How to Read Body Language in the Workplace'. Search for it and see what else you find.

TEST YOURSELF

1 a Look back at the charts and graphs that provide information about Acme Fitness Centre. Marisha Jordan has asked you to identify TWO facts about membership and ONE trend so that the business can use this information to try to increase membership.

  b Acme Fitness Centre have arranged for a famous gymnast, Carey Holden, to give an exhibition two weeks today. Invent any other relevant details about Carey and prepare a short press release to publicise this event and a notice that could be placed in the reception area of the Centre.

Now check your answers against those on the accompanying CD.

EXAM TIP

Try to identify both positive and negative factors so that Marisha can assess where they need to focus their efforts.

Making choices

LEARNING OUTCOMES

By the time you have completed this section you should be able to:

- identify factors affecting the selection of communication media
- select appropriate types and sizes of stationery for a variety of uses.

Methods of communication

Oral methods
Interviews, meetings and conferences, radio and television, telephone

Electronic methods
Teleconferencing and videoconferencing, telecommuting / telemarketing, computer, internet, World Wide Web, email, fax, text and picture messaging

Written methods
Letters, memos, meeting documents, questionnaires, itineraries, notices, press releases, adverts

Visual methods
Pictures, charts and graphs, signals, multimedia presentations, body language

| **Figure 2.6.1** | Different methods of communication |

KEY TERMS

The word **media** is the plural of 'medium'. **Communication media** are simply different means of communication, for example radio and television. The term **new media** is used for electronic methods such as the internet and websites.

Selecting communication media

Overview of communication methods

You know that communication methods can be divided into four different types. These are summarised in Figure 2.6.1.

The best type of communication to use in a situation will depend upon several factors.

- **The degree of urgency**. Electronic communications arrive more quickly than those sent by traditional methods. Sending original documents quickly can be expensive, especially if a courier is used. Other methods of instant communication include the telephone, text messages, videoconferences and internet links.
- **The genre**. This refers to the **type** of communication – in this case whether it is oral, written or visual.
  - **Oral methods** are best when you want to have a discussion, to find out someone's views and when you need instant feedback.
  - **Written methods** are better for complex information or if you need a record for future reference.
  - **Visual methods** are ideal for communicating structures, relationships and ideas that are difficult to describe.
- **The level of confidentiality**. Faxes are easily seen by other people, therefore an email is preferable as it goes to a person's private inbox. Confidential letters or memos must be put in a sealed envelope that is marked 'Confidential'.
- **The location and time zone**. Phone calls, videoconferences and teleconferences should be prearranged to take account of any time difference. Emails and text messages can be accessed and answered at any time. Business letters can be sent overseas.
- **Cost, efficiency, effectiveness**. It costs more to phone abroad than to email, and sending an original document by courier is more expensive than airmail. Sending a document as an email attachment costs nothing.

Choosing paper and envelopes

You need to know the types of paper and envelopes that you can use and decide which is best for your needs.

Paper

Types of paper include the following.

- **Bond paper**: this is commonly used for letterheads and memos. It is available in different weights. The heavier the weight, the thicker the paper.
- **Parchment**: this is heavier and more expensive because it is made from animal hides. One type of parchment is vellum. It is sometimes used for important diplomas and certificates.

- **NCR paper**: this is specially coated so that a copy is made without using carbon paper. The letters mean 'no carbon required'.

Sizes include the following.

- A4 (8¼ in × 11¾ in): the most popular.
- A5 (half of A4) and A6 (half of A5).
- A3 (double A4); A2 (double A3); and A1 (double A2).
- Legal (8½ in × 14 in) paper: this is larger than A4.
- Letter paper (8½ in × 11 in): this is slightly smaller than A4.

Envelopes

Envelopes may have a gummed flap or be self-sealing. They include the following.

- White envelopes: these are mainly used for correspondence.
- Window envelopes: these have a transparent panel where the address shows through if it is accurately positioned.
- Other varieties include heavy-duty envelopes, airmail envelopes and padded bubble envelopes to protect fragile items.

Sizes include the following.

- C4 envelopes: these take A4 paper flat or A3 folded once. C5 is half this size and C6 is smaller still.
- DL: this is the main size used for letters and takes A4 paper folded twice.

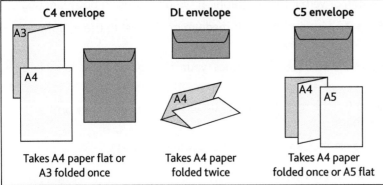

C4 envelope	DL envelope	C5 envelope
Takes A4 paper flat or A3 folded once	Takes A4 paper folded twice	Takes A4 paper folded once or A5 flat

Figure 2.6.2 Envelopes come in different sizes

DID YOU KNOW?

The best method of communication is always the most cost-effective one that will efficiently serve your purpose.

DID YOU KNOW?

Paper has a wrong and right side. Hold a sheet of bond paper up to the light. If you are looking at the correct (smooth) side then you will be able to read the watermark.

FIND OUT MORE

Check out the websites of some office suppliers and/or look around your local store to see the different types of paper and envelopes that are stocked. One useful website is www.brydensxpress.com.

TEST YOURSELF

1 You work for a realtor with branches across the Caribbean and an office in Miami.
   a Suggest THREE economical methods you could use to communicate documents or photographs to other branches.
   b Identify THREE factors you would take into consideration when choosing which method of communication to use.
Now check your answers against those on the accompanying CD.

EXAM TIP

Always remember to identify first whether the recipient is internal or external, as this will affect your choice of method.

LEARNING OUTCOMES

By the time you have completed this section you should be able to:

• discuss the barriers to effective communication.

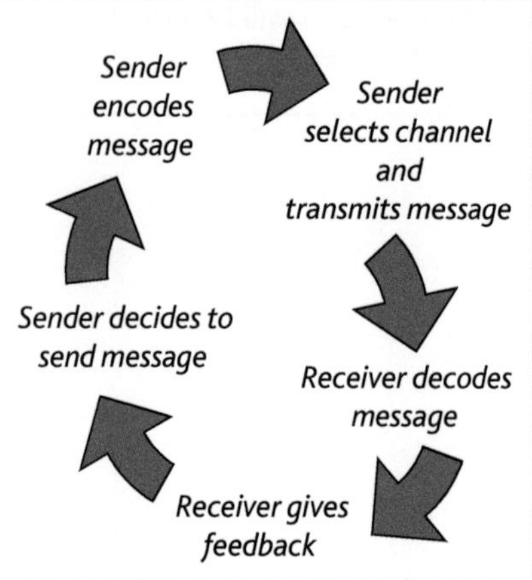

Figure 2.7.1 | The communications cycle

(Sender encodes message → Sender selects channel and transmits message → Receiver decodes message → Receiver gives feedback → Sender decides to send message)

DID YOU KNOW?

In some countries of the world shaking your head means 'yes', not 'no', so it would be easy to send the wrong message!

KEY TERMS

Bias is a strong feeling or prejudice that influences your response to a situation.

Not all communications go smoothly. Despite the best attempts of people and organisations to communicate promptly and accurately, things can go wrong. To understand why, it is helpful to know what actually happens when you communicate with someone, either verbally or in writing.

THINK ABOUT IT!

How many times has something gone wrong with one of your communications? Think of occasions when there might have been a misunderstanding between you and your family or friends, such as conflict over what time or day you were seeing them. What went wrong? Can you identify why it happened?

The communications cycle

This is the process or sequence that takes place when you communicate with someone. A problem, or barrier, can occur at any stage.

Steps in the cycle

Step 1 – you decide to send a message

Step 2 – you 'encode' your message. This means putting it into written or verbal forms, graphical symbols or using body language.

Step 3 – you decide which medium or channel to use and then transmit your message.

Step 4 – the receiver 'decodes' your message and tries to make sense of it.

Step 5 – the receiver clarifies understanding (or not) by giving feedback.

The cycle then starts again with another message.

What can go wrong?

Several common barriers to effective communication are summarised below.

Bias – perceptual, cultural and personal

Every message that you send and receive is affected by the way you see the world. This is affected by your upbringing and your experiences.

• **Perceptual bias** are the perceptions you have, the positive and negative opinions that you hold and how these affect your behaviour. For example, you may love a certain radio station but your parents might think it is just a lot of noise!

• **Cultural bias** means that you make judgements based on your own culture, which is what you are used to. So, for example, if you think that only local food is tasty, you will ignore foreign dishes listed on a menu.

- **Personal bias** is your own beliefs and responses. Young people may have a certain opinion on older people, but equally, older people may have a certain opinion on younger people. This will influence how they react to each other.

Language and semantics

When a message is encoded, this must be in a language – or symbols – that will be understood by the receiver. Using the wrong vocabulary, technical jargon or local expressions may mean that the message cannot be understood.

Literacy skills

This is the ability of the sender or receiver to write or understand the written word. If you do not know what to say, or struggle with your spelling, this will affect the quality of your message. If your recipient has a limited vocabulary, this will affect their ability to understand you.

Figure 2.7.2

Time constraints

Sending a message at the wrong time – when someone is too busy to read it, when they are doing something else or are otherwise distracted, for example – will also affect their ability to understand it and respond.

DID YOU KNOW?

KISS stands for 'Keep It Short and Simple'. It is a good rule to follow for all of your communications!

Overcoming barriers to communication

You can overcome barriers by following the golden rules shown in Table 2.7.1.

Table 2.7.1   Overcoming communication barriers

Communication stage	Rules to follow
Overcoming bias on the part of the recipient	Think about the recipient(s) – who they are and how best to communicate with them Consider the opinions held by the recipient and their culture, and how these could affect their understanding of the message Check that you have a clear understanding of the information
Overcoming language or literacy problems	Keep it short and simple Avoid jargon, complex words or slang Check there are no errors or ambiguities Use a written method for long or complex information
Overcoming time constraints	Choose the best time to get the recipient's attention and give them time to respond Use an electronic method for urgent information, or a courier Check that the message has been received and read
Overcoming your own personal bias/ language issues	Listen carefully and do not interrupt Do not jump to conclusions or make assumptions Query any parts of the message that are not clear

TEST YOURSELF

1 List THREE barriers of communication that can occur, and for each one state the action you would take to overcome it.

Now check your answers against those on the accompanying CD.

How businesses are structured

By the time you have completed this section you should be able to:

• identify the various forms of business structure.

Figure 2.8.1 There are many decisions to be made in business every day

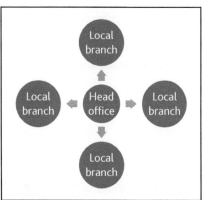

Figure 2.8.2 A centralised structure

DID YOU KNOW?

Scotiabank is an organisation with a centralised structure. Major decisions are made at head office so that customers will receive the same information and services wherever they hold an account.

Business structures and decision making

Decisions are made every day in business. Who makes them can often depend upon the type of business structure.

• **Strategic decisions** are important decisions that affect the future of the company, such as location, numbers of staff, pay rates, what products to make or sell.

• **Operational decisions** are day-to-day decisions, such as how much stock to order, how to handle a customer complaint, when to hold the next staff meeting.

In Section 1.2 you learned that offices are organised so that work is completed efficiently by staff. You also met the terms **centralised** and **decentralised**. These terms can also apply to the way the whole business is organised.

Centralised structures

In a **centralised structure**, the senior management or the owner will usually make most decisions and pass down instructions to other parts of the business, for example:

• when an **entrepreneur** starts and controls their own small business, such as a small taxi company run by the owner

• when a larger organisation has a head office that makes all of the major decisions and controls the way that other parts of the business operate.

KEY TERMS

In a **centralised structure** most decisions are made by management and are passed down to other staff.

In a **decentralised structure** staff are involved more in decision making.

An **entrepreneur** is a person who starts their own business or enterprise. It is a French word, meaning 'to undertake'.

Decentralised structures

A **decentralised structure** is the opposite of a centralised structure. Staff can make more decisions, such as a supermarket chain where the branch managers can stock the foods that suit local tastes.

• A **pyramid structure** shows an organisation that has progressively more people at each lower level. Strategic decisions will be made by senior managers at the top, but day-to-day decisions will be made by staff lower down the pyramid.

• A **matrix structure** is often found in organisations that deal with special 'one-off' projects. These companies may be working on several projects at once, such as building a hotel, a sports facility and a shopping centre in different Caribbean territories. An expert team is responsible for seeing each project through and needs the support of the major functions of the organisation, such as finance, HR and production. The project managers discuss issues such as costs, staffing and design with these departmental heads. The project team works on a project until it is complete. It is then disbanded and a new team is formed to work on a new project.

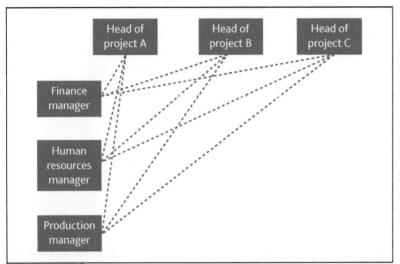

Figure 2.8.4 | A matrix structure

- **An independent structure** exists when individuals can make their own decisions about their operations, even if they work as part of a larger enterprise. For example, franchisees who run their own store or gas station but obtain support and information from the larger franchisor, which allows them to trade under that name. A similar arrangement applies to independent entrepreneurs who have a concession in a major store, such as at Cave Shepherd in Barbados.

Figure 2.8.3 | A pyramid/hierarchical structure

DID YOU KNOW?

A **hierarchical organisation** has many levels whereas a **flat organisation** has only two or three. Staff are usually more involved in decisions if there are fewer levels.

DID YOU KNOW?

Creative industries need the input of all of their staff in order to do a good job. Companies such as Google and Pixar have decentralised structures and encourage staff to collaborate as much as possible.

TEST YOURSELF

1 Kevin Alleyne is the General Manager of Island Tours. He set up the business six years ago and made all of the decisions himself. As the business became more popular he employed more staff and now has an office manager, a transport manager, three clerks and four drivers.

  a Did Island Tours originally have a centralised or a decentralised structure? Give a reason for your answer.

  b Draw an organisation chart to show the current structure.

  c Identify TWO ways in which decision making at Island Tours will have changed as it has grown larger.

Now check your answers against those on the accompanying CD.

FIND OUT MORE

Golden Krust's vision is to 'provide the taste of the Caribbean to the world'. Read its mission statement and values on its website at www.goldenkrustbakery.com then find out about being a franchisee and opening a Golden Krust kiosk yourself. What decisions could *you* make, and what decisions would they help you to make?

Sources of information

LEARNING OUTCOMES

By the time you have completed this section you should be able to:

• select relevant sources of information.

Figure 2.9.1 | What information would you find in these reference books?

DID YOU KNOW?

If you are using Word on your computer then you can use the dictionary and thesaurus within the software. If not, you can access these online, for example www.oxforddictionaries.com.

FIND OUT MORE

Many gazettes are now searchable online. For Trinidad and Tobago see the e-Gazette at www.news.gov.tt. For Jamaica see http://jamaicagazette.gov.jm/content/about-us and for the Virgin Islands see www.bvigazette.org. Check out your territory and see what you can find out about *your Official Gazette*.

Sources of reference

No one who works in an office can possibly know or remember all of the information they might need to do their job. What they should know, however, is where to find the facts and figures they need.

FIND OUT MORE

What types of reference books and materials does your school keep in the library? Which would be helpful to an office administrator? Visit your library to find out.

Types of reference materials

A dictionary and a thesaurus

• A **dictionary** provides more than just a list of words, their spellings and their meanings. You can also check the pronunciation of words and the meaning of commonly used abbreviations.

• A **thesaurus** provides lists of alternative meanings (synonyms) for a wide range of words. Most also include one or two opposite meanings (antonyms) as well.

Official Gazettes

The *Official Gazette* is a government publication. It is produced by many Caribbean territories on a weekly or monthly basis and includes information such as Acts of Parliament, government notices, public appointments and lists of bankruptcies.

Telephone directory

This contains the names, addresses and telephone numbers of subscribers in alphabetical order. There are often separate sections for individuals, businesses and government offices. The Yellow Pages section contains a list of businesses. These are classified according to the type of business and then listed in alphabetical order.

Maps

Maps are available at different scales. Large-scale maps show more detail. A road map is better for a business person than one showing geographical features. Maps are useful for reference, but many business people now prefer to use a satellite navigation system when they are driving somewhere new.

DID YOU KNOW?

You can quickly check the distance between two places in Google or Bing Maps. You can also find out how long the journey will take.

Schedules

Schedules provide a list of planned events in the order in which they will occur. Travel schedules are produced by transport companies such as airlines and ferry operators. They show arrival and departure times on different days, the routes and the terminals involved. In business, meetings and appointments are also scheduled. A time period is allocated for each one to ensure maximum efficiency.

Post Office Guide

This provides information on post office services including postal regulations for inland and overseas post, postal rates, delivery times, the opening and closing times of different branches, and other services such as money transfer and savings accounts.

Trade journals

These are specialist magazines, published at regular intervals and aimed at a particular trade or profession, such as ventilation experts or dentists. They contain articles, features and adverts so that people can read about developments in their industry and even change job, as there is often a classified section that includes job vacancies.

Hansard

Hansard provides a daily and weekly **verbatim** report of proceedings in Parliament.

The internet

The internet enables you to find lots of information, in different formats, as long as you know what you are doing. This means:

- You know how to use a good **search engine**, such as Google, Yahoo! or Bing.
- You double-check your information to make sure it is up to date.
- You only rely on official websites, such as government sites or those of reputable organisations.
- You can find your way around a website and use the site map.
- You are wary of Wikipedia and blogs that are written by individuals.
- You avoid technical websites and scholarly papers that contain information that you do not understand.

Figure 2.9.2 Do you use a bus schedule?

DID YOU KNOW?

Many countries are putting postal information online, such as the Barbados Postal Service at www.bps.gov.bb.

FIND OUT MORE

Check out a variety of trade journals at www.thenewmagazinecity.com/categories-trade---professional-journals.html.

KEY TERMS

Verbatim means 'word for word' – so every single word spoken is recorded.

TEST YOURSELF

1 Identify TWO types of information that you would find in each of the following.

  a A thesaurus   c An airline schedule

  b A trade journal   d The telephone directory.

Now check your answers against those on the accompanying CD.

EXAM TIP

Check that you can accurately describe the key information to be found on these pages.

Telephone techniques and services

Using the telephone effectively in an office requires three skills:

- receiving and making calls in a professional manner
- taking a clear message
- knowing what communication services are available.

Telephone techniques

- These relate to the way you receive information and relay messages by telephone.

Telephone etiquette

- The main points to note are given below.

Table 2.10.1	Telephone etiquette when you are receiving or making calls
Receiving calls	**Making calls**
• Answer promptly with your organisation's standard greeting • Identify yourself or your department • Sound pleasant and cheerful and listen carefully. • Have a pen and notepad to hand • Write down the name of the caller, the person they want to speak to and the reason for their call • If you cannot help, pass the call to a colleague or take a message • Ask the caller to spell their name if it is unusual • Check you have the caller's number before you ring off • Say 'Thank you for calling' at the end of the call • Pass any message on promptly	• Check you know the reason for making the call • Write down the information you must give or find out • Introduce yourself and explain why you are calling • Do not use slang or jargon such as 'OK' or 'Bye' • Do not gabble. Ask the other person to slow down if they speak too quickly • Ask people to spell unusual words • Say figures in *pairs* as they are easier to understand, for example, 12-78-97, *not* 127-897 • If you mishear something, never say 'What?' Say 'Sorry, could you please repeat that?' • Write down the information you receive

LEARNING OUTCOMES

By the time you have completed this section you should be able to:

- describe the proper techniques for receiving and relaying messages by telephone
- describe the services offered by communications service providers.

KEY TERMS

Telephone etiquette relates to the correct way to answer the telephone in a business environment.

Figure 2.10.1 What skills do you need to use a telephone at work?

DID YOU KNOW?

Smiling during a telephone conversation reflects in your voice. You sound friendlier and more pleasant to deal with.

DID YOU KNOW?

You should *never* answer the telephone when you are chewing.

FIND OUT MORE

Find out what the standard telephone greeting is in your school office. Then listen to those used by other organisations, such as: 'Good morning' (or afternoon), 'Acme Fitness Centre, Zara speaking. How may I help you?'

Recording systems

These enable callers to leave a message when the office is closed. The main options are as follows.

- **Voicemail**. Employees have their own voicemail box that answers calls to their extension with a personal, pre-recorded message if they are unavailable. Stored messages can usually be retrieved remotely if required.
- **An answering machine** on which callers can leave a recorded message and their telephone number.
- **Answering services** that receive calls and take messages on someone's behalf. They are mainly used by small businesses where the owner is often away.

DID YOU KNOW?

Some businesses prefer to use a system that gives pre-recorded information to incoming callers about the company products or services and opening hours.

Receiving and delivering messages

Messages are taken if the person that the caller wants to speak to is not available. The main points to note are shown in Table 2.10.2.

Table 2.10.2	Golden rules for message taking

1 Write out the message as you are listening. Redraft it afterwards with the key information in the correct order.

2 Listen carefully. Ask the caller to repeat anything you do not understand.

3 Check you have the **key facts** that you need, such as:
  a the person's name (check the spelling)
  b the name of the organisation or the caller's address
  c the caller's telephone number and dialling code
  d the main points relating to the message, such as:
    i the reason for the call
    ii details of any information requested
    iii details of any information you are given
    iv action to be taken.

4 Double-check dates, times, place names, prices and any numbers. You cannot guess these later!

5 Read the message back to the caller to check it is correct.

6 Write out the message neatly with the key facts in a logical order.

7 Add your own name and the date and time of the call.

8 Pass urgent messages on immediately – give them to your supervisor if the recipient is away.

DID YOU KNOW?

All messages must always be checked regularly and callers should receive a prompt response.

FIND OUT MORE

Listen carefully to messages that you hear when you phone a business out of hours. Then decide what message Acme Fitness Centre should leave on its phone system to respond to callers.

Figure 2.10.2	Why is it a good idea to use preprinted message pads?

DID YOU KNOW?

Preprinted message forms help you to remember the key points to include when taking a message.

EXAM TIP

Using words like 'tomorrow' or 'yesterday' in messages can be confusing for the reader as they may not read the message on the day it was taken. So, write the date and day instead.

DID YOU KNOW?

Many messages are passed on quickly by text or email to a cellphone.

FIND OUT MORE

Check your own directory, then your local online Yellow Pages. You can find the Jamaica Yellow Pages at http://jamaicayp.com. Use this to go to the pages for your territory and check the information that is included.

DID YOU KNOW?

If the company directory is on the computer system staff will need special authority before they can alter any data.

DID YOU KNOW?

Pagers are more reliable than cellphones because they communicate by satellite and do not rely on mobile phone signals.

DID YOU KNOW?

If you do not know the number you need to call, it can be cheaper to search online than to ask for operator assistance.

Using a telephone directory

Many directories categorise information into businesses, private individuals and government offices, agents and services. Additional information may include:

- other telephone services and international codes
- emergency numbers
- information about the telephone company itself.

Maintaining a personal and a company directory

Personal directories can be held on paper or stored electronically on your cellphone or computer. Software is available especially for this purpose.

Company directories may be issued on paper, but they are usually held electronically, often on the company intranet (see page 24). Sometimes staff may help to keep this up to date by adding information on new contacts, such as the person's name, the name of the organisation, the address, telephone number(s) and email address.

Functions and operations of automated switchboards

Traditional switchboards need an operator to receive and connect incoming calls. Outgoing calls are usually made direct by the extension users.

An automated switchboard does not have an operator. An automated voice greets callers and offers a menu of options, for example: 'To hear your balance press 1. To make a payment press 2.' Callers select the options they need and, in some cases, they never speak to a human being.

This system enables the business to process several calls simultaneously without employing an operator. But callers may be irritated if the options do not match their needs or if they are placed in a long queue to speak to someone. This gives a poor impression of customer service.

Paging devices

Pagers are small, hand-held devices on which people can be reached quickly and easily. The simplest pagers bleep to tell the user to ring the switchboard or a certain number. Some bleep or flash and vibrate and give the user a message. Others allow two-way communication including email.

Pagers are used when cellphones could cause problems or be unreliable, for example in hospital complexes, high-level military installations and remote locations.

Communication services

In order for a telephone to work it needs the services of a communications service provider (CSP). These services are summarised in Table 2.10.3.

Table 2.10.3 Communication services

Services offered	Features of the service
Local, long-distance and overseas calls	Charges vary depending upon the company and the contract. Local calls to **subscribers** in your own area may be free. Long-distance calls are those to other area codes. International calls are preceded by another country code and are more expensive
Station-to-station, person-to-person calls	A station-to-station call means that you speak to whoever answers at the subscriber's location. If you must speak to one particular person you can book a person-to-person call with the operator. You are only charged when that person responds, which is better for expensive international calls
Collect calls	Calling 'collect' means you ask the operator to check if the subscriber will pay for the call. If they refuse, the operator ends the connection
Conference calls and videoconferences	See page 22. Look back now and refresh your memory
Call waiting	If you are on a call, the system alerts you when someone else is trying to call you. You can ask the current caller to wait while you speak to the new caller
Call forwarding	This allows you to divert a call to another number, such as sending your home calls to your cellphone
Voicemail	See page 45
Speed dialling	You can store your most frequently used numbers as codes in your telephone and enable quick dialling
Caller ID	This retrieves the caller's identity from the phone memory and displays it to show you who is calling
Phone cards	Prepaid phone cards enable calls to be paid for in advance rather than in cash or on a bill. You dial the service number and enter your PIN before dialling the number. They are useful for anyone who makes long-distance telephone calls when they are travelling because they do not need cash to make calls, nor do they need to use expensive hotel telephones
Electronic top-up machines	These enable you to increase the credit on a cellphone. You enter your number and the amount you are paying. The machine then communicates the transaction to your CSP and prints a receipt
Cell/mobile phones; text messaging	Cellphones (or mobile phones) enable you to make and receive calls and text messages when you are away from home. Smartphones enable you to connect to the internet and send emails, though roaming rates for cellphones that are used abroad are high
Voice over IP (VOIP)	This enables you to make calls over the internet. Providers include Skype, MagicTalk and Google Call. Computer-to-computer calls are usually free, but subscribers can also use the service to make telephone or cellphone calls at a much reduced rate

TEST YOURSELF

1 a List FOUR aspects of telephone etiquette that you would demonstrate when you answer the telephone.
  b Identify THREE additional factors that you would bear in mind if you had to take a message.

Now check your answers against those on the accompanying CD.

KEY TERMS

The **subscriber** is the person or organisation who has signed the contract with the CSP and pays for the service.

LEARNING OUTCOMES

By the time you have completed this section you should be able to:

- describe the services available for despatching mail
- outline procedures for sending and receiving parcels
- outline procedures for dealing with incoming and outgoing mail in large and small offices.

Figure 2.11.1 What are the advantages of using a courier?

DID YOU KNOW?

Many small businesses use SkyBOX (or an equivalent service) to buy IT supplies quickly and cheaply from international companies such as Amazon.

Figure 2.11.2 What items do you think SkyBOX handles the most?

Introduction to the mail room

Vast numbers of documents are sent by mail from business organisations every day. Administrators need to know how to process incoming mail and outgoing items for despatch, and the different services that are available.

Mail services

There are several services to choose from, depending upon:

- whether the item is valuable, urgent or very important
- whether you need proof of posting and/or delivery
- the type of item and its destination.

Courier services

Some services are local, others operate throughout the Caribbean and/or overseas. They ensure that items arrive promptly, regardless of size or weight. Local packages are delivered immediately. Overseas deliveries usually take 24 hours within the Caribbean and to North America, and 2–3 days to Europe. Items are tracked and the sender is compensated if there is loss, damage or late delivery.

The high cost is often considered worth paying because it is speedy and safe for urgent or important items. It is also convenient and confidential, and there is a door-to-door delivery and collection service.

FIND OUT MORE

Check your Yellow Pages for local couriers. Then research Caribbean services, such as www.laparkan.com or www.liatcargo.com. Compare these with international operators, such as Fedex, DHL or UPS.

Postal services

When you are choosing a postal service you must consider the following points.

- How urgent or important is it? This will affect the **class of mail**.
- How do you want it to arrive? This will affect the **delivery options**.

The options available are shown in Table 2.11.1.

SkyBOX

This service is available to everyone in the Caribbean. It means that people can buy goods online in the US and have them delivered to their home in the Caribbean even if the seller does not deliver outside the US. The goods are sent to a Miami address and then despatched to the purchaser's home address. Similar services are offered by other firms, such as Laparkan.

Table 2.11.1 Classification of mail and delivery options

Classification of mail		Delivery options	
Express	The fastest but most costly way of sending mail. All items are tracked	Registered	Used for money and valuables. The cost depends upon the value. The item is insured against theft, loss and damage. The recipient must sign on delivery
Priority	Registered and recorded delivery takes priority over ordinary mail, so it is used for valuable or important items	Express delivery	This has priority over other deliveries
First class	This mail usually arrives the next day, so it is used mainly for correspondence, invoices and small packages	Recorded delivery	Used for important documents, such as legal papers, when proof of delivery is required
Standard	The cheapest method. Mail takes 2–3 days to arrive, so it is used for routine items and mailshots	Poste restante	This mail 'rests' at a named post office until collected by the addressee. If it is not collected it is returned to the sender

FIND OUT MORE

Decide on TWO occasions when the poste restante service would be used. Then find out how to complete a poste restante envelope.

Procedures for sending and receiving money and parcels

Regulations relating to money and valuables

Money and valuables are sent by courier or by **registered post** and they are insured. It is better to post a money order than cash, but if it is necessary to send cash (and your postal system allows it) make sure the envelope is secure, no banknotes are visible and never indicate that money is enclosed.

If you take delivery of a valuable item then you will probably have to sign for it. Check that the package is undamaged. Then take it to your supervisor immediately *without* opening it.

Parcel post

This is used for items that are too heavy or bulky to go by letter post. Overseas parcels can go by airmail or surface mail, which takes longer but is cheaper. The total cost will depend upon the service used, the size and weight of the parcel and the destination. You can obtain a certificate of mailing to prove that the item was sent. For an extra charge you can track delivery and obtain a signature upon arrival. A customs declaration form, stating the contents, must be completed for overseas parcels.

Parcels are often delivered to the workplace. If you have to collect one from the post office take some ID, any documentation you have received (such as the advice note) and some money in case there are any duties payable.

EXAM TIP

Check that you can differentiate between different postal services and know the benefits of using a courier. And remember how to spell 'poste restante'!

DID YOU KNOW?

Coins should never be sent by mail as they can be damaged by the sorting equipment.

DID YOU KNOW?

Some items are prohibited, such as drugs and alcohol. Others are restricted. You can check the list of restricted items in the *Post Office Guide*.

Table 2.11.2 Packaging checklist

✓	Use a box large enough for the contents and strong enough for their weight
✓	Wrap fragile items individually with bubble plastic or foam sheeting
✓	Fill any gaps with polystyrene chips or scrunched paper
✓	Use wide carton-sealing tape, not sticky tape
✓	Address the parcel clearly and include your own name and address as the sender
✓	If appropriate, add 'Fragile' or 'This way up' labels

DID YOU KNOW?

The main difference between mail handling in small and large organisations is automation. Large firms may have a centralised mail room with specially trained staff and equipment that processes mail automatically.

KEY TERMS

Remittances are payments, such as cheques or money orders.

DID YOU KNOW?

Empty envelopes are normally retained for 24 hours in case of queries about missing enclosures.

Packaging

Good packaging means parcels arrive intact (see Table 2.11.2).

Procedures for dealing with incoming and outgoing mail

Incoming mail

The sequence of events for handling incoming mail is as follows.

- **Receiving mail**. Mail is delivered, or collected from a post office box, each morning. It is then **pre-sorted** and 'Personal' or 'Confidential' items are set aside to be delivered unopened. Envelopes are usually opened using a **letter-opening machine**.
- **Recording mail**. Some businesses, such as solicitors or accountants, record every item of received mail in a special mail register. Most commercial firms do not.
- **Stamping mail**. All mail, other than financial or legal original documents, is date stamped.
- **Remittances and registered mail** are always recorded. The date and time received are noted. The remittance book records the amount received. The record for registered mail states the recipient's name.
- **Enclosures** are checked and attached to the main document by a staple or a paper clip. Any omissions are noted on the document and initialled.
- **Circulars**, such as journals, may need to be seen by several staff. A circulation slip is attached, which lists the names of those who need to see it and the office to which it must be returned.
- **Routing of mail**. Mail is sorted into departments with 'Urgent' or 'Personal' items on the top to be delivered promptly.
- **Archiving** means storing items that are no longer referred to regularly – such as a journal that everyone has seen. This is covered on page 68.

Outgoing mail

The procedures for despatching mail are as follows.

- Mail is sorted into different categories for despatch, for example, first class, second class, parcels and special items, such as express, registered or recorded delivery. Urgent and important items are processed first and the correct forms are completed. All items should be sealed or securely fastened.
- Envelopes and parcels are weighed and the postage rate is calculated before a stamp is affixed or the envelope goes through the franking machine (see Table 2.11.3).
- The mail is collected or taken to the post office.

Mailing lists

These are names and addresses of customers and/or suppliers that are usually stored on a computer so that labels can be printed quickly and easily. Letters can be addressed quickly by **mail merge** when the text of a letter is combined with selected names from the mailing list.

Postage books

These are used to record the amount spent on outgoing mail each day so that a business can keep track of its postage costs. They are not usually needed if a franking machine is used as these automatically keep a postage record (see Table 2.11.3).

The automation of mailing activities

Many small businesses use a franking machine and create mailshots by mail merge. Automated equipment is likely to be used when bulk mail is prepared regularly, such as by banks and insurance companies.

DID YOU KNOW?

Franked mail is never put into an ordinary mail box. It goes in a special envelope and is handed over the post office counter.

Table 2.11.3 Mailing equipment, its functions and benefits

Item	Function	Benefits
Letter openers	Automatically opens mail by taking a thin slice off the top of each envelope	Opens a large number of envelopes quickly without damaging the contents
Mail merge	Combines word-processed documents with the mailing list	Enables mailshots to be produced quickly
Addressing machine	Prints addresses onto envelopes automatically	Speedy method of addressing multiple envelopes
Postage scales	Weighs and calculates postage accurately	Digital scales are programmed with the latest postage rates and calculations are done by pressing a button
Franking machines	Puts a printed impression on each envelope and prints labels for parcels	No need for stamps. A printed impression can include the company logo and return address as well as the postage rate. The machine keeps a record of postage costs
Collating machines	Combines several pages into a multi-page document	Saves assembling a long document manually. (Note: collators are now a common feature of office photocopiers)
Folding, inserting and sealing machines	These functions are often combined into one machine that feeds the contents towards an envelope, folds the contents, inserts them and seals the envelope automatically	Automatically processes bulk mailings quickly and easily

TEST YOURSELF

1 a   Identify FOUR steps in the procedure for handling incoming mail.
   b   Recommend THREE types of mail room equipment that would help a business to process outgoing mail more easily.

Now check your answers against those on the accompanying CD.

EXAM TIP

Always read the question carefully! In question 1 the second part is about outgoing mail. So answering 'A letter opener' would not gain you any marks.

SECTION 1: Multiple-choice questions

1 A telephone caller is phoning his bank at 11am. The greeting he should hear is:

  a   Hi, this is Jerome, what can I do for you?

  b   Hello there, who do you want?

  c   Hi there, how can I help you today?

  d   Good morning, Island Bank, Jerome speaking.

EXAM TIP

Remember – you should only choose one right answer for each question here.

2 A telephone salesperson works from home and is connected to head office by computer. This is an example of:

  a   Teleconferencing.

  b   Videoconferencing.

  c   Telecommuting.

  d   Telemarketing.

3 Benefits of VOIP include:

  i   Cheaper calls than cellphone service providers.

  ii   Can use video as well.

  iii   Can use when away from the office.

  iv   Free for computer-to-computer calls.

  a   i, ii and iii only

  b   ii, iii and iv only

  c   None of the above

  d   All of the above

4 The best type of visual communication to show the percentage of money spent on different types of equipment (such as mail room, reprographic, filing and IT) is:

  a   A pie chart.   c   A bar chart.

  b   A line graph.   d   A histogram.

5 Misunderstanding information because the message included several regional or local expressions is a communication barrier caused by:

  a   Cultural/personal bias.

  b   Semantics/language.

  c   Time constraints.

  d   Literacy skills.

6 To wrap a large parcel correctly you need to:

  i   Use a strong box.

  ii   Ensure the contents cannot move around inside.

  iii   Put packing signs or signals on the outside.

  iv   Tie up the parcel with string.

  a   i and ii only   c   i, ii and iii only

  b   iii and iv only   d   All of the above

7 A characteristic of a matrix organisation is:

  a   There are many staff and they work at various different levels.

  b   Staff often work in project teams and are involved in decision making.

  c   Most decisions are made by head office and passed on to branch managers.

  d   The manager is independent and can make their own decisions.

8 A travel schedule will usually include:

  i   The price of a ticket.

  ii   Times of departure.

  iii   Times of arrival.

  iv   A map showing the destination.

  a   i and ii only   c   ii and iii only

  b   iii and iv only   d   All of the above

9 To fit A4 paper into a DL envelope it should be:

  a   Folded once – in half.

  b   Folded twice across the centre.

c Folded twice – first in half, then in half again.

d Kept unfolded.

10 Benefits of using a franking machine include:

  i No need to buy stamps.

  ii Envelopes are sealed automatically.

  iii There is an automatic record of postage costs.

  iv The postal impression can include a return address.

a i, ii and iii only

b ii, iii and iv only

c i, iii and iv only

d All of the above

Further practice questions and examples can be found on the accompanying CD.

SECTION 2: Short answer questions

1 Describe TWO types of telephone calls for which you would ask the operator to assist you.

2 A recent visitor to your business, Samuel Fisher, has just phoned to say he left several business documents in a red folder and some gold cufflinks in his hotel room. He stayed at the Blue Water Hotel from Monday to Wednesday last week. Write a telephone message for your office administrator summarising his call. His cellphone number is (001) 5103 794484.

3 Describe THREE items of equipment that you would expect to find in an automated mail room.

4 Identify TWO benefits of using email to communicate with overseas offices.

5 Identify the best way to despatch each of the following.

  a Send an expensive watch for specialist cleaning.

  b Return a passport urgently to a visitor at a nearby hotel who is leaving tomorrow.

  c Send a copy of a travel schedule to a colleague working at home.

  d Send mail to a representative who will be visiting Guyana next week.

6 Draft a memo to a new office employee, Tamika Goodman, in which you identify TWO benefits and TWO problems with using the internet as a source of reference.

7 Identify FOUR steps in the procedures for handling outgoing mail.

8 Your school has received a letter from Phillip Moore, an expert in internet business communications who travels around the Caribbean. He met your head teacher at a social event recently and, as a result of their conversation, has now offered to come and talk to your class about his work. He would prefer to come during the morning on a Thursday or Friday next month, when he is visiting your area. Decide on a suitable time and date for his visit and draft a letter, on behalf of your head teacher, to accept his offer. His address is: 14 Harbour Road, Holetown, St James, Barbados.

9 Draft a memo to your office administrator in which you identify TWO benefits and TWO drawbacks of automated switchboards.

10 Write an email to your friend, Sophie King, who has just moved to your territory from the UK, describing SkyBOX and the benefits of using this service.

Further practice questions and examples can be found on the accompanying CD.

3 Recruitment and orientation

3.1 Finding job information and seeking employment

LEARNING OUTCOMES

By the time you have completed this section you should be able to:

- identify sources of information for job opportunities.
- outline factors to be considered when seeking employment.

Introduction to recruitment and orientation

Whenever you apply for a job there are certain factors to bear in mind to make sure that you only target suitable vacancies. This unit covers all of these aspects, as well as appropriate sources of information so that you can start your job hunt in all of the right places.

Sources of job information

There are many sources where you can find information on specific career opportunities as well as general information to help you find the best job for you. You can obtain help to prepare a good résumé and to find out how to look your best and perform well at an interview. These are summarised in Table 3.1.1.

Table 3.1.1 Sources of job information

Source of information	Brief description
Newspaper	Your regional newspaper will often display job advertisements and job listings in the Classified section. Some also publish special employment features for job seekers and advertise job vacancies online, for example www.tntcareernet.com/TrinidadGuardian
Employment bureau/agency	The Ministry of Labour for many territories provides free help to job applicants. Private employment agencies are listed in your local Yellow Pages and online. These agencies normally do not charge applicants for finding them a job. Many also offer temporary or seasonal employment
Electronic media	Your regional Ministry of Labour may provide information online including a searchable job database. Many businesses advertise job vacancies on their website
Personal contact	You may hear about a vacancy from someone you know – a neighbour, friend, relative or your teacher. This is often called **networking** – using people you know as resources to help you
Trade journals	These contain advertisements for job vacancies in specific trades
Company newsletters	These may be given to employees as hard copies or may be available on the staff intranet. Some vacancies may be restricted to internal applicants
Magazines	General magazines give guidance on looking your best, such as http://caribbeanbelle.com

KEY TERMS

Networking means using your contacts to find out information.

FIND OUT MORE

Keniesha lives in Antigua and has listed the *Antigua Observer*, the website www.searchantigua.com/classifieds and the Notices section of the government website as sources of job information. Make a similar list for your territory and include at least one employment agency. If you live in Antigua, check that Keniesha's list is up to date and add three more sources of your own.

Factors to consider when seeking employment

You should be able to assess job opportunities to ensure that you will be doing a job you enjoy, earning enough money to live and working in a location that suits you. This means carefully considering the factors listed in Table 3.1.2.

DID YOU KNOW?

LinkedIn (at www.linkedin.com) is a social networking site for professionals who want to keep in contact with people in their own industry.

Table 3.1.2   Factors and considerations

Factor	Considerations
Career interest	What career do you want to follow? How do you see yourself in five years' time? What jobs will act as stepping stones to help you to achieve your goal? As an administrator you could work for the government or a private business, in areas as varied as retail and banking. You could work in several different areas, for example, reception, information management, sales, human resources or accounts
Job description	The job description will identify the duties and responsibilities of the job holder and state the minimum qualifications and experience required for the job. Check that you meet these. If you do not, it is unlikely that you will be given an interview
Personal taste	Are you shy and prefer to work behind the scenes, or would you enjoy helping customers? Are you happy to be behind a desk or would you prefer a job where you travel around? Would you prefer to do more specialised work in a large organisation or work in a small business where you know everyone?
Training and qualifications	What qualifications do you have now? What additional qualifications do you need to achieve your goals and when/where can you obtain these? Can you train on the job or would you be able to study part time?
Salary, **fringe benefits**	What salary is being offered – and can you live on it? Are there any fringe benefits, such as medical care, dental treatment, free uniforms or discounted shopping?
Location	How long will it take you to get to work and how much will your travel cost? Will you be near to your friends and family, or will you have to move away from home? If you have to move, what would your living costs be?
Image of the firm	Does the business have a good reputation? Will you be proud to say you work there? How well known is it in your area? What do people say about the working conditions?
Career advancement	If you work hard, will there be opportunities for promotion? Will the job give you a chance to develop and improve your skills and knowledge? Or is it a dead-end job with few prospects for improvement?

TEST YOURSELF

1 Your friend Kareen has seen a job advertisement for a hotel receptionist. Suggest FIVE factors she should consider before she makes an application and, for each one, suggest TWO questions she should ask herself.

Now check your answers against those on the accompanying CD.

KEY TERMS

Fringe benefits are additional items paid for by the employer, on top of salary.

LEARNING OUTCOMES

By the time you have completed this section you should be able to:

• prepare applications for a job.

DID YOU KNOW?

Many organisations produce a **job description** that lists the main elements of a job and the duties of the job holder. This will give you more insight into the tasks you would be doing.

Figure 3.2.1 Why should you practise on a photocopy of the form?

DID YOU KNOW?

You can often save an online form before you send it. You can then ask someone to check it with you first.

DID YOU KNOW?

Many application forms contain a special section where you have to say why you want the job. This is similar to the type of information you would put in a job application letter (see page 59).

Procedures for making applications

At some stage you will make your first job application. You are likely to find that there is quite a formal procedure to follow, because the organisation is making a considerable commitment if it hires you. It therefore wants to be certain that, as far as possible, you are the best person for the job. Knowing the procedure to follow increases your chances of success. So, too, does knowing about the job itself, because this means you can target your application more effectively.

Application forms

Many organisations send standard application forms to applicants and some make these available online. Job applicants often make silly mistakes when completing them, from scruffy writing to writing the current date instead of their date of birth. This can eliminate them right from the start! The main points to note are shown in the checklist in Table 3.2.1.

Table 3.2.1	Checklist for completing an application form
✓	Photocopy the form and practise on the copy
✓	Collect all of the information you need before you start, for example, examination results
✓	Read the form through before you start, and note any parts that you must leave blank
✓	Check what type of pen you must use and whether BLOCK CAPITALS are required
✓	Write neatly and *think* about what you are doing
✓	Check if you need to include names of referees – and get their permission first
✓	Think about your answers in relation to the space you are allowed
✓	Double-check your spelling, grammar and punctuation
✓	Ask someone, whose advice you respect, to check your practice form
✓	Complete the original form slowly and carefully and take a photocopy before you post it
✓	If you make a mistake, check the form to see if there are instructions about what to do. If not, use a *tiny* amount of correction fluid rather than cross out lots of text
✓	Reread the form before you go for interview to remind yourself what you said

FIND OUT MORE

Check out Scotiabank's recruitment process online by following their Careers link at www.scotiabank.com. You can also find hints and tips on how to prepare for an interview.

A curriculum vitae or résumé

There is very little difference between these documents at this stage of your career. Both summarise your achievements to date.

- A **CV** is the longer document. It is divided into specific sections, such as your personal details, education, professional qualifications, employment details/experience and personal attributes. This information is obviously limited if you have not yet worked anywhere or if you have only a few qualifications.
- A **résumé** is a brief summary about you. It is normally one page long and focuses on the most relevant and important aspects of your qualifications and experience to the job you are applying for.

Both documents are your adverts, about yourself, to an employer, so they must look professional and be error free.

Cover letters

You should never send a CV or a résumé to an employer without a cover letter. See pages 59–60 for how to write these.

See pages 59–60 for how to write these.

DID YOU KNOW?

You can download a variety of résumé and CV templates if you use Word.

FIND OUT MORE

Find samples of CVs and résumés online at the Green Light Project website (http://greenlightscholarships.com/career-advice) and tips for writing one at the National Employment Service of Trinidad and Tobago website (www.nes.gov.tt).

DID YOU KNOW?

Employers often ask questions about claims on a CV or résumé and they may ask for proof. So *never* lie or exaggerate about what you have done!

TEST YOURSELF

1 Practise writing a résumé by preparing your own. Use the template shown in Figure 3.2.2 as your guide.

Now check your answer against the one on the accompanying CD.

YOUR NAME
Address
Home and mobile telephone numbers
Email address

Education
- Name of high school, dates attended.

Qualifications
- Give date taken and state if you are awaiting results.

Work experience
- Include any part-time work or internships you have had.
- Put these in date order and summarise your duties.

Other achievements
- Include any certificates, diplomas or awards you have gained, for example, leadership awards, sporting trophies or school prizes.
- Add any volunteer work that you are regularly involved in.

Personal interests and hobbies
- Do not just put computer games or watching TV. It will not make you sound very interesting to an employer.

Additional skills
- List any computer or language skills that you have.
- Add any other job-related personal skills.

DO NOT SIGN YOUR RÉSUMÉ! IT IS NOW COMPLETE.

Figure 3.2.2 | Template for a student résumé

Writing letters

By the time you have completed this section you should be able to:

- prepare applications for jobs
- prepare other types of letters.

Writing job application letters

You first saw how to write and set out a letter on page 27. Look back at that page now to refresh your memory.

There are two types of letter that you may have to write when you apply for a job.

- A **job application letter** is sent if there is no application form and you have not been asked to send a CV or résumé.
- A **cover letter** is sent if you are attaching a CV or résumé. Less information is needed than for a job application letter, because most of it is in the document you are sending with the letter.

Table 3.3.1	Checklist for writing letters to an employer
✓	Always use business layout (see opposite) and put your home address at the top
✓	Then put the current date, in full, for example 29 April 2012
✓	Put the title, name and address of the person you are writing to
✓	Start with an appropriate salutation, for example, 'Dear Mrs Isaacs'
✓	Put a heading – such as the job title or vacancy number if you are applying for job
✓	Write three or four paragraphs using standard business phrases: • The *first* paragraph introduces the topic. Get to the point! • The *second and possibly the third* paragraphs go into more detail • The *final* paragraph concludes the letter
✓	End with the appropriate complimentary close (for example 'Yours sincerely'), then put your name
✓	Put 'Enc' if you are enclosing something, such as your résumé

The content of a job application letter

Points to note

- If you do not know the name of the person to send it to, address your letter to the Human Resources Manager and start 'Dear Sir or Madam'. Then remember to end it with 'Yours faithfully'.
- The letter should be fairly short, normally three or four paragraphs.
  - The *first* paragraph should say where you saw the advertisement (or found out about the job) and state that you would like to apply for the position.
  - The *second* paragraph should give general background information about yourself at school or college. Then go into more detail about your qualifications and any work experience you have done.
  - The *third* paragraph should say why you want the job or would like to work for this organisation – or anything else to make your application different and interesting.
  - The *final* paragraph should say that you are available for interview at any time or state when you are not available.

Notice how in Figure 3.3.1 Tamika uses the information that the job was in the sales department and that team-working skills were required to target her application.

278 Clifton View
St John
BARBADOS
Tel: (246) 283 4837
Email: tamika.260@hotmail.com

6 July 2012

Ms Rachel Clarke
Human Resources Manager
WPD Financial Services Ltd
Hastings Square
BRIDGETOWN
B10110

Dear Mrs Clarke

TRAINEE ADMINISTRATION ASSISTANT

I would like to be considered for the position of trainee administration assistant in your sales and marketing department, which was advertised in the *Barbados Advocate* last Friday.

In June I took eight CXC qualifications at Westmere School and I am now awaiting the results. The subjects I took were: English A, Mathematics, Principles of Business, Spanish, Office Administration, Electronic Document Preparation and Management, Information Technology and Music. I was a conscientious student in all of these subjects and I am predicted to achieve good grades.

I would very much like to be considered for this job for several reasons. I have thoroughly enjoyed studying Office Administration and IT, and these were two of my best subjects at school. Last year I took part in our school's Youth Internship programme during my summer vacation. I worked in the office of the Everysports Store in Hastings, assisting the administrator, and I helped with the filing and photocopying. I also answered the telephone and took messages, and prepared documents using Word as part of a sales campaign they were doing at the time. I found this work very interesting and really enjoyed helping customers, too. This made me decide that working in a sales department as an administrator would be my ideal position.

I am a keen and conscientious worker. I am also used to working in a team – both at Everysports and as a member of the school concert band.

I can attend for interview at any time.

Yours sincerely

Tamika Haynes

Tamika Haynes

| **Figure 3.3.1** | A job application letter |

Cover letter

Points to note

- The layout of the cover letter is exactly the same as for a job application letter – internal address, date, etc.
- Again, put the job title as a heading and include any reference number.
- This time, aim for four paragraphs.
  - The *first* paragraph should be the same as an application letter.
  - The *second* paragraph should give some general background information and refer to the CV or résumé that you are enclosing.

DID YOU KNOW?

There is an easy way to write all letters – look at Table 3.3.1.

EXAM TIP

Always use the information given in the scenario that accompanies the examination question to help focus your letter. In real life, always use the information in a job advert to target your application more precisely.

- The *third* paragraph can mimic the job application letter – summarise why you really want this job and would be the ideal candidate.
- The *fourth* paragraph can be the same as the job application letter.
- Do not forget an appropriate complimentary close, your name and put 'Enc' below, because you are enclosing something.

More letters

Follow-up letters

Once you have submitted an application various things can happen.

- Nothing. You do not know whether the application has been received, so you decide to find out.
- You are told there are no current vacancies or the vacancy has been filled. So, some time later, you decide to see if there is a new vacancy.
- You attend an interview, are offered the job and decide to accept it.
- You attend an interview, are offered the job and decide you do not want it, so you have to write and say so.

Table 3.3.2 | Example content of follow-up letters

The opening paragraph introduces the main topic.	
No reply to application/ No vacancy at the time	On [date] I wrote to you about the above vacancy [this relates to your heading] and enclosed my résumé.
Acceptance/Non-acceptance of job	Thank you for your letter of [date] offering me the position of trainee administrative assistant in your sales department.
The second paragraph goes into more detail. If there is a lot of information, split this into two paragraphs.	
No reply to application	I have not yet had any response to my application and I was concerned that it may have been lost in the mail. [Then say how much you want to work for them, and why.]
No vacancy at the time	At the time, you contacted me to say that the position had been filled and there were no further vacancies. As this was more than six months ago, and as I have always been very keen to work for your organisation, I wanted to contact you again to see if the situation had changed. [Add a third paragraph if you have improved your qualifications or experience and want to mention this.]
Acceptance of job	I am delighted to accept your offer [confirm salary, benefits and other main terms and conditions] and can start for work, as agreed, on [day and date].
Non-acceptance of job	I regret that since attending the interview my circumstances have changed and I am therefore unable to accept your kind offer. [Or you might state this is because you have decided to accept an alternative job.]
The closing paragraph is often just a simple, appropriate ending that relates to what will happen or the action now expected.	
No reply to application/ No vacancy at the time	I would be very grateful if you could let me know. [You could also offer to resend the information that you sent previously.]
Acceptance of job	I very much look forward to becoming a member of your organisation.
Non-acceptance of job	I would like to take this opportunity of thanking you for the courtesy you showed me during the interview.

Other types of letters

Once you start work you still may need to write a letter as an employee:

- because you decide to resign from the job
- because you want to apply for special leave, for example, to travel or study
- to acknowledge a special opportunity or invitation.

The trick to writing different types of letters is to understand how letters are structured and to know a few appropriate phrases to use. If you also know how to set out a letter (you already know this) then you can use these skills no matter what type of letter you may have to write. Use Tables 3.3.2 and 3.3.3 to help you.

DID YOU KNOW?

Although letters must be polite, it is not a good idea to overuse the word 'please'. Other phrases such as 'I would be grateful' are often better.

Table 3.3.3 Example content of other types of letters

The opening paragraph	
Resignation from job/ Application for leave	For the past 12 months I have worked as an assistant administrator in the sales department.
Acknowledgement letter	I refer to the recent award I received as most promising new employee, together with a cheque for $50.
The second paragraph	
Resignation from job	During that time I have enjoyed my work and the opportunity it has given me to develop my skills. As a result, I have now been offered a more senior position at another organisation and would therefore be grateful if you would accept my resignation.
Application for leave	I have recently been offered the opportunity to join a group who will be trekking in the Andes for six weeks to raise money for a children's charity. As this is longer than my annual leave entitlement, I would be grateful if you would consider allowing me unpaid leave to enable me to take part.
Acknowledgements	I was delighted to receive this award and very moved that my efforts over the last few months have been recognised.
The closing paragraph	
Resignation from job	I will, of course, miss everyone very much and would like to take this opportunity to thank you for all the help, guidance and support you have given me since I started work here.
Application for leave	I hope you will be able to look kindly on my request and look forward to hearing from you.
Acknowledgement letter	Please accept my personal thanks for supporting me.

TEST YOURSELF

1 Your boss, Quincy Jones, the sales manager at WPD Financial Services, has agreed that you can go trekking in the Andes and you are delighted. How would you draft out the letter to acknowledge and thank him? Note that all of the information you need is included in this section (the address is shown in Figure 3.3.1).

Now check your answer against the one on the accompanying CD.

Job interviews

LEARNING OUTCOMES

By the time you have completed this section you should be able to:

- explain factors to be considered when preparing for a job interview.

DID YOU KNOW?

Be aware that a phone call could be the unofficial start of your interview. Use your best business technique when you answer the phone (see page 44).

FIND OUT MORE

Look back at the checklist for job interviews on page 20 to refresh your memory of the key points.

Figure 3.4.1 You do not have to look drab to look businesslike

Factors to consider

The aim of making a job application is to achieve an interview. If you are successful you will then receive a letter or telephone call inviting you to attend on a certain date. Meanwhile you should prepare well so that you make the best possible impression.

Selection of attire

Well before the interview you should decide what to wear. This will give you time to ensure that your outfit is freshly laundered. If you do not own any suitable clothes, you need to go shopping or borrow something. Remember, an interview is a formal event, so dress conservatively but not as though you are attending a funeral. Check out modern business clothes in a magazine. Remember that your grooming will also be on show, so use the checklist in Table 3.4.1 to ensure you look your best.

Table 3.4.1	Interview attire and grooming checklist
✓	Choose clothes that are loose fitting and crease resistant
✓	If you are female, check that your skirt is below your knee and that you do not show any cleavage
✓	A suit in a muted colour, or a skirt/loose trousers and blouse/shirt is ideal. Men should also wear a tie
✓	Shoes should be clean and businesslike – no trainers or sandals! Women should wear black or brown smart shoes with a moderate heel
✓	Well-cut, neat, freshly washed hair is essential
✓	Restrict jewellery to a watch and (for women) one pair of earrings
✓	You need clean, manicured/trimmed nails. Any polish, if you are female, should be muted. Make-up should be subtle
✓	Choose light perfume or aftershave and use sparingly

Deportment

Your deportment and conduct at the interview will be observed by everyone – including the person who greets you. Never be late or chew gum. Check how long your journey will take. Other important things that you *should* do are listed below.

- Switch off your cellphone before you enter the building.
- State your name and who you have come to see. Smile and answer questions pleasantly. Try to strike a balance between giving a full answer to the question and not talking too much or providing irrelevant information.
- Breathe deeply to conquer your nerves, and do not fidget or keep checking your watch.

- Be prepared to shake hands with the interviewer by carrying your bag or folder in your left hand.
- In the interview room, sit up straight, smile and make eye contact.
- Answer questions honestly. If you do not know the answer, say so.
- Prepare to respond to the question: 'Is there anything you would like to ask?'
- At the end, thank the person for seeing you and gather your belongings. Close the door quietly. Say goodbye to the secretary or receptionist as you leave.

Research the organisation

Find out about the organisation. Where is it situated? What does it do? How long has it been in existence? How many people are employed? Is it global, regional or local? What is its mission statement? Have you seen its advertisements?

Start by looking online and checking the website. Visit the library to see if it has been mentioned in newspapers or journals. You might know someone who works there – but allow for personal opinions that may not relate to the job you have applied for.

Types of questions

Questions that an interviewer may ask include the following.

- Why did you decide to apply for this job?
- What interests you about this job?
- What subjects did you enjoy most at school/college?

If you have a gap in your résumé then your interviewer will want to explore this, so be ready with an explanation.

Questions that you could ask the interviewer include the following.

- Will I be able to continue to develop my IT skills?
- What are the exact hours of work?
- If I worked hard, could you say what my promotion prospects might be?

Portfolio, evidence of qualifications

You may decide to take evidence of your work or achievements relevant to the job to your interview. This could include portfolio assessments from on-the-job training, your examination certificates from CXC or other qualifications and relevant references or testimonials. Place everything neatly in a folder.

DID YOU KNOW?

List everything you have done that proves you work hard or can do a good job. If you mention some of these during the interview you will increase your chances of getting the job.

FIND OUT MORE

Check whether your handshake is too limp, too violent or just right by shaking hands with your teacher or a family member and asking for feedback.

DID YOU KNOW?

Finding out about an organisation often gives you an insight into the work you will be doing. You can then think about the type of skills that you should stress that you have.

DID YOU KNOW?

It is not a good idea to ask questions about pay rises and annual leave.

TEST YOURSELF

1 You have just been offered an interview. Draw up a checklist of SIX things that you should do to prepare for the interview.

Now check your answers against those on the accompanying CD.

The work environment

LEARNING OUTCOMES

By the time you have completed this section you should be able to:

• demonstrate knowledge of the requirements of the work environment.

International Labour Organization

Figure 3.5.1

FIND OUT MORE

Check out the ILO website at www.ilocarib.org.tt to see the labour laws that apply to your territory. Find out more about ILO in the Caribbean.

DID YOU KNOW?

One key difference between school and work is that at work you have a legal and contractual obligation with your employer. Your employer will agree to pay you a specific rate for doing a specific job and you will agree to do it to the best of your ability in order to earn that money.

Knowledge of the work environment

There are two aspects that you need to know about: labour laws, and the difference between the culture of school and the culture of the organisation or work environment.

What are labour laws?

Laws cover most of the main aspects of employment. They can be divided into the following main areas.

• Health and safety (see also page 129).
• Equal opportunity and discrimination.
• Industrial relations, including the recognition of trade unions and employer organisations.
• Relations between employer and employee, and conditions of employment, including the minimum wage.

Labour laws and the ILO

All Caribbean countries are members of the International Labour Organization (ILO), which aims to promote the concept of decent work and fair wages throughout the region. The ILO promotes four fundamental aims in the workplace.

• Freedom of association and the right to collective bargaining. This means workers have the right to join a trade union.
• Elimination of forced and compulsory labour.
• The elimination of discrimination in the workplace. This means workers cannot be treated unfavourably for reasons unconnected to the job, such as race, sex, religion, nationality or social origin.
• The abolition of child labour.

Labour laws and CARICOM

Caribbean workers can live and work in any CARICOM country. As a result, the ILO and CARICOM have worked to harmonise labour laws throughout the region. CARICOM has devised four model labour laws that provide a basis for individual territories to develop their own legislation based on ILO standards. These model laws cover:

• equality of opportunity and treatment in employment and occupation
• occupational safety and health in the working environment
• registration status and recognition of trade unions and employers' organisations
• termination of employment.

Culture of school versus the organisation

Everyone remembers their first day at school – and most people remember their first day at work too. This is because they are apprehensive and anxious about what to expect and what will happen. They want to make a good impression and do their best, right from the start, but realise they know very little about the organisation or what they will have to do.

To help, most organisations have an **induction** or **orientation** programme for new recruits. This may last one or two days and covers all of the key aspects that new employees need to know, such as company rules, the layout of the organisation, their rights and responsibilities as employees and the requirements of their new job.

You will also settle down more quickly if you are already aware that there are some key differences between the way your school operates and the way a commercial organisation works. Their expectations of you will be different too. Some of the major differences are shown in Table 3.5.1.

KEY TERMS

Induction or **orientation** is a short programme during which new employees are given the essential information they need to know about the organisation and their new job.

FIND OUT MORE

Talk to someone who works and compare their start and finish times, and their holiday, with those at your school. Ask them what other differences they have noticed between work and school.

Table 3.5.1 Main differences between school and work

School	Work
Bells summon you to class, teachers remind you about homework and project deadlines, and encourage you if things are difficult to do	You are expected to arrive on time, work late if necessary, organise your work and meet deadlines without being constantly supervised or reminded
You will be told which skills you need to develop and how to do this. Your teachers will push you to succeed and also monitor your welfare	You are likely to be expected to take an active interest in your own self-development and welfare, and link this to the aims of the business
You will know everyone and probably chat freely with your classmates at break and sometimes in class. You will also talk about school with friends and family at home	Discretion and confidentiality will be expected about sensitive work-related matters. There will be less opportunity for idle chatter apart from breaks and lunchtimes
If you break school rules you will get a warning, but your teachers will probably want to give you a second chance	If you break company rules you will also get a warning, but for some offences you could be summarily dismissed (sacked)
If you feel ill and you miss a day, it may affect your studies but it is unlikely to inconvenience other students	If you are absent then your colleagues could be badly affected. You should never take unauthorised absence or stay away without good reason
If you dislike someone at school, you may be quite childish in how you deal with this and what you say to them	At work you are paid to get on with your colleagues and work alongside them cooperatively, regardless of your personal feelings
Fundamentally, you are a student and you are at school to learn with people of a similar age to yourself	Fundamentally, you are now an adult, earning a living, and you will be treated as a mature and responsible person by a wide range of colleagues

TEST YOURSELF

1 List FIVE key differences between the culture of your school and a commercial organisation. For each one, explain how you would change your behaviour as a result.

Now check your answers against those on the accompanying CD.

SECTION 1: Multiple-choice questions

1 An example of a fringe benefit is:
   a Your basic pay.
   b Commission on sales you make.
   c Overtime payments.
   d Subsidised meals at lunchtime.

2 You would apply for special leave if you:
   a Want time off at Christmas.
   b Want time off over and above your annual leave allowance.
   c Want to visit family abroad.
   d Feel ill.

3 Suitable documents to put into a portfolio are:
   i   Course attendance certificates.
   ii   Photographs of yourself.
   iii Examination certificates.
   iv   References.

   a i, ii and iii   c i, iii and iv
   b ii, iii and iv   d All of the above

4 Appropriate methods of researching an organisation include:
   i   Looking on the website.
   ii   Phoning the receptionist.
   iii Checking newspaper and magazine articles.
   iv   Listening to local radio.

   a i and iii only   c iii and iv only
   b ii and iv only   d i and ii only

5 An example of discrimination is:
   a Teasing someone and hurting their feelings.
   b Not speaking to someone because you dislike them.
   c Treating someone differently because of their race or colour.
   d Paying different wages to different members of the workforce.

6 A legal right of all employees is:
   i   To be able to join a trade union.
   ii   To get an annual pay increase.
   iii To be paid at or above the minimum wage.
   iv   To work in a safe environment.

   a i, ii and iii only   c i, iii and iv only
   b ii, iii and iv only d All of the above

7 The best way to respond at the end of an interview is to say:
   a Thank you for seeing me.
   b When will I hear from you?
   c Have I got the job?
   d Give me a call if you want to know anything else.

8 You receive a letter offering you a job, but you have decided it is not what you want. The action to take is:
   a Send a text turning them down.
   b Ring them up and turn them down.
   c Accept and see how it goes.
   d Write a letter explaining that you cannot accept.

9 The main role of the International Labour Organization (ILO) is:
   a To find jobs for people who want them.
   b To represent Caribbean territories at international conferences.
   c To encourage Caribbean people to work hard.
   d To promote decent working conditions and wages for everyone.

10 Your friend has listed the following differences between school and work. Identify those that are correct.
   i   You are expected to work harder at school than at work.
   ii   You work longer hours at work than at school.

  iii You have to schedule and manage your own time at work.

  iv You can wear anything you want when you go to work.

  a i and ii only   **c** iii and iv only

  b ii and iii only   **d** i and iv only

Further practice questions and examples can be found on the accompanying CD.

SECTION 2: Short answer questions

1 List FOUR sources of information that you could use to find out about job vacancies.

2 An advertisement for an HR administrator offers additional training, career advancement, fringe benefits and a central location. Explain how each of these factors would influence your decision about whether to apply for the job and add ONE further factor of your own choice that would be important.

3 Identify FOUR types of information that you would include in your résumé.

4 Clearly explain the difference between a job application letter and a cover letter.

5 A new local radio station opened a few months ago – RX100. The address is 15 Main Street, Hopeville. At the start they were advertising for an administrator and a receptionist. You sent in a résumé and a letter, but by then the jobs had been filled and you were told there were no vacancies but to try again another time. You would love to work there as listening to music is one of your top hobbies. Write a follow-up letter, addressed to Julian Barnes, the station manager, to see if the situation has changed.

6 Identify FIVE items of information that it would be useful to know about an organisation before you went for an interview.

7 Explain THREE important issues that are covered by labour laws in CARICOM countries.

8 You have just read the advertisement shown opposite. Write a letter under an assumed name to apply for the position.

 SEABOARD INSURANCE BROKERS LTD

JUNIOR ADMINISTRATIVE ASSISTANT

An excellent career opportunity exists for a junior administrative assistant in our HR department.

The successful applicant will have a good secondary education with at least five (5) CSECs including English and Mathematics, as well as a proven interest in Office Administration. Proficiency in Microsoft Word is essential.

Good interpersonal, oral and written skills are vital, as is the willingness to commit to continued professional development through LOMA e-learning, and/or part-time study for a Private Secretarial Certificate or Business Administration degree.

Apply in writing, quoting reference AA10, to Mr Jerome Adams, HR Manager, Seaboard Insurance Brokers Ltd, Warrens, St Michael, Barbados.

9 Prepare a checklist of SIX steps that you would take to make sure you completed an application form as accurately as possible.

10 List FOUR important differences between the culture of school and the culture of an organisation.

 Further practice questions and examples can be found on the accompanying CD.

4.1   What is records management?

LEARNING OUTCOMES

By the time you have completed this section you should be able to:

• describe the characteristics of an information management system.

Introduction to records and information management

All businesses receive and produce information daily in letters, memos, emails, contracts, invoices and other documents. This information must be stored safely and accurately so that it can be retrieved quickly and easily whenever it is needed. Because many people do these tasks every day, there are normally special procedures in place to make sure they do them in the same way, otherwise important information could easily be lost or mislaid. Information that is no longer required must also be dealt with in order to free up space. Again this must be done correctly.

In this unit you will learn about different ways of storing information and how this is classified, as well as the equipment that is used and the difference between manual and electronic methods of storing information.

Information management systems

Information management systems aim to ensure the efficient control of **records** – both paper and electronic – throughout their life. This means from the time they are created or received until they are disposed of. These systems aim to ensure that records are kept securely and in good condition, and that they can be retrieved easily. When they are no longer needed they are thrown away or **archived**.

Figure 4.1.1   What type of information do you think your school must store?

EXAM TIP

The easy way to remember the cycle is with the following words: 1 Create, 2 Sort, 3 Store, 4 Use, 5 Retain (or Discard).

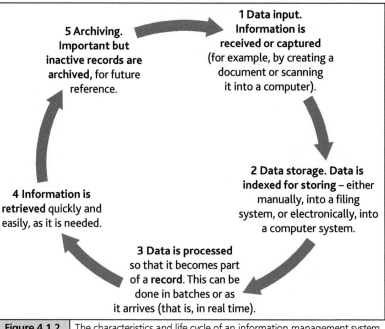

5 Archiving. Important but inactive records are **archived**, for future reference.

1 Data input. Information is received or captured (for example, by creating a document or scanning it into a computer).

2 Data storage. Data is indexed for storing – either manually, into a filing system, or electronically, into a computer system.

3 Data is processed so that it becomes part of a **record**. This can be done in batches or as it arrives (that is, in real time).

4 Information is retrieved quickly and easily, as it is needed.

Figure 4.1.2   The characteristics and life cycle of an information management system

Characteristics of an effective records management system

Major aims of records management relate to finding information quickly and keeping documents in pristine condition. Other key characteristics are listed below.

Table 4.1.1   Characteristics of an effective records management system

Characteristic	Meaning
Access	Levels of access determine which grades of staff can obtain the files. Some files will be available to everyone, others (such as HR records and sensitive financial documents) may be available only to supervisors or managers. Access to confidential electronic files is controlled by using **passwords** that are known only to certain levels of staff
Security	Files must be stored securely. Filing cabinets should be locked at night. Some have special combination locks for added security. These are used for confidential papers and are kept locked all of the time. An electronic filing system must also be kept secure. This means ensuring it is backed up every night and storing the backup copy off the premises
Accountability	Someone must be responsible for the system and for ensuring it operates smoothly. Users must follow the rules and procedures that apply. This prevents unauthorised access and ensures that any files that are borrowed can always be traced
Expansion	The system must be capable of expansion without major disruption. Most successful businesses store more documents over time, not fewer

KEY TERMS

Records are sets of information on a particular topic. For example, a customer record will include all recent enquiries and transactions.

Archiving means removing inactive files from the system. These may be destroyed or moved to long-term storage (see page 76).

DID YOU KNOW?

An **information system** refers to the methods and equipment used to store documents, either manually or electronically. You will learn more about electronic records on pages 70–71.

FIND OUT MORE

Anyone planning a records management system must think about the worst that could happen, such as a fire or flood. The best filing cabinets are fire and impact resistant so that they will not split open if there is an explosion or if they are thrown out of the building in an emergency. Electronic systems should be backed up every night and the backup copy should be stored off site. Find out what precautions are taken by your school or college to ensure that records are kept securely and would be protected in an emergency.

TEST YOURSELF

1 List FOUR steps in the cycle of a records management system and, for each one that you identify, give a brief explanation of what happens at this stage of the cycle.

Now check your answers against those on the accompanying CD.

Maintaining records management systems

LEARNING OUTCOMES

By the time you have completed this section you should be able to:

• describe the duties of a records management clerk.

DID YOU KNOW?

If you save documents that you create in folders on your computer, then you operate your own electronic filing system. If you add tags and keywords to photographs that you store or share online, you are already classifying information electronically.

DID YOU KNOW?

Many digital photocopiers can also be set to scan and index documents automatically into an electronic filing system.

THINK ABOUT IT!

Which documents do you prefer as hard (paper) copies and which do you save on computer. What are the advantages and disadvantages of each of these? Thinking about this should give you an insight into the benefits and drawbacks of having an electronic system.

Manual and electronic records management systems

Every organisation has paperwork that it needs to keep for future reference. Some businesses have a manual system and store documents in folders in lockable filing cabinets (see page 78). Other businesses scan documents that they receive into an electronic records management system. This reduces the amount of paper that they need to keep and so cuts down the space required for the filing system.

You need to understand the differences and similarities between manual and electronic systems and the advantages of using electronic systems.

Table 4.2.1 The main differences between manual and electronic information systems

	Manual information system	Electronic information system
Equipment and supplies	Filing cabinets, file folders, dividers, out sheets or charge-out cards (see also page 75)	Computer, scanner, document management software, storage media
Storage method	Documents are indexed according to the classification system in use; they are sorted and placed in file folders	Documents are scanned into the system, then indexed by the use of keywords, customer numbers, dates and geographic area
Retrieval method	A clerk locates the file folder in the system and removes it, replacing it with an out sheet or charge-out card (see page 75)	Users of the system can search for a document by inputting keywords or the approximate date of inputting
Archiving	Inactive files can be preserved on microfilm or microfiche, or moved to archive boxes in another area, for example, the basement	There is less need for archiving given the storage space available – up to 20,000 A4 documents can fit on one 650 MB CD-ROM

Table 4.2.2 The advantages and disadvantages of electronic filing

Advantages
It saves space, and money too, if less office space is needed
There is less chance of misfiling a document because the system will query any misspellings
Passwords make different user access levels easy to set up
Documents never get tatty or torn, and can be seen by all network users with access to read them

Disadvantages
Set-up costs (equipment and staff training) may be quite high for small businesses
It is less easy to flick through a set of files on a particular topic
Documents *must* be shredded after scanning, or little space will be saved
Documents cannot be seen without access to a computer

Incoming mail is scanned as images.

Images are processed by an administrator on a computer system and stored as index data.

Figure 4.2.1 Processing mail using an electronic filing system

Duties of a records management clerk

The records management clerk will be involved in every stage of information processing, whether the system is manual or electronic.

Table 4.2.3 The duties of a records management clerk

	Manual system	Electronic system
Preparing documents	Checking multi-page documents are complete and in the right order Removing paper clips and stapling the documents (to prevent other papers getting hooked up with them) Repairing any torn papers Punching papers centrally using the ruler on the punch or the central notch as a guide	Scanning received documents into the system Adjusting, changing or enhancing the image as required
Processing data	Indexing documents and classifying these according to the system used Securing documents into the correct folder	Entering key indexing words so that the document can be found easily Setting access levels for each document
Managing records	Making out cross-reference cards Controlling access to the files Ensuring that borrowed files are returned promptly Identifying inactive files and arranging for the disposal or archiving of those records	Ensuring documents are scanned into the system promptly Processing the paper document after scanning (usually this is shredded) Ensuring the system is backed up every day
	Ensuring legal requirements relating to the storage and security of information are met	
Retrieving documents	Obtaining records as requested for authorised users Tracking and obtaining borrowed files that are overdue for return	Locating documents as requested Printing or emailing documents as requested Assisting users who need help to retrieve documents

TEST YOURSELF

1 Identify THREE duties of a records management clerk, and for each one describe TWO tasks that would be carried out if a manual system was in use. Then explain how ONE task would be different if the organisation changed to an electronic system.

Now check your answers against those on the accompanying CD.

EXAM TIP

Make sure you can list two or three tasks for each of the main duties carried out by a records management clerk.

Classification systems

Methods of classification

All records are kept in a particular order. The order chosen will depend upon the type of record and which aspects of it are the most important.

Table 4.3.1	Classification systems	
Method	**Main use**	**Examples**
Alphabetical by name	When the *name* is the most important factor	Customer files Staff (HR) records
Geographical	When the *place* is the most important factor	Branch office files Overseas contacts
Subject	When the *topic* is the most important aspect	A manager's personal files
Numerical	When the files have a unique reference number	Customer files in a large organisation
Chronological	When the *date* is the most important factor	Birth certificates Travel files

Using alphabetical filing systems

These are most suited to small businesses and to a manager's personal files. This is because they cannot be expanded very easily. Some letters are particularly popular ('B' is one example) and soon become congested. Then all of the files have to be reorganised to make more space.

The main advantage is that these systems are *direct*. If you know the name, place or topic then you can go straight to the file that you want. A disadvantage, particularly with subject filing, is that you may need to file papers in more than one place because they relate to more than one topic. In this case you must know how to cross-reference a file (see page 74).

It is important that everyone who uses the system knows the rules for filing alphabetically, and there is more to this than just knowing your alphabet. These rules are summarised below.

Filing alphabetically by name

Indexing order

Your first task is to put each name into its correct **indexing order**. This is because the order used for indexing is not always the same as the usual order. For example:

- Mr Jacob Kent would be indexed as 'Kent, Jacob Mr'.
- The Department of Justice would be indexed as 'Justice, Department of'.

Table 4.3.2 has more examples and shows how these are then put into alphabetical order.

LEARNING OUTCOMES

By the time you have completed this section you should be able to:

- maintain a records management system by electronic and other means.

DID YOU KNOW?

Geographical and subject files are also stored in alphabetical order. So, knowing the rules for alphabetical filing is very important.

DID YOU KNOW?

The danger with classifying by subject is that topics may be repeated by accident (for example, 'staff', 'employees' and 'personnel'). This can be prevented by having a master index that lists all of the topics that are used.

KEY TERMS

Indexing order is the sequence of words, or indexing units, written in priority order for filing.

Table 4.3.2 The rules for alphabetical filing

Rule to follow	Example of indexing order	Rule to follow	Example of indexing order
People		**Organisations**	
Surname first	Adams, Kate	Ignore the word 'The'	Broad Street Journal, The
Short names before long	Adams, Kate Adamson, Joanne	Treat numbers as words	Three Steps Restaurant Two Sisters gift shop
For identical names, follow first name(s) or initial	Adamson, Joanne Adamson, Martin	If names are identical use place to decide the order	Caribbean Airlines Ltd, Tobago Caribbean Airlines Ltd, Trinidad
Initials always come before full names	Ambrose, M Ambrose, Marsha	Initials come before full names (ignore 'and' and '&')	KPMG (St Lucia) K & Z Consultants Kentucky Fried Chicken (St Lucia) Ltd
Treat 'Mac' and 'Mc' as 'Mac' and file before 'M'	MacDonald, T McKay, M Murray, T	Treat 'Saint' and 'St' as 'Saint'	Sagicor Financial Corporation St James Hotel Sea Freight Services Ltd
Ignore apostrophes	O'Sullivan, B Ottey, J	File public bodies under name, or place if the names are identical	Education, Ministry of, Barbados Education, Ministry of, Jamaica
Treat a prefix as part of the name	De Silva, P Dujon, M		

DID YOU KNOW?

If there are too few documents to warrant a new file, odd papers may be put into a 'Miscellaneous' file. There may be just one for the whole system or one for each letter of the alphabet.

Geographical filing

This is used to store records **by area**.

- You must use alphabetical order within each region and subregion, for example:

  Barbados – St John *before* St Joseph

  Belize   – Cayo *before* Corozal

Subject filing

This is used to store records **by topic**.

- Subjects are filed in alphabetical order, for example:

  Canaries *before* Cats

- Broad subjects are usually subdivided, for example:

  Footwear – Boots *then* Sandals *then* Slippers *then* Trainers

FIND OUT MORE

Check your local phone book and Yellow Pages to see how the names of people and businesses are indexed and listed there.

TEST YOURSELF

1 a Put the following names into their correct indexing order: Dr Vivien Jamieson, St John's Primary School, The Judges House, Johnson & Carruthers, Mr Benjamin Johnson, St John's Hospice. Then put them into alphabetical order.

  b List the parishes, districts and/or counties where you live. Put these into indexing order, then put them into alphabetical order. Check you were right by clicking on www.citypopulation.de/America.html, find your own country and look at the order in which they are listed.

Now check your answers against those on the accompanying CD.

LEARNING OUTCOMES

By the time you have completed this section you should be able to:

- maintain a records management system by electronic and other means.

DID YOU KNOW?

Traditionally small cards were used for indexes as they could also be used to keep small amounts of information, such as customer contact details. Today many indexes are held on computer.

FILE NAME	REFERENCE NUMBER
Air Jamaica Ltd	11804
Ambrose and Wilson Ltd	16809
Asgarali Clive	12004
Associated Paint Products Ltd	6090

Figure 4.4.2 An extract from an alphabetical index for a numerical filing system

DID YOU KNOW?

Documents are always stored in date order in a file with the most recent at the top.

Numerical filing systems

Many large organisations store files **by number** because the system can be expanded easily. No reshuffling is needed when all you do is allocate the next available number to a file.

The problem is that you cannot go direct to a file unless you know the number. It is therefore *indirect*, so you need an alphabetical index to help you find a file – or you need the reference number. This is why many organisations quote a reference number on their documents. This helps staff to file the copy in the right place.

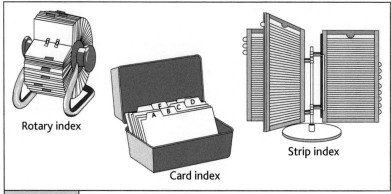

Rotary index

Card index

Strip index

Figure 4.4.1 What type of information would be held on these index cards?

Chronological filing

This is used to store files **by date** and is only suitable for certain types of documents, such as bank statements or petty cash vouchers, where the key identifying feature is the date. In an electronic system the date must be entered in the same format each time. You also need to know whether to use the American system (6.12.2013 = 12 June 2013) or the British system (6.12.2013 = 6 December 2013).

Indexing: methods and procedures for cross-referencing

Cross-reference cards

These are used for files that could be placed under two (or more) names, so that they can be found quickly. A card is made out and stored in the *opposite* place to the file. So if Roxanna Brown changed her business name to Headstart Hair Salon you should:

- rename the file and move it to 'H' in the system
- put a cross-reference card under 'B' which reads as shown in Figure 4.4.3.

> **BROWN Roxanna**
>   See under Headstart Hair Salon

Figure 4.4.3 A completed cross-reference card

Out sheets (or charge-out cards)

These are used to keep a check on borrowed files. They enable the records management clerk to monitor the frequency with which files are borrowed, where they have gone, when they are due back and whether they are overdue for return.

An **out sheet (or card)** replaces a borrowed folder and states who took it and when. A sheet can be attached to the front of each folder stating its title or number. If the folder is removed, the name of the borrower and the date is entered on the sheet, which remains in the filing cabinet. Alternatively, a charge-out card is made out when a folder is borrowed and the card is put in the position in the cabinet where the folder is normally kept. This card may be reused several times for different files. The purpose in both cases is to say where the file has gone. A duplicate card is placed in a tickler file so that the clerk can monitor the return of the folder.

DID YOU KNOW?

One problem with borrowed files is the backlog of papers that cannot be filed until they are returned, so some out cards include a pocket to hold these documents while the folder is missing.

OUT SHEET			
File name:	J D Watson Ltd, Chartered Surveyors		
Date borrowed	Name of borrower	Department	Date returned
24 January	Grace Gaskin	Finance	1 February

Figure 4.4.4 | Example of an out sheet

KEY TERMS

A **tickler system** is used to 'tickle' or jog your memory.

Tickler files

A **tickler system** reminds you what needs doing – in this case, which files are due for return. Each time a file is borrowed a card is placed in the system under the date the file is due to come back. It is then easy to check the cards and chase up any overdue files.

Card indicators

These separate cards and file folders into separate sections (alphabetical or numerical) so that they can be found easily (see the index cards in Figure 4.4.1). In a filing cabinet, the guide cards lead you to specific sections.

Colour coding

File folders, charge-out cards, guides, card indicators and even filing cabinets can be purchased in different colours. If colour is used to denote different types of files then this can make finding files much easier. It also makes it obvious if a file is returned to the wrong place.

Searches and shared databases

Many indexes are created and maintained on computer because the information can be entered and edited easily, and entries can be found quickly by searching on specific criteria. An index list can be created on a word-processing package or more detailed records held on a database.

TEST YOURSELF

1 a Explain TWO benefits of using:

   i   out cards
   ii a tickler system
   iii colour-coded files.

  b A firm of solicitors has changed its name from Richards, Martin and Manley to Manley and Partners. Explain what action you would take and draw up a cross-reference card to cover the change.

Now check your answers against those on the accompanying CD.

Dealing with inactive files and legal stipulations

LEARNING OUTCOMES

By the time you have completed this section you should be able to:

• outline the procedures for dealing with inactive files

• describe the main legal stipulations governing access to, and retention of, documents.

KEY TERMS

Inactive files are those that are no longer used.

DID YOU KNOW?

Solicitors and accountants archive most files because they do not know when a legal case may be reopened, or a tax investigation may take place in the future.

Dealing with inactive files

Over time, cabinet drawers can become full, with no room for new files and no space for more cabinets in the office. It is therefore important that the system is reviewed regularly so that **inactive files** are identified and removed from the main system.

This does not mean that the file can be thrown away. Many need preserving for several reasons.

• There are legal requirements that state how long some documents must be kept, such as tax records.

• The file contains important papers that might be needed in the future, such as documents relating to a legal case that could be reopened.

• The file contains papers of historical interest, for example, government or parish records.

For these reasons, archiving decisions are normally made by a supervisor or manager. The possible options are listed below.

• **Microfilming** preserves documents and reduces the storage space needed. Paper documents are converted into tiny microfilm or microfiche images that can be viewed on a special reader. Microfiche is better because images do not have to be viewed sequentially on a roll of film.

• **Retention periods** govern the length of time certain types of documents must be kept. They take into account the legal requirements relating to documents such as accounts and tax records, payroll information and accident reports, which must all be kept for a minimum number of years. Documents that may be needed in the future will also be retained. These files may be archived, but they must not be destroyed.

• **Disposal of files** is possible for those that are unimportant and inactive. Documents containing sensitive information about staff, customers or financial data should be shredded so that their content is unreadable.

• **Archiving** means putting inactive files in long-term storage. Files must be kept in good condition and clearly labelled. Special archive boxes are available for this purpose.

• **Backing up to external storage media** means scanning archived documents on to CDs or DVDs.

DID YOU KNOW?

Some organisations operate a manual system for current files but arrange for a specialist firm to scan their archived files onto DVDs.

| **Figure 4.5.1** | Why are special storage boxes used for keeping archived files? |

Legal regulations relating to documents

The additional stipulations that should be known by records management staff are summarised in Table 4.5.1.

Table 4.5.1 Legal stipulations and their meanings

Stipulation	What this means
The right of access, and limitations on this right	This is your ability to find out information about yourself or your government. Under a Freedom of Information Act you can obtain information about government activities by requesting a copy of certain documents. Refusal is only possible for specific reasons, for example, if access would threaten national security. In most countries employees can ask to see their own staff record, and only documents containing sensitive information can be withheld. You also have the right to see your own credit reference and correct it if it is wrong, and you can check other information held on you by businesses that you deal with
Infringement of copyright	Copyright laws limit the action that can be taken with an original work (for example, a book, song, film or computer program) that someone else has created. If the business allows this to be copied or distributed freely it will be breaking the law, whether it is found on the internet or in printed form. Organisations can ask the creator for permission or apply for a licence from an appropriate agency, for example, to cover a newspaper article it wants to copy and circulate in a report
Defamation	Defamation law aims to prevent anyone writing or saying false or malicious statements about another individual or organisation. If these are contained in company documents or files then the organisation itself could be sued. This includes emails sent by staff, the content of the website, as well as documents in the company records
Breach of confidence	This occurs if sensitive information is disclosed to a third party, such as someone's medical condition or financial details. Organisations that deal with personal information, such as banks, hospitals and schools must ensure that only authorised individuals can access this. HR departments are responsible for ensuring that staff details remain private
Parliamentary privilege	This enables Members of Parliament to speak freely about issues without worrying that they may be sued for defamation or breach of confidence. This is to enable them to raise questions that they may otherwise not be able to raise
Secrecy provisions	Many organisations have 'trade secrets' or future business plans that they want to keep to themselves. Employees who know about these are usually asked to sign a non-disclosure clause in their contract to prevent them talking about this to anyone. Some suppliers may also have to sign special contracts

TEST YOURSELF

1 You work as a records clerk in the HR department of a large organisation. Explain how legal stipulations relating to the following could affect your work:
   a the right of access
   b defamation
   c breach of confidence.

Now check your answers against those on the accompanying CD.

LEARNING OUTCOMES

By the time you have completed this section you should be able to:

• explain the use of equipment and supplies in records and information management.

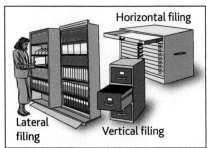

| Figure 4.6.1 | Which types of cabinet have you seen being used? |

EXAM TIP

If you are asked to list filing equipment do not forget to say that for an electronic system you would need a computer and scanner.

DID YOU KNOW?

Box files are ideal for storing papers that cannot or must not be hole punched.

Filing equipment

A manual information system needs a variety of equipment and supplies to ensure that documents are stored correctly and kept in good condition. Three main types of cabinet are used to store files.

• **Vertical filing cabinets** are the most commonly found cabinets in offices. They have between two and five large drawers, although four is the most popular number. They may be made of metal or wood, they are lockable and fitted with a safety mechanism to prevent more than one drawer being opened at once (to stop the cabinet tipping forward onto the user).

Inside the drawers there are usually suspension pockets that hang from side to side, often in a continuous row. Each pocket has a tab at the front, giving the name of the file folder that it contains.

• **Lateral filing cabinets** are wider and not as deep. They are like large open cupboards with a sliding door or blind that can be pulled down when the cabinet is not in use. Instead of shelves there are rows of suspended pockets, each with tabs on the side. File folders are inserted sideways, usually to the right of the tab.

• **Horizontal filing cabinets** are used for documents that are very large or must not be hole punched, such as drawings, maps and photographs. They are often found in an architect's or surveyor's office.

FIND OUT MORE

Filing cabinets are available in a range of colours and can be chosen to match an office colour scheme. Lateral files can be used to divide up space in an open-plan office area. Look around you when you visit your school office or any building where files are kept and note the type of equipment that is being used to store them.

Storage materials and other supplies

A variety of storage materials and supplies are available for holding documents and maintaining the system.

• **File folders** are used to store most papers. They are available in a variety of colours and with optional fastenings. In most organisations the papers are fastened into the folders. In others, it depends upon the type of information being stored.

• **Index cards** are used to record small items of information – turn back to page 74 to see what these look like.

• **Minute sheets** are usually secured to the inside front cover of a folder. They enable people using the file to make comments and requests or record short notes. The minute sheet can also record the movement of the file from one person to another.

FILE MINUTE SHEET
File name/reference number: Travel file for Linford Richards: trip to New York

Date	Comment	Referred to	Date	Initialled
22.4.2013	Costings obtained from Worldwide Travel – agree with Finance.	JT	22.4.2013	PT
23.4.2013	Costings approved.	PT	23.4.2013	JT
10.5.2013	LR now attending meeting before conference – travelling two days earlier – Worldwide Travel rearranging flights.	JT	13.5.2013	PT

Figure 4.6.2 File minute sheet

- **Charge-out cards**   you learned about these on page 75. Can you remember what they are and why they are used?

- **Dividers** separate files so that they are easier to find. You might use dividers yourself in a ring binder to keep your notes neatly.

- **Treasury tags** are one method of securing hole-punched papers together. They are pieces of string with metal or plastic bars at the ends, and they are available in different lengths.

- **Fasteners** are available in plastic or metal for securing papers inside a file folder. Papers can also be secured together temporarily using paper clips or bulldog clips.

- **Microfilm and microfiche** was explained on page 76. To convert documents a special camera is required, as well as a processor and a supply of film (or fiche) or aperture cards. A microfilm/fiche reader and printer is also needed to read documents and/or print them out.

- External **storage media** is used to store documents electronically. CDs, DVDs and USB flash drives are commonly used for this purpose, but larger systems will use external hard-disk drives, CD-ROMs or have the option to store documents on a remote server.

THINK ABOUT IT!

If you were working with two colleagues on a project and you were all gathering information and keeping it in one folder, how helpful would a minute sheet be? What type of comments do you think you might add to it?

DID YOU KNOW?

The latest electronic information systems enable businesses to store their data off site. It is held on a secure server, maintained by a specialist organisation.

FIND OUT MORE

Visit a local office supplier or check out the website of one online, for example, www.brydensxpress.com in Barbados, www.bosstrinidad.com or www.sos.com.jm and see for yourself the type of supplies that they keep.

TEST YOURSELF

1 Identify TWO items of equipment and THREE types of supplies that you would use if you worked as a records clerk. For each one you identify, explain its purpose.

Now check your answers against those on the accompanying CD.

Centralised and decentralised records management systems

LEARNING OUTCOMES

By the time you have completed this section you should be able to:

• differentiate between centralised and decentralised records management systems.

DID YOU KNOW?

'The registry' is the term used for a department that holds records. For example, the Land Registry holds land records.

Figure 4.7.1 A centralised system ensures that everyone's files are stored and maintained properly

Centralised or decentralised?

Organisations have a choice whether to allow each department to maintain its own files (a decentralised system) or whether to set up a central department that is responsible for all aspects of records management. This is known as a centralised records management system.

Whether this is a good idea will depend upon several factors. These include:

• the size of the business and whether it is small or large scale
• the number and type of records that it needs to keep and maintain
• whether the business is situated in one central location or in several small offices
• the number of people who need to access different records.

There are advantages and disadvantages with both systems.

Advantages and disadvantages of centralised systems

Table 4.7.1	Centralised systems – advantages and disadvantages

Advantages
Specialist staff can be employed and trained to operate the system Specialist equipment and supplies can be purchased Major decisions about archiving, retention and access levels can be made and enforced, and will be consistent throughout the organisation Procedures are the same for everyone to follow All documents are kept in one place, which reduces duplication

Disadvantages
It may be more expensive, in terms of staff and space requirements It may be difficult to obtain a file quickly, even in an emergency The equipment and methods of storage may not be appropriate for specialist departments Highly confidential files may still need to be kept in a separate location If a file is lost, there may be no backup or alternative records available

Advantages and disadvantages of decentralised systems

Table 4.7.2	Decentralised systems – advantages and disadvantages

Advantages
Records can be accessed quickly because they are close at hand Equipment and procedures can be appropriate to the type of documents stored, and their use Departmental staff will automatically update their knowledge as they file and retrieve papers in the system Confidential matters remain within the department

Disadvantages
Some departments may keep records efficiently, others may not
There may be duplication of paperwork and records between departments
If a file goes missing, everyone may deny responsibility
Filing procedures and policies about archiving, retention and access levels may vary from one department to another
More equipment and storage space is likely to be needed

THINK ABOUT IT!

Some organisations use a combination of systems. At CXC, most documents are stored and maintained by the Registry, but HR records are kept separately by the HR department. Can you think why?

Small- and large-scale businesses

The most suitable type of records management system will also depend upon the size of the business.

- **Small businesses** will hold a limited number of records and these will be needed by the majority of staff. Therefore they should be easily accessible. The usual method is to locate filing cabinets near to the staff who need access to the files they contain. So, financial records will be kept near to where the accounts staff work, and customer records will be sited near to sales staff or in the sales department.

  As a business grows in size this system can be maintained or changed. It will depend upon the nature of the business. A hotel or a department store will not need to keep as many records as an insurance company or a hospital, for example. So, in a hotel or store it may be quite easy to store all of the records in one area, such as reception or in the administration office.

- **Large-scale businesses** may prefer to introduce a centralised system as this will give better control and accountability. This is why most hospitals store patient records centrally, as a missing record could cause serious problems.

  Some large organisations are choosing to introduce electronic document management systems. The latest systems enable staff from all departments and locations to access any document quickly via the company intranet or even using a web-based system. The staff do not even need to be on the premises to gain access to the files. This is ideal for businesses with offices in many locations.

DID YOU KNOW?

Web-based email systems, such as Gmail or Hotmail, keep your documents safely because they are stored on the Google or Hotmail server until you access them again.

Figure 4.7.2 Can you give two reasons why it is helpful to colour code filing folders – especially in a large, centralised system?

TEST YOURSELF

1 A telecommunications company that operates throughout the Caribbean decides to introduce centralised records management at its head office in Jamaica. Identify THREE advantages and TWO disadvantages of this decision.

Now check your answers against those on the accompanying CD.

SECTION 1: Multiple-choice questions

1 A useful method of securing loose papers is to use:

   a A divider.   c A card index.

   b A treasury tag.   d A folder.

2 Documents that are filed in date order are stored:

   a In subject order.

   b In numerical order.

   c In geographical order.

   d In chronological order.

3 Duties of a records management clerk include:

   i   Monitoring borrowed files.

   ii Filing documents.

   iii Keeping the filing area tidy.

   iv Retrieving documents.

   a i, ii and iii only   c i, iii and iv only

   b i, ii and iv only   d All of the above

4 You keep your customer records in alphabetical order by name. Documents about Professor John McKay should be filed under:

   a P   b J   c M   d K

5 Access is likely to be restricted to files that have information containing:

   i   Future business plans.

   ii Customer names and addresses.

   iii Supplier invoices.

   iv Staff salaries.

   a i and ii only   c i and iv only

   b i and iii only   d ii and iii only

6 Large drawings or artwork should be stored in:

   a A vertical, four-drawer cabinet.

   b A lateral cabinet.

   c A card index cabinet.

   d A horizontal cabinet.

7 Supplier and employee contracts sometimes include a clause to prevent them telling anyone about the work they are doing. This is an example of:

   a Secrecy provisions.

   b Parliamentary privilege.

   c Breach of confidence.

   d Copyright.

8 A tickler system is devised to:

   a Make you work more quickly.

   b Remind you about things to check.

   c Make you laugh.

   d Help you find what you need.

9 A business that could find geographical filing helpful is:

   i   A pan-Caribbean company with offices in many territories.

   ii A large school or college.

   iii An exporter who operates on a global scale.

   iv A multinational banking corporation.

   a i, ii and iii only   c i, iii and iv only

   b i, ii and iv only   d All of the above

10 Scanning and saving documents for access by computer is called:

   a Centralised filing.

   b Electronic filing.

   c Decentralised filing.

   d Automated filing.

Further practice questions and examples can be found on the accompanying CD.

1 Put the following folders into subject order for filing:

Seminars

Publicity – Open Days

Personnel – Training

Publicity – Leaflets

Travel

Publicity – Displays

Presentations

Publicity – Exhibitions

Personnel – Health and Safety

Conferences

Personnel – Welfare

2 Explain the difference between indexing order and alphabetical order.

3 A news agency has several documents to file. Identify the most suitable filing system for each of the following.

  a Supplier details

  b Expenses invoices

  c Correspondence kept on various topics

  d International travel articles by journalists

4 a Change the following list to chronological order using the consistent date style of dd/mm/yy.

Name	Date of birth
Orla Hunte	19 Nov 94
Carl Gibbs	04.11.1993
K Duvalier	March 4 1994
Mia Harper	18 August 1993
Vincent Hunter	Dec 3 1993
Aimee de Freitas	13:03:94

  b Now change the list so that it is in alphabetical order by name.

5 a Suggest THREE actions that could be taken with inactive files that are no longer required.

  b Give TWO reasons why some files may need to be preserved.

6 The following files must be arranged using the geographical system. Rearrange them so that they are in the correct order.

Trinidad and Tobago –	Port of Spain
	Chaguanas
	San Fernando
	Arima
Jamaica –	Kingston
	Port Antonio
	Ocho Rios
	Montego Bay
Barbados –	Bridgetown
	Oistins
	Holetown
	Speightstown

7 Identify THREE types of files that would be classed as containing sensitive or confidential information. Then state TWO ways in which this information should be protected.

8 Identify THREE characteristics of an effective records system.

9 Suggest THREE advantages and ONE disadvantage for a business that decides to change its method of filing from a manual system to an electronic one.

10 Explain the main purpose of each of the following filing systems and give an example of when each one might be used: alphabetical by name, subject, geographical, numerical, chronological.

Further practice questions and examples can be found on the accompanying CD.

5 Reception and hospitality

5.1 The importance of reception

By the time you have completed this section you should be able to:

- assess the contribution of the reception desk to the welfare of the organisation.

Introduction to reception and hospitality

The receptionist is often the first point of contact for visitors and, therefore, influences their perception of the whole organisation. This unit covers the skills and attributes needed to give a professional image, as well as the duties and responsibilities of a receptionist.

Inexperienced receptionists may struggle to appear efficient *and* friendly and helpful, particularly on busy days. This unit will show you how to do this, as well as how to manage appointments and use different reminder systems.

Contribution of the reception desk

Many organisations spend thousands of dollars on an impressive reception area to impress visitors and demonstrate how successful they are. This is ruined if the receptionist gives the opposite impression by being scruffy or uncommunicative.

Organisations with a constant stream of visitors need a dedicated receptionist, so many banks and large insurance companies have a front-of-house person, or receptionist, to greet callers and provide information and guidance. In this case the receptionist(s) will be fully occupied ensuring that each person is dealt with promptly and properly.

Figure 5.1.1 What skills do you think a professional receptionist needs?

Small organisations and businesses with fewer personal callers will expect receptionists to do other administrative duties too, such as maintaining the office diary or appointments book, answering the telephone and responding to email enquiries.

However, anyone who works in this area must carry out the two major roles of reception. These are:

- maintaining effective **interpersonal relationships** between the organisation and members of the public
- promoting goodwill and a positive image of the business.

Maintaining effective interpersonal relationships

A receptionist must greet all visitors in a friendly, professional and helpful manner to create a good first impression of the organisation. They must then help visitors with their individual needs. If they have a simple request, this is straightforward. It is more difficult if the visitor is tired, impatient or not sure what they want.

DID YOU KNOW?

If people are treated courteously and efficiently in reception, they gain a good impression of the business as a whole.

KEY TERMS

Interpersonal relationships are the relationships between yourself and each person that you deal with.

Table 5.1.1	Ten tips for maintaining effective interpersonal relationships
1	Make people feel welcome by making eye contact and smiling when they arrive, even if you are dealing with someone else or are on the telephone at the time
2	Greet a visitor by saying 'Hello', 'Good morning' or 'Good afternoon' and ask how you can help
3	Greet regular visitors by name whenever you can
4	Find out a new visitor's name tactfully. Say 'Could you give me your name please?' not 'What are you called?'
5	If a visitor's arrival needs to be recorded in a visitor log, provide a pen and show the visitor where to write the information
6	If the visitor has an appointment, promptly notify the person they are seeing
7	Talking about neutral topics, such as the weather or the journey, often breaks the ice and helps a visitor to relax
8	If there will be a short wait, tell the visitor about the facilities that are available, such as newspapers, magazines, the water cooler and/or coffee machine
9	If the visitor has travelled some distance, be prepared to point out where the toilets are situated
10	Always check how long visitors have been waiting and, if necessary, remind the person they have come to see

DID YOU KNOW?

Many receptionists work in a team. In this case it is important to be cooperative and helpful to your colleagues, rather than competitive.

DID YOU KNOW?

Goodwill is important because it encourages customers to keep returning to an organisation.

DID YOU KNOW?

In one organisation a rather scruffy gentleman was treated disdainfully by the receptionist. Unfortunately for her he was the president of the company who called in on his day off. These days you cannot assume VIPs are always dressed formally – so beware!

Promoting goodwill and a positive image

Promoting goodwill and being positive is simple when everything is going fine. But if you are stressed, if a colleague is difficult or a visitor is impatient then it is easy to get flustered or grumpy.

Conversely, if you are the new recruit then you may try too hard to be friendly. Chatting to visitors informally can easily appear unprofessional. Remember that a professional receptionist is welcoming and articulate and also tactful and discreet.

Table 5.1.2	Goodwill and positive image checklist
✓	Many receptionists wear a uniform in the corporate colours of the organisation. Otherwise choose clothes that reflect the image that the organisation wants to give to its visitors
✓	Be well groomed at all times and look pleasant, cheerful and welcoming
✓	Check that your desk and the area around you is clean and tidy – so magazines are neatly stacked and dirty glasses or cups are promptly removed
✓	Always be polite and courteous no matter how busy you are
✓	Do not judge your visitors by their appearance. Treat everyone the same
✓	Never make tactless comments about anyone, or discuss other customers or staff with a visitor

TEST YOURSELF

1 List FOUR ways to ensure that you promote a positive image of your organisation when you are dealing with visitors in reception.

Now check your answers against those on the accompanying CD.

The duties, responsibilities and attributes of a receptionist

LEARNING OUTCOMES

By the time you have completed this section you should be able to:

• identify the duties and attributes of a receptionist.

Figure 5.2.1 What information do you need to obtain when a visitor arrives?

KEY TERMS

Procedures are the correct steps to take to carry out a task.

When you **screen** a visitor you ensure they are authorised to be there. This is done by checking that they have an appointment, are on a guest list or have a reservation.

Figure 5.2.2

Duties and responsibilities

This section focuses on the duties and responsibilities that relate to all receptionists.

Receiving and screening visitors

The first stop for all visitors should be the reception desk:

• so they can receive prompt attention and assistance

• for safety and security purposes.

Most business organisations ask visitors to sign a reception register, identifying themselves and the reason for their visit. Visitor badges prove that a visitor is authorised to be on the premises. However, visitors are not usually permitted to roam around unless they are accompanied by a member of staff – and some parts of the building may still be off limits.

The names of visitors are listed in a register. When visitors leave, they sign out and return their badge. This ensures that if there was a roll call in an emergency, they would not be overlooked.

The **procedures** to ensure that you **screen** visitors properly are given in Table 5.2.1.

Table 5.2.1	Procedures for receiving and screening visitors
Type of visitor	**Action to take**
All visitors	Greet each person promptly Ask if you can help them and find out the reason for their visit
Visitors with an appointment	Ask for their name and check their appointment on your system Note down their arrival Tell the person they are meeting that they are in reception Ask them to complete the reception register and then to be seated Point out any reading materials and/or facilities to obtain a drink
Visitors without an appointment	If the visitor has no appointment, find out the reason for their visit Ask them to be seated while you find out whether someone can see them. If no one is available, ask your supervisor for advice The action to take will usually depend on what the visitor wants, who they are and the organisational policies. Some organisations are pleased to see casual callers, others insist that a formal appointment is made for a future date

Visitors who want information or advice	Know which information and literature you can give to callers and which is confidential or restricted. If you have any doubts about providing information, ask the visitor to be seated, then ask a supervisor for advice

Coping with problems

Occasionally a visitor may arrive but there is no record of an appointment – possibly because someone forgot to list the appointment or the visitor has got the date wrong. Ask the person to be seated while you check your system for a solution, such as a different time or date. Even if the misunderstanding is the visitor's fault, it is helpful to check whether someone can see them now so that their trip will not have been wasted.

Another problem may arise owing to a long delay before a visitor can be seen. You should be tactful but honest. Apologise, explain the reason for the delay and give the visitor the option of waiting, returning later or rearranging the appointment for another day.

Introducing visitors

Visitors arrive in reception for various reasons. They may be attending or making an appointment, making an enquiry, asking for information, paying a bill or arriving for an interview. The reasons vary depending on the organisation.

Sometimes you need to ask a visitor to wait while you find the best person to help or notify the person they are meeting. When your colleague arrives in reception, you should point out the visitors that are waiting. You may have to make a formal introduction. This is not scary providing you get the names right. There are many rules about social introductions, but in business just remember to start with the most important person's name. This is usually the person who has the most senior job title, for example, chief executive, president or director. For example:

'Mr Lewis, this is Mr Jake Solomon, the IT consultant from Devine Associates. Mr Solomon, this is Mr Abraham Lewis, our IT director.'

DID YOU KNOW?

If you are handed a business card (see pages 88–89), this will tell you the visitor's name and title and the organisation they represent. Otherwise, write the visitor's name on your notepad so you do not forget it.

Maintaining the reception register

You already know that a reception register keeps track of all visitors to the organisation. It may be kept in paper form (as a visitor's book) or electronically on computer. Your task is to make the entry on

DID YOU KNOW?

Some visitor badges have emergency evacuation procedures on the reverse so that if the alarm sounds the visitor knows what to do and where to assemble.

FIND OUT MORE

Find out the steps taken by reception staff at your school when visitors arrive. Do visitors sign a reception register? If so, what information are they asked to provide and why?

DID YOU KNOW?

It is sensible to have information available for callers. That is why banks have financial leaflets and hotels keep tourist information and street plans in their reception areas.

EXAM TIP

Simply remember the first sentence as 'Mr Important, this is Mr Unimportant who does xxx.' Then reverse it.

DID YOU KNOW?

The more you know about the organisation, how it operates and who does what, the easier it is to help a visitor or deal with a problem.

DID YOU KNOW?

Entering the car registration number means that visitors can be found more easily if their vehicle needs to be moved.

EXAM TIP

Remember that a reception register is always completed in chronological (date and time) order.

Figure 5.2.3 Some reception areas are more difficult to maintain than others

DID YOU KNOW?

If something is obviously damaged on delivery, this should be noted by the receptionist on the delivery form that is signed to confirm receipt.

the relevant system by obtaining the information that is needed. If there is a paper-based reception register, some receptionists ask the visitors to make the entries and then check the columns have been completed correctly. You also need to record the time of departure when each visitor leaves.

RECEPTION REGISTER Date: 4 June 2013					
Time of arrival	Name	Organisation	Car registration	To see	Time of departure
0920	Jake Solomon	Devine Associates	H2108	Abraham Lewis	1015
0930	Tina Holland	Sunny Supplies	X7080	Trixie Bishop	1000
0945	Valerie Rae	Prompt Printworks	P5098	Ross Birkett	1030

Figure 5.2.3 Extract from a reception register

Operating a switchboard

Many receptionists also operate the switchboard. The two jobs are often combined because reception must contact all departments to inform them about visitors who have arrived, parcel deliveries and to answer other queries that callers may have.

Switchboards and telephone systems were covered in Unit 2, see page 46.

Receiving letters and parcels

The morning mail will be handled by the mail room. However, during the day other items may be delivered or arrive by courier. The receptionist should sign to confirm the item has been received and arrange for collection for, or by, the addressee. This should be done immediately for urgent items.

Managing and maintaining the reception area

All reception areas must always look clean and tidy, even during busy periods. Hotel reception areas, where people are trying to check in or out, need a porter on duty to move luggage out of the way quickly. Basic reception tasks include:

- keeping the desk area tidy by putting paperwork away promptly, removing cups or glasses that people have used, keeping magazines and newspapers neatly stacked
- ensuring all information and notices are up to date
- arranging for any spillages to be cleaned up promptly.

Receiving and filing business cards

Many business callers will provide a business card on arrival. This will give their name, job title and the name and contact details of the organisation where they work.

The task of the receptionist is to:

- note the visitor's name and company, and give these details correctly to the person they are seeing
- use their name, title and company in any introductions that are made
- hand the card to the person they are visiting or file it, depending upon organisational policy.

The attributes of a receptionist

The personal qualities, or **attributes**, needed are usually specified in job advertisements and these include enjoying meeting and helping other people. Other attributes are shown in Table 5.2.2.

Table 5.2.2	Attributes of a receptionist
Personal appearance	This focuses on good grooming and not good looks. Hair should be tidy and freshly washed, nails must be clean, clothes must be freshly laundered and pressed. If there is no official uniform then the clothes and shoes must be appropriate for the job (no short skirts, tight trousers, T-shirts or low-cut tops). Jewellery should be subtle and make-up restrained
Good temperament	This means having a positive attitude and being even tempered – even on a bad day. Being positive means that you are a 'can do' person and are able to overcome minor difficulties or problems. Being even tempered means that you stay calm in a crisis, even if you have to count to 10 under your breath
Willingness to use initiative	This means being positive and seeing difficulties as a challenge, not a problem. It also means that you will find a way around an issue to help someone. You will think about all of the options and suggest an acceptable solution, or compromise, to solve a problem
Tact	Tactful people do not make statements or comments that would hurt or distress someone. The remarks they make are positive and helpful, and make people feel good about themselves
Articulate	Being articulate means that you speak clearly and use appropriate words to describe or explain a situation. People usually understand you easily. Otherwise, you have the skills, patience and ability to rephrase your statement to help them understand more easily

FIND OUT MORE

Many receptionists wear uniforms designed in the corporate colours of their organisation. Is this a good idea? Check out different types of reception uniforms and decide which you prefer or would like to wear yourself.

KEY TERMS

Attributes are personal qualities and skills that a person possesses.

EXAM TIP

Make sure you are clear about the difference between duties and attributes. They are not the same thing.

TEST YOURSELF

1 List FOUR duties of a receptionist and, for each of the duties that you identify, describe TWO tasks that you would carry out to do your job effectively.

Now check your answers against those on the accompanying CD.

Appointments and reminder systems

LEARNING OUTCOMES

By the time you have completed this section you should be able to:

• manage appointments for an executive using electronic or manual systems

• explain the importance and use of electronic and manual reminder systems.

Managing appointments

Many receptionists have the task of making appointments for one or more executives. This may be done using a manual (paper) system or electronically.

Paper-based appointment systems

These consist of preprinted diaries and appointment books. Some organisations have standard diaries used by all executives. The important thing is that the diary is of adequate size to enter appointments neatly, such as the 'page a day' type. It is also helpful to have preprinted time indicators.

Electronic systems

There are several types of electronic systems available, such as Microsoft Outlook as well as specialist software for use by hairdressers, dentists and doctors. There are several advantages to using an electronic system.

• It is easy to enter, access, store and update information.
• Daily printouts can be made.
• Recurring and routine appointments need to be entered only once.
• Executives can check their updated diary and appointments using their mobile phone.
• On a networked system colleagues can check each other's diaries and make appointments with each other.
• Double bookings are impossible.

The only disadvantage is that if the computer system fails there can be chaos until it is restored. This is why it is useful to take a printout of the following day's appointments the evening before.

Making and cancelling appointments

There are two types of appointments that you will make.

• Those for visitors and customers who want to see an executive. These may be made face to face with a caller or over the telephone.
• Those where an executive wants to visit someone else. These are more likely to be arranged over the telephone or by email.

In both cases there a certain key items of information that must be discussed and agreed.

DID YOU KNOW?

Some electronic systems will send automatic text message reminders to clients and customers a day or two before their appointment.

DID YOU KNOW?

All appointments *must* be entered or amended in the diary promptly, otherwise they can easily be forgotten.

Table 5.3.1 | Making and cancelling appointments

MAKING AN APPOINTMENT

Key information

1 The day and date (you need *both* as a double-check)

2 The time

3 The full name of the other person (spelt correctly) and preferably their job title. If the visitor is a business person coming to you, you also need the name of the organisation they represent

4 A contact telephone number in case arrangements need to be changed

5 The length of time allotted for the appointment

6 The full address, if the executive is making the visit

Procedure to follow

1 Note down which dates and times would be suitable

2 Talk to the other person and agree which would be best

3 Write the appointment in the diary and check that you know all of the key information listed above

4 Be prepared to ask for/give directions, if necessary

5 Confirm the arrangements in writing, if requested

Special note

If the appointment is **provisional** then write it in *pencil* in a manual system. It is entered in ink only when it has been confirmed.

CANCELLING AN APPOINTMENT

Procedure to follow

1 Check if the executive wants to cancel the appointment completely or wants you to reschedule it to a different date/time

2 Contact everyone involved and tell them about the cancellation. Give the reason for cancelling, if this is not confidential

3 Apologise for any inconvenience. If you are rescheduling it, agree an alternative date

4 Erase the pencil entry if it was provisional. Clearly cross through the entry if it is in ink. Delete it from any electronic systems

5 Enter any new arrangements in the diary

Maintaining a diary

If you are responsible for maintaining an executive's diary then you need to know:

- their routine commitments, for example, a weekly departmental meeting. These must be entered in the diary for weeks ahead so that the time is always allocated for this purpose
- any holidays they have scheduled
- their personal preferences, such as 'quiet time' when they do not wish to have appointments made (for example, the first half hour of the morning, when they are reading the mail, or the last hour of the day) and whether they like a regular lunch break or are prepared to have a working lunch
- the general timing of appointments, for example, whether these should be made in one block or spread out over the day

Figure 5.3.1 | What information would you enter in an appointments diary?

DID YOU KNOW?

It is always better to allow a bit too much time for an appointment than too little.

• the length of time to be allocated to different types of appointments

• whether you are also expected to use the diary as a reminder system (see pages 92–93).

You are then in a position to make entries in the diary. Follow the checklist shown in Table 5.3.2.

Table 5.3.2	Checklist for maintaining a diary
Note that items 1, 3 and 4 apply only to paper-based diaries	
✓	**1** Your handwriting must be clear and the names of non-regular visitors should be printed
✓	**2** Always include all additional details, such as the contact telephone number and the visitor's status or title
✓	**3** Remember that provisional appointments should be written in pencil and only inked in when they have been confirmed
✓	**4** Leave enough space between appointments so that, if one is cancelled, you can write in a new appointment underneath
✓	**5** At the end of each day review the entries to make sure that: • the day's events have gone to plan and you have no outstanding issues or reminders to carry forward • you know what is happening tomorrow and the important tasks that must be done
✓	**6** At the start of each day, glance down the entries so that you know what to expect during the day

Rescheduling

This means changing an appointment to a different time and/or date. Your tasks are to ensure that:

• the original appointment is cancelled in the system

• all of the key information is transferred to the new agreed appointment time or date

• everyone involved is aware of the change.

The importance and use of reminder systems

Reminder systems are invaluable aids when you have many priorities and tasks to carry out. They jog your memory and, if you have set them up properly, they remind you about deadlines, appointments, meetings, conferences and other commitments, as well as when people will be away on leave or absent at social functions. They also remind you about tasks you have to carry out, such as obtaining foreign currency for a trip abroad or checking that new magazines have been delivered for the reception area. The aim is to ensure that you never forget anything and always have sufficient warning to enable you to complete tasks on time.

There are various systems that you can use and these are summarised in Table 5.3.3.

| Figure 5.3.2 | What attributes are useful when you are rescheduling or cancelling appointments? |

Table 5.3.3	Reminder systems

System	Description
Tickler files	This is a file set up to jog your memory. (See page 75 for tickler systems and filing.) A tickler system is comprised of notes, or index cards, that remind you about upcoming events. The guide cards, or dividers, should indicate days of the week (or months of the year) with reminders behind the appropriate day or number. For example, if an executive is attending an important meeting on 23 March, you could place a note in your file for 16 March to remind you to collect all of the papers that will be used
Diaries	The diary can be used to record reminders as well as appointments. So the note for 16 March would now appear on the diary page. It is important to make certain that you separate clearly the reminders from the appointments in a paper-based diary. A useful method is to use a different colour ink. In an electronic system, your reminders about key tasks appear on your screen with your calendar showing today's date. You can even set an alarm to remind you to do a task at a specific time of the day
Calendars, wall planners and charts	Calendars and wall planners are available to show the next month or the next 12 months. They enable you to enter information as written notes or by using magnetic symbols. These provide a constant aide-memoire of upcoming events and commitments

DID YOU KNOW?

An electronic diary can also be used as a reminder system with an alarm to notify you when something must be done.

EXAM TIP

Remember that when you are entering information in a reminder system, you do this ahead of when it is needed, not on the actual day of the event.

TEST YOURSELF

1 You maintain the diary for Grace Lara, an architect. She is a partner in a busy practice and frequently visits clients. The following activities are planned for 25 April between 9 am and 5 pm.

   a Routine partners' meeting for one-and-a-half hours at start of working day.

   b One-hour working lunch with Martin Garvey about plans for new hotel.

   c Two hours needed to attend interviews for new secretary.

   d One hour to visit new client, Marsha Gibbs, to discuss potential project.

   e Half an hour to read and deal with incoming mail.

   f Half an hour to sign outgoing mail.

   Prepare a diary page for 25 April and organise the activities into the most appropriate time slots.

   Now check your answers against those on the accompanying CD.

SECTION 1: Multiple-choice questions

1 An appropriate greeting by a receptionist to a visitor is:

  a   Good afternoon, can I help you?

  b   Hi, great to see you.

  c   Hello, who have you come to see?

  d   What do you want?

2 Useful reminder systems for a receptionist include:

  i   A tickler system.   iii   A diary.

  ii   A wall planner.   iv   A calendar.

  a   i, ii and iii only   c   i, iii and iv only

  b   i, ii and iv only   d   All of the above

3 The first thing that a visitor is most likely to notice about a receptionist is:

  a   What they are wearing.

  b   Whether they are attractive or not.

  c   Whether they have an accent.

  d   Whether they are friendly and welcoming.

4 The role of the receptionist in maintaining the reception area may include:

  i   Cleaning the floor.

  ii   Arranging for parcels or cases to be moved.

  iii Replacing old magazines and keeping them tidy.

  iv Clearing away dirty glasses and cups.

  a   i, ii and iv only   c   ii, iii and iv only

  b   i, iii and iv only   d   All of the above

5 You maintain the diaries for three executives in your organisation. When someone telephones to make an appointment the first fact that you try to ascertain is:

  a   What day they want to come.

  b   What time they want to come.

  c   Who they want to see.

  d   Why they want to make an appointment.

6 A visitor is becoming annoyed because although he arrived in good time for his 10 am appointment, it is now 10:15 am and he is still waiting in reception. In this situation the action you would take is to:

  i   Apologise for the delay.

  ii   Offer him another drink.

  iii Telephone the person he is seeing to remind them.

  iv Ask the visitor to return another day.

  a   i and ii only   c   ii and iii only

  b   i and iii only   d   iii and iv only

7 A courier arrives with an urgent package that has been damaged in transit. It is addressed to a senior manager who you know is in an important meeting and it is marked urgent and confidential. As receptionist you would:

  a   Refuse to accept it.

  b   Open it immediately to check the damage.

  c   Call the manager to come to reception.

  d   Accept it but write a note about the damage on the delivery slip that the courier asks you to sign.

8 An advertisement for a receptionist emphasises the need to be articulate. This is:

  a   The attribute of being able to express your thoughts clearly.

  b   The skill of being able to draw accurately.

  c   The art of being able to do two things at once.

  d   The desire to work hard and do well.

9 The need to screen visitors and only allow authorised people beyond the reception area is the main reason why:

  i   The reception desk must never be left unattended.

  ii   Only visitors with an appointment are welcome.

  iii Some organisations spend a lot of money on their reception areas.

  iv All visitors must enter their details and time of arrival in the reception register.

  a   i and ii only   c   i and iv only

  b   i and iii only   d   ii and iv only

10 A visitor who is waiting in reception asks about your job and what it is like to work in your organisation. Do you:

a Happily answer their questions.

b Tell them that you cannot respond because the information is confidential.

c Ignore them.

d Answer in general terms and then ask them about their journey instead.

Further practice questions and examples can be found on the accompanying CD.

SECTION 2: Short answer questions

1 a Identify THREE types of information usually found on business cards.

  b List THREE benefits of being given a card by a business visitor.

2 Give an example of how a receptionist could demonstrate each of the following attributes:

  a tact   b initiative

  c good temperament.

3 List THREE actions you would take if you were rescheduling an appointment for a manager.

4 List THREE ways in which you, as a receptionist, can help to maintain effective interpersonal relationships between your organisation and members of the public.

5 a Identify FIVE steps you should take to receive and screen a visitor who has an appointment.

  b Explain what you would do differently if the visitor had no appointment but wanted to see someone.

6 Your boss (Mrs Beverley Foster, the marketing director) is expecting a visitor at any moment. He is Mr Juan Cozier, the sales manager of Diablo Products. She has never met Mr Cozier before and wants you to make the introductions. Write down how you will do this, and what you will say.

7 List FOUR ways in which you would ensure that your personal appearance was appropriate for working on reception.

8 a Design a simple reception register with appropriate headings.

  b Record these visitors who arrive today:

  i Mrs J Duval from Safety Plus Ltd arrived at 09:15 to see Dr Hershall, the HR manager. She stayed until 11:00.

  ii Mr P Phillips from Target Associates arrived at 15:00 to see Edna Price, the sales manager, and stayed an hour.

  iii Miss Jessie Hendricks from JL Caterers arrived at 11:30 for a meeting with Dr Hershall. She left after 45 minutes.

  iv Sonny Campbell arrived at 14:00 and stayed until 15:30. He is from Hitronics Software and he saw Amy Roach, the IT manager.

9 Explain the procedures that you would follow if you were:

  a making an appointment for an executive

  b cancelling an appointment.

10 a List THREE types of reminder systems and explain the use of each one.

  b Identify FOUR types of events that you would note in this system.

Further practice questions and examples can be found on the accompanying CD.

6 Meetings

6.1 Meetings in business organisations

LEARNING OUTCOMES

By the time you have completed this section you should be able to:

• list the various types of meetings.

Figure 6.1.1 Does this meeting look formal or informal?

KEY TERMS

The **minutes** of a meeting are the official record of the proceedings.

FIND OUT MORE

When the South Trinidad Chamber of Industry and Commerce wanted to change its name to the Energy Chamber of Trinidad and Tobago it held an extraordinary general meeting (EGM) because the membership had to be allowed to vote for or against the change. Find examples of EGMs held in your own region by searching on the internet.

Introduction to meetings

Meetings are held by all business organisations. Some are short, informal affairs where a group of staff discuss work-related issues. Others are more formal. Some are a legal requirement and external people, such as shareholders, may be invited. An example is the annual general meeting (AGM) of a public limited company. A record – called the **minutes** – is kept because there must be evidence of the decisions made. Minutes are useful for informal meetings, too, as they remind everyone what they said and agreed to do.

You need to understand the different types of meetings, the main terms that are used and what they mean. You need to know how to organise an effective meeting and take follow-up actions afterwards, such as circulating the minutes. This unit summarises the facts you need to do all of these tasks.

Types of business meetings

Business meetings can be **formal** or **informal**. The difference between the two, and the different types of formal and informal meetings, are summarised below.

Formal meetings

A meeting that is a legal requirement, concerns strategic (long-term and important) issues relating to the organisation, and involves the sharing of information with governors, trustees or shareholders, will be formal. This means:

• its rules and procedures are clearly specified and set out for reference

• a formal record (the **minutes**) is kept of the proceedings. These must be kept safely because the organisation has a legal responsibility to hold certain meetings and disclose certain types of information.

DID YOU KNOW?

If an organisation uses public money to run its operations (such as a charity, government body or public limited company), the rules and procedures for a meeting are usually set down by law and the minutes must be made public.

Table 6.1.1	Types of formal meeting
Type of meeting	**What it is**
General meeting	A regular meeting of a company, society, association or union to which members are invited. General meetings held by companies include AGMs and EGMs, described below
Annual general meeting (AGM)	An important yearly meeting to which all members or shareholders are invited. It is held by many types of organisations but it is a legal requirement for all public limited companies under the Companies Act (see page 99). All shareholders must be invited and must be sent a copy of the report and accounts
Extraordinary general meeting (EGM)	A meeting held to transact any business with shareholders that cannot wait until the next AGM. It may be called by the directors or the shareholders and is usually held to discuss important changes or developments, such as financial issues
Board and committee meeting	A board meeting is held regularly by company directors to discuss organisational policy and decide future action. The first one must be held soon after a company is **incorporated**. All company directors must attend. The board of directors may delegate specific powers and duties to a **committee** to carry out certain tasks and report back to the board. Committees are also formed to run associations, clubs and societies. They are often responsible for certain areas of government work, such as transport or planning, or particular areas in a company, such as safety
Statutory meeting	This is a meeting that must be held between a company and its shareholders soon after a company is incorporated (in some countries this should be no later than three months afterwards). It is held to discuss the statutory report, which includes a short account of the company's finances since incorporation and its business plan

Informal meetings

Informal meetings are usually easier to arrange as there are no formal rules to follow, except those devised by the organisation itself. Some meetings are held on a regular basis, such as a weekly departmental meeting to discuss new developments. Others are held for a particular purpose or to solve an urgent problem. In this case, a **task group** may be formed to decide what to do.

The main types of informal meetings are:

- **staff meetings** between employees in the same, or different, departments. There may be a meeting of the entire staff to give them important information
- **departmental meetings**, which are held between a manager and their staff.

KEY TERMS

A company is **incorporated** when it is officially formed and legally registered in accordance with the Companies Act.

A **committee** is an official group of people who meet to carry out certain delegated tasks.

TEST YOURSELF

1 Briefly explain the difference between a statutory meeting, an annual general meeting and an extraordinary general meeting.

Now check your answer against the one on the accompanying CD.

DID YOU KNOW?

Task groups are cross-departmental teams that get together to do a particular job or investigate certain issues.

6.2 Legal requirements of annual general meetings

LEARNING OUTCOMES

By the time you have completed this section you should be able to:

• discuss basic legal requirements of annual general meetings.

KEY TERMS

Auditors check that the accounts of an organisation are completely accurate.

EXAM TIP

Check that you can list four items of business that take place at an AGM and three documents that would be prepared beforehand.

DID YOU KNOW?

The by-laws of many private associations, such as clubs or societies, often state that an AGM must be held each year.

More about annual general meetings

An annual general meeting (AGM) is held between the directors and shareholders of a company each calendar year. No more than 15 months must elapse between one AGM and the next. The business of the meeting is usually concerned with:

• receiving the report and accounts
• declaring a final dividend
• electing directors
• reappointing the **auditors** and agreeing their remuneration.

All shareholders are invited. They are given advance notification of the meeting. This must include:

• the **notice** of the meeting and the **agenda** stating the business to be discussed
• the auditor's report
• any other documents to be presented at the meeting (such as the director's annual report)
• **proxy forms** for shareholders who cannot attend in person (see page 99).

On the day of the AGM an attendance register is kept to record those who attend, even though only the overall number is noted in the minutes. Voting papers are also required.

NOTICE OF MEETING
Notice is hereby given that the fifth annual general meeting of Nichols and Webb Inc. will be held at Dominion Hotel, Seascape, St Jude's on Tuesday, 23 October 2013 at 15:00 hours.

AGENDA
1. Welcome and opening remarks
2. To receive and consider the directors' report and financial statements for the year ended 31 March 2013 and the auditors' report
3. To declare a final dividend of 12 cents per share
4. To re-elect Mr J T Michaels, director
5. To appoint auditors for the ensuing year
6. Any other business

BY ORDER OF THE BOARD OF DIRECTORS
Nicole Drakes
Secretary
Registered Office: Brightwater Towers, Seascape, St Jude's
10 September 2013

Figure 6.2.1 Notice and agenda for a company AGM

Annual general meetings and the law

The basic legal requirements that constrain the way in which AGMs must be held are summarised as follows.

The Companies Act

This is the main law that regulates annual general meetings. It distinguishes between private and public limited companies. A private company is privately owned and is often a family-run business. A public limited company sells its shares on the stock exchange. These shares are bought by institutional and private investors who become **shareholders**.

The management of companies

The law states that the board of directors has formal responsibilities towards the shareholders, the employees and the company as a whole. The board comprises executive directors who work for the organisation and are its senior managers. Non-executive directors, who do not work for the company, may also be recruited for their expertise.

Officers and shareholders

The law also recognises 'company officers' with specific responsibilities. These include the company secretary, senior management, the accountant and auditor. The shareholders are expected to approve the appointment of directors and officers and oversee their activities, and they have the power to dismiss them.

Meeting proxies

All shareholders have the right to vote at an AGM or EGM. If they cannot attend then they can appoint a **proxy**, a person who attends and votes on their behalf.

Corporate records

Minutes *must* be taken at all general meetings, all directors' meetings and any managers' meetings. They must be signed by the chairperson and kept available at the registered office. All members or shareholders are entitled to receive a copy.

The Articles of Incorporation and by-laws

The Articles of Incorporation (and/or the by-laws) list the internal and administrative rules that apply to the way the organisation conducts its business. They also stipulate the conduct and business of directors' meetings. They specifically cover:

- the notice to be given for general meetings. Generally, notice amounting to 21 **clear days** is required for an AGM
- the procedures to be followed (for example, the **quorum** and method of **adjournment** – see page 101)
- the rights of members when voting, including the right to appoint a proxy
- the nature and frequency of directors' meetings.

DID YOU KNOW?

Company shareholders have one vote for every share that they own. So, someone with many shares has more power than someone with only a few.

KEY TERMS

A **proxy** is someone who attends a meeting and votes on someone else's behalf.

Clear days are the days between issuing the notice of a meeting and the meeting being held.

TEST YOURSELF

1 You are helping the secretary to prepare for the AGM on 24 June.
  a Why is the date you put on the notice and agenda important?
  b Identify THREE other documents that will have been prepared.
  c List THREE items of business that would be included on the agenda.

Now check your answers against those on the accompanying CD.

The importance of effective meetings and understanding terms and procedures

LEARNING OUTCOMES

By the time you have completed this section you should be able to:

• define terms associated with meetings.

Figure 6.3.1 There are many reasons for holding meetings

DID YOU KNOW?

A committee that is set up for a particular purpose and then disbanded is called an **ad hoc** committee.

The importance of meetings, their purpose and benefits

All meetings are held for a reason, often because they are an excellent way for people to get together and communicate on matters of mutual concern or interest.

Reasons for holding meetings include:

• to give or share information
• to obtain views and opinions
• to decide on action to be taken
• to solve problems
• to dispel rumours and provide accurate, up-to-date information
• to generate ideas and suggestions
• to coordinate activities to be undertaken by different people
• to report upon or evaluate an event or activity
• to discuss current issues of mutual concern
• to broaden participation and involvement in a project
• to obtain assistance
• to organise special events or occasions.

If they are effective then several benefits are likely:

• **An exchange of information** takes place, so that each person learns from their colleagues.
• **Time is saved** as key issues can be debated among a group of people all concentrating on the same item at the same time.
• **The best possible conclusion is reached** because a range of information, expertise and experience is on hand at the same time.
• **Everyone involved is committed to achieving the agreed purpose** and carrying out the tasks required to ensure success.
• **People understand and appreciate each other's views more.**

However, not all meetings are effective. Only well-planned, appropriately organised and properly controlled meetings achieve their objectives.

Understanding meeting terms

Meetings must be well organised. This means that there must be an effective **chairperson** and a competent **secretary**, and any rules (sometimes called **standing orders**) that apply must be followed. For this reason there is normally a set procedure that is followed, especially at formal meetings. Understanding this will help you to remember the terms that are used and what they mean.

• The meeting must be correctly called or **convened**. Everyone who is entitled to attend must be sent a notice of the meeting, in accordance with the required **clear days,** giving the time, date and venue. An **agenda** may be included, which lists the topics to be discussed (see page 104).

- Before the meeting starts, a **quorum** must exist. This is the minimum number of people required for the meeting to be valid. If insufficient people attend then the meeting cannot be held. The quorum must continue to exist throughout, so if several people leave part-way through, the meeting may have to be **adjourned** until another date.

- The **chairperson**, who is in charge of running the meeting, will open the proceedings, and the secretary will note those attending and record those who have sent their apologies. Some members may be **ex officio**. This means that they are entitled to attend because of their position or status in the organisation.

- The chairperson should explain clearly each topic for discussion. A member may propose that something is done or action is taken. At a formal meeting a proposal is often called a **motion**.

- Once a motion has been discussed it may be put to the vote so that a decision can be made. Some members may **abstain**, which means they do not cast a vote. If there is a tie, then the chairperson has the **casting vote**. This is an extra vote to prevent a deadlock.

- The secretary will take the minutes. These are usually a summary of the discussions and decisions made. Occasionally a **verbatim** record is made. This is when every spoken word is recorded.

Avoiding ineffective meetings

If meetings are ineffective then very little is achieved. People will find excuses not to attend, or may not do the tasks allocated to them. These problems can usually be solved if:

- the chairperson runs meetings effectively (see page 102)
- anyone who cannot attend the meeting gives a reason for their absence
- anyone who regularly fails to attend is asked to resign and is replaced by someone else
- all participants observe meeting protocol (see page 102)
- the secretary efficiently organises the meeting and issues the minutes promptly afterwards
- the minutes contain an action column, so people can see what they have agreed to do, or a separate action sheet is circulated (see page 107)
- before the next meeting, the secretary contacts people who have to carry out certain tasks to remind them of their responsibilities.

TEST YOURSELF

1 a List FOUR benefits to be gained by having effective meetings.
  b Explain each of the following meetings terms: quorum, proxy, motion.

Now check your answers against those on the accompanying CD.

DID YOU KNOW?

A meeting may be adjourned for other reasons, such as insufficient time to discuss everything that day or some relevant information not being available.

KEY TERMS

Adjourning a meeting means discontinuing a meeting that has already begun.

DID YOU KNOW?

Hansard is a verbatim record of the proceedings of a parliament. See page 43.

EXAM TIP

Check that you can define each of the following terms: agenda, ad hoc, verbatim, quorum, proxy, casting vote, chairperson, ex officio, adjourn and motion.

FIND OUT MORE

There are various methods of voting. Sometimes there is a **show of hands**, or there may be a secret **ballot** so that people can vote without anyone knowing their choice. Find out why people often prefer this method and why it is believed to produce a fairer outcome.

Organising meetings and understanding follow-up procedures

LEARNING OUTCOMES

By the time you have completed this section you should be able to:

- organise different types of meeting
- outline the follow-up procedures related to decisions made at meetings.

DID YOU KNOW?

If the meeting is held in an external venue the chairperson will usually outline 'housekeeping arrangements', including the position of the restrooms and the nearest emergency exit.

FIND OUT MORE

You will see Robert's Rules of Order in practice if you watch a parliamentary debate on television or on YouTube. You can also find out more on the website at www.robertsrules.org.

DID YOU KNOW?

Today, as part of meeting protocol, many chairpersons ask that all mobile phones are switched off or put on silent mode for the duration of the meeting.

The duties of the chairperson

A good chairperson makes all the difference to the running of the meeting, the amount of business it gets through, the atmosphere that prevails and the ease with which the secretary can prepare for the event. Ideally a chairperson is nominated because of his or her expertise and skill in managing people. The duties of a chairperson involve the following:

- to know the rules, regulations and procedures relating to the meeting – particularly what is allowed and what is not
- to start the meeting on time
- to ensure that apologies are recorded from people who cannot attend
- to ensure that all participants know each other and to introduce any new participants
- to state the 'ground rules' that apply and follow meeting protocol (see below)
- to follow the agenda (see page 105)
- to provide relevant background information on a topic and encourage discussion
- to ensure that everyone has the opportunity to put forward their views, but not to talk for too long
- to summarise the discussion and put forward the action to be taken
- to arbitrate – using their casting vote – if there is deadlock between members
- to close the meeting properly and on time
- to check, approve and sign the minutes afterwards.

Robert's Rules of Order and meeting protocol

Robert's Rules of Order was devised to enable parliamentary debates to run smoothly. The aim was to ensure that people were courteous and did not interrupt each other, and that each motion was debated properly and then voted upon. Only then would the next topic be introduced. In addition, all comments had to be addressed through the Speaker. Individuals could not chat to each other as this would lead to chaos.

These rules are very sensibly adapted for formal business meetings. So, for example, all members must always **address the chair** rather than each other. This prevents different conversations breaking out around the table and it means that the chairperson is aware of all aspects of the discussion. Other aspects of protocol, that are appropriate for both formal and informal meetings, are summarised in Table 6.4.1.

Table 6.4.1	Meeting protocol
✓	All participants should arrive punctually. Anyone who cannot attend should send their apologies to the secretary or chairperson
✓	The chairperson should sit in the most commanding position and be clearly visible to everyone. This is usually at the head of the table or in the middle of the long side of a rectangular table. The next most important person usually sits to the chairperson's right and the next to his or her left
✓	Participants should put their point of view clearly, succinctly and courteously, and listen to the views of others without interrupting
✓	All participants should address the chair, not each other
✓	Discussions at the meeting should remain confidential unless it is agreed otherwise
✓	All participants must abide by the decision of the majority when a motion is put to the vote

Duties of the administrator

The administrator has the task of organising the meeting. This involves:

- obtaining the necessary supplies and equipment
- booking the room and ordering refreshments
- preparing the notice, agenda and chairman's agenda, and sending these out
- making other preparations in advance of the meeting being held
- assisting the chairperson on the day of the meeting
- completing appropriate follow-up procedures after the meeting.

Supplies and equipment for different meetings

There are very few meetings at which no supplies or equipment are required. At the very least, people are usually provided with a pen and paper, and there is a jug of water and glasses on the table. Most people wish to record decisions or ideas on a whiteboard or flip chart. Anyone giving a formal talk or presentation will usually expect audio-visual equipment to be available.

DID YOU KNOW?

Many participants take their own laptop computers to meetings and expect WiFi access to be available. Photocopier facilities are also useful.

EXAM TIP

Make sure you know the difference between supplies and equipment, and only select those items that would be appropriate for the type of meeting described in the question.

Table 6.4.2	Meeting supplies and equipment
Supplies	**Equipment**
Stationery, that is, paper and pencils/pens File folders	Laptop or computer with presentation package
Spare copies of the agenda	Projector (overhead, slide or multimedia) and projection screen
Copies of documents to be discussed	CD player/DVD player and television
Coloured markers (non-permanent) for a whiteboard	Microphones (roving or radio microphones enable the presenter to walk around)
Flip chart and markers	Laser pointer

Meetings documents

Three documents are prepared before a meeting: the notice, the agenda and the chairman's agenda.

Notice and agenda

In many cases the notice and agenda are combined into one document, as illustrated in Figure 6.4.1. The purpose of this document is to tell people when and where the meeting will be held. The agenda lists the order of business to be discussed.

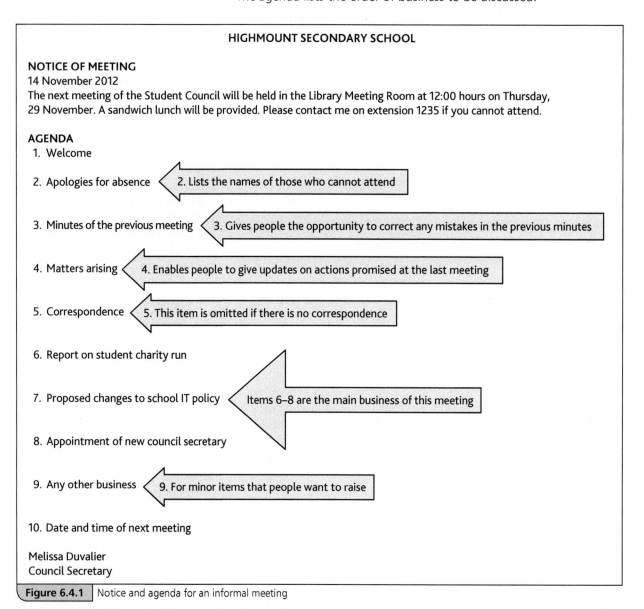

HIGHMOUNT SECONDARY SCHOOL

NOTICE OF MEETING
14 November 2012
The next meeting of the Student Council will be held in the Library Meeting Room at 12:00 hours on Thursday, 29 November. A sandwich lunch will be provided. Please contact me on extension 1235 if you cannot attend.

AGENDA
1. Welcome
2. Apologies for absence — 2. Lists the names of those who cannot attend
3. Minutes of the previous meeting — 3. Gives people the opportunity to correct any mistakes in the previous minutes
4. Matters arising — 4. Enables people to give updates on actions promised at the last meeting
5. Correspondence — 5. This item is omitted if there is no correspondence
6. Report on student charity run
7. Proposed changes to school IT policy — Items 6–8 are the main business of this meeting
8. Appointment of new council secretary
9. Any other business — 9. For minor items that people want to raise
10. Date and time of next meeting

Melissa Duvalier
Council Secretary

Figure 6.4.1 Notice and agenda for an informal meeting

EXAM TIP

Items 1–4 and 9 and 10 on the agenda in Figure 6.4.1 are standard items for most meetings. Make sure you know these.

Chairperson's agenda

This is a separate agenda prepared for the chairperson. There are two main reasons for doing this.

- Additional notes can be included to act as an aide-memoire for the chairperson.
- An additional column is included for the chairperson to add further notes during the meeting. These may be helpful to the secretary when the minutes are being prepared.

An extract from the chairperson's agenda for the Student Council meeting is shown in Figure 6.4.2.

DID YOU KNOW?

The item 'call to order' is sometimes put at the start of an agenda. This is to get everyone's attention before the official welcome.

HIGHMOUNT SECONDARY SCHOOL
CHAIRPERSON'S AGENDA
Meeting of the Student Council, 12:00 hours, Thursday, 29 November 2012,
Library Meeting Room

AGENDA ITEM	NOTES
1. Welcome and opening	1
New member, Nadine Kent	
2. Apologies	2
Received from Adam Bewley	
3. Minutes of the previous meeting	3
4. Matters arising	4
5. Correspondence	5
Letter of thanks recieved from	
Animal Shelter	
6. Report on student charity	6
To be given by Shanice Dandas	

Figure 6.4.2

Other preparations

Most administrators prefer to work to a checklist before a meeting, and on the day itself. This ensures they do not forget anything. An example checklist is shown below.

Table 6.4.3   Checklist for preparing for a meeting

Before the meeting		On the day	
✓	Prepare and send out notice and agenda and any other paperwork	✓	Put up signs and check the room for tidiness, temperature, space, etc.
✓	Prepare chairperson's agenda	✓	Check that all equipment is working, that supplies are adequate and that spare agendas and other papers are to hand
✓	Check who is coming and who has sent apologies	✓	Help to greet participants and show any new members where to sit
✓	Book the meeting room	✓	Record attendance and note any apologies received
✓	Inform reception if external visitors are expected	✓	Circulate the minutes of the last meeting and take minutes
✓	Obtain any supplies and equipment required	✓	Read any correspondence
✓	Arrange for refreshments to be available	✓	Help to serve refreshments if requested
✓	Arrange car parking spaces for external members	✓	Help to tidy the room when the meeting has ended and return borrowed equipment

Minutes of the meeting

The next step is to prepare the minutes. Those for the meeting at Highmount secondary school are shown in Figure 6.4.3.

HIGHMOUNT SECONDARY SCHOOL

MINUTES OF MEETING
A meeting of the Student Council was held in the Library Meeting Room at 12:00 hours on Thursday, 29 November 2012.

PRESENT

Annika Hall (Chair)
Shanice Dandas
Melissa Duvalier
Nadine Kent
Samuel Williams

Action

1 Welcome
The Chair, Annika Hall, welcomed all present and introduced Nadine Kent, the new member.

2 Apologies for absence
Adam Bewley sent his apologies.

3 Minutes of the previous meeting
These were agreed as a true and correct record and signed by the Chair.

4 Matters arising
Shanice Dandas said that Copyshop had quoted $80 to print the posters to advertise the Christmas Fayre and agreed to obtain two further quotations to see if a cheaper price was possible. SD

5 Correspondence
The Chair read a letter of thanks received from the Animal Shelter following the recent volunteer project. This had been very popular and it was agreed to repeat it in 2013. Melissa Duvalier said she would organise it again. MD

6 Report on student charity run
Shanice Dandas reported that 74 students had taken part in the charity run on 6 October and over $1,000 had been raised so far. Money was still being collected and she agreed to report the final total at the next meeting. SD

7 Proposed changes to school IT policy
Samuel Williams circulated a paper containing the proposed changes. After some discussion it was agreed that members would study the paper in more detail and identify the likely implications and report back at the next meeting. All

8 Appointment of new council secretary
Shanice Dandas agreed to take over this role when Melissa Duvalier left Highmount school at the end of 2012. SD

9 Any other business
There was no other business.

10 Date and time of next meeting
The next meeting will be held at 12:00 hours on Thursday, 13 December 2012.

Signed .... (Chairperson)   Date ....

Figure 6.4.3 Minutes of a meeting

Minutes are important for several reasons.

- They are the official record of the discussions that took place and the decisions that were made.
- They are a legal requirement for some meetings.
- They are sent to people who attended to remind them what took place and to those who did not attend to update them on what happened.
- They often include an **action column** or **action sheet**, which identifies the action that a person said they would take before the next meeting. This prompts people to do what they promised.

Points to note

- The Chairperson is listed first under those present. The other members are then listed in alphabetical order.
- The headings are identical to those in the agenda.
- The minutes are written in the past tense and specific dates are given (not 'tomorrow' or 'next year' as this could be confusing).
- The minutes are usually simply a summary. Details of discussions and conversations are not included.
- The important item to record is the action that has been agreed.

Follow-up procedures

The final sequence of events that the administrator needs to carry out is shown in Table 6.4.4.

Table 6.4.4	Checklist for follow-up procedures
	After the meeting
✓	Draft out the minutes and ask the chairperson to check and sign them
✓	Check that the date of the next meeting is in everyone's diary
✓	Prepare a final copy of the minutes incorporating any comments or amendments made by the chairperson
✓	Send a copy of the approved minutes (and any separate action sheet) to all members
✓	Ensure that a copy of the minutes is placed in the meetings file or minute book, and note this insertion in the index
✓	Deal with any other paperwork that has been asked for at the meeting and carry out any other tasks or follow-up actions that are your responsibility

FIND OUT MORE

Writing minutes is a useful skill to have. You can find out more about how to do this at www.ehow.com. The layout is easy if you download one of Microsoft's Word templates to use. You can also ask your tutor to show you samples from school.

DID YOU KNOW?

The minutes must usually be officially confirmed as being a correct record at the start of the next meeting. See agenda item 3, page 104.

TEST YOURSELF

1 Identify THREE tasks that you would carry out as administrator for a meeting:
   a before it is held
   b during the meeting
   c after it has ended.

Now check your answers against those on the accompanying CD.

SECTION 1: Multiple-choice questions

1 Your school sets up a committee to organise the Christmas fair. The committee will be disbanded after the fair has been held. This type of committee is called:

  a An ad hoc committee.

  b An ex officio committee.

  c A statutory committee.

  d A shareholders' committee.

2 A meeting that has been adjourned has been:

  a Cancelled.   **c** Postponed.

  b Completed.   **d** Suspended.

3 The initials EGM stand for:

  a Extra general meeting.

  b Extra governors meeting.

  c Extraordinary general meeting.

  d Emergency general meeting.

4 Standard items in meeting agendas include:

  i Any other business.

  ii Minutes of last meeting.

  iii Apologies for absence.

  iv Date and time of next meeting.

  a i, ii and iii only   **c** ii, iii and iv only

  b i, ii and iv only   **d** All of the above

5 An action sheet is prepared to:

  a Remind the chairperson what to do.

  b Remind the administrator or secretary what to do.

  c Remind the meeting participants what they agreed to do.

  d Remind the chairperson when to give everyone a break.

6 The chairman's main task after the meeting has ended is to:

  a Approve and sign the minutes.

  b Prepare the chairman's agenda.

  c Chat to participants.

  d Write up the minutes.

7 A shareholder cannot attend an AGM in person but still wants to vote. He or she needs to complete:

  a A ballot paper.

  b A proxy form.

  c An agenda.

  d An attendance sheet.

8 Appropriate equipment for a presenter at a meeting could include:

  i A flip chart and marker pens.

  ii A laptop and projector.

  iii A photocopier.

  iv A whiteboard.

  a i, ii and iii only   **c** ii, iii and iv only

  b i, ii and iv only   **d** All of the above

9 The HR manager is entitled to attend all meetings of the safety committee because of his or her senior position in the organisation. This means the HR manager is:

  a An executive director.

  b An ex officio member.

  c An ad hoc member.

  d A chairperson.

10 The role of the chairman at a meeting includes:

  i Calling the meeting to order.

  ii Introducing new members.

  iii Ensuring the rules are kept.

  iv Having the casting vote.

  a i, ii and iii only   **c** ii, iii and iv only

  b i, ii and iv only   **d** All of the above

Further practice questions and examples can be found on the accompanying CD.

1 List FOUR tasks you would undertake after a meeting to ensure that the minutes were dealt with efficiently.

2 Write a short definition for each of the following meeting terms: verbatim, motion, proxy.

3 Identify TWO differences between a formal and an informal meeting.

4 a Explain the relevance of Robert's Rules of Order to business meetings.

  b List FOUR aspects of meeting protocol that a chairperson should insist on.

5 Two people leave a meeting part-way through and it becomes inquorate (there is no longer a quorum). Explain what this means, what action the chairperson must take and why.

6 Explain the difference between a board meeting, a committee meeting and a staff meeting.

7 a Draft out the notice and agenda for the sales meeting to be held next Tuesday at 11 am in Room 204. Include the standard items that you would find on an agenda. The main business items that the chairperson wants to discuss are: the spring sales conference; the new format for representatives' reports; and sales figures for the previous month. There is no correspondence.

  b Explain TWO ways in which the chairperson's agenda would differ from the main agenda.

8 a Suggest FOUR reasons why departmental meetings are held.

  b Identify FOUR resources (supplies or equipment) that would be useful at these meetings.

9 List FOUR responsibilities of the chairperson during a meeting and FOUR responsibilities of the administrator or secretary.

10 Explain the main business carried out at an annual general meeting and the importance of taking minutes at this event.

Further practice questions and examples can be found on the accompanying CD.

7 Travel arrangements

7.1 Information and services required for business travel

LEARNING OUTCOMES

By the time you have completed this section you should be able to:

• outline the types of information and services required for travel.

DEPARTURES ✈

TIME	DESTINATION	STATUS
12:55	New York	Last call
13:15	Port of Spain	Boarding
14:05	Grenada	On time
14:35	London	On time
16:20	Miami	Delayed

Figure 7.1.1 Where would you like to visit?

DID YOU KNOW?

The budget may be larger for directors and other senior staff, who may travel business class and have better accommodation.

Introduction to business travel

Making travel arrangements is an interesting task, and knowing how to do this is a useful skill for your private life too. Good administrators obtain all of the key information that they need before choosing the best option. This also helps to keep the costs down. Understanding the available services, planning a schedule and knowing about travel documents and money for foreign trips are invaluable skills. This unit covers all of these tasks.

Information and services required for travel

Before you make any arrangements you must know the options available. Start by establishing some important facts.

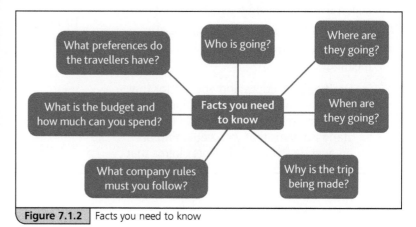

Figure 7.1.2 Facts you need to know

You can then identify:

• the best method of travel
• the type of accommodation and facilities required
• how much you can spend and the company rules that apply.

Additional factors to consider, particularly for long-haul trips, may include:

• essential travel documents – such as passports and visas
• monetary issues – such as which foreign currency to take
• other considerations – such as climate, business customs and public holidays
• time zones and the possibility of jet lag.

Next, you need to know the basic facts about making travel arrangements.

Tickets and e-tickets

Tickets enable us to enter an event or travel on a vehicle or aeroplane. Losing a paper ticket may mean that we are refused access, which is why electronic tickets (or e-tickets) are better. They are now used by most airlines and confirm that a specific passenger reservation is held on their computer system. An e-ticket receipt can be printed, but it is not essential as the passenger's passport confirms their identity and enables a boarding pass to be issued. Many airlines operate a web check-in system so passengers can print their own boarding pass and go to a rapid luggage drop-off counter or straight to the gate if they only have hand luggage. Business travellers prefer shortcuts like this that reduce queuing – though they must ensure that they only carry permitted items in their hand luggage through security.

Key facts about buying tickets

- First obtain all essential information, such as dates, times and places.
- Compare prices online (for airlines try www.skyscanner.net unless you are only checking out one particular airline). For complicated or multi-city trips, ask a specialist agency for help.
- Different conditions apply for different types of tickets, so you should balance cost and convenience. A long delay between flights or an enforced stay on a Saturday night may be cheaper but unacceptable. You should also know whether to buy a flexible ticket (that is, one that can be changed) or a non-flexible, cheaper one.
- Air passengers can travel economy, premium economy or business class (first class is too expensive for most business travellers) and you can select the seats online.
- Spell each traveller's name correctly – so that it matches their passport – to avoid any problems at check-in.
- Check that the details are correct on any tickets you receive, then put them in the travel folder (see page 113). Note the airport name (there may be several in a major city) and terminal number. These are essential if you are booking a taxi transfer to the hotel.

Preparation of itineraries

An **itinerary** summarises the essential information that the traveller needs during the trip. Sometimes a shortened version is prepared on a postcard for quick and easy reference.

Key facts about itineraries

- The heading should state the traveller's name, the destination(s) and the dates.
- All entries should be in date and time order.
- Use the 24-hour clock to avoid confusion (see page 115).
- The itinerary should include all travel arrangements, from the start of the trip to the end, details of all accommodation, meetings, transfers and documents needed.

DID YOU KNOW?

If an executive is a member of an airline frequent flier club or hotel honoured guest scheme you must enter the membership number when you make a booking with that airline or hotel.

Figure 7.1.3 | What do you need to know before you buy a ticket?

DID YOU KNOW?

The seat pitch in an aircraft is the distance between a seat and the one in front. Most executives prefer a generous seat pitch if possible.

FIND OUT MORE

Check the differences between different airlines (including food served and seat pitch) at www.airlinequality.com. You can find local travel specialists by looking in Yellow Pages.

DID YOU KNOW?

A good itinerary provides key information for the traveller in a logical order.

FIND OUT MORE

Find out about the benefits of being a member of the Caribbean Club at www.caribbean-airlines.com. You can find the information under 'Products & services'.

THINK ABOUT IT!

Check that the itinerary contains all of the information needed to get Bethany Williams to Barbados and back without any problems. Then decide why her outgoing flight appears to take longer than the return flight (see page 114 for the answer).

DID YOU KNOW?

You learned how to make and cancel appointments in Unit 5. Look back at pages 90–91 to refresh your memory.

An example is shown below. Bethany Williams is a Kingston-based interior designer who is travelling to Bridgetown next Tuesday.

BETHANY WILLIAMS
Club Caribbean Membership No.1028933ABC
Visit to Bridgetown, Barbados, 20–22 May 2013

Monday, 20 May 2013

10:00	Taxi booked from home to airport (J D Supercars, cellphone 02938 173812)
10:45*	Check in at Norman Manley International Airport, Kingston, e-ticket no. 302939273049
12:45	Depart Caribbean Airlines flight BW415
16:20	Arrive Grantley Adams International Airport, Barbados (take airport taxi to hotel)

Accommodation reserved at White Sands Hotel, Hastings, tel (1-246) 438-0204. Confirmatory email attached

Tuesday, 21 May 2013

08:30	Taxi booked from hotel to Watts and Copley, Architects, Manor Road, St Michael (Rapid Taxis, (1-246) 238-3729)
09:00	Planning meeting with Jasper Copley For relevant papers, see folder 1
16:30	Meeting ends, taxi to hotel (arrange direct with Rapid Taxis)
18:00	Taxi booked from hotel to Women in Business seminar and dinner at Fairgrove Hotel, Bridgetown (Rapid Taxis) For programme, see folder 2
21:00	Taxi to hotel. Arrange direct with Rapid Taxis

Wednesday, 22 May 2013

06:45	Taxi booked from hotel to airport (Rapid Taxis)
07:25*	Check in at airport
09:25	Depart Caribbean Airlines flight BW414
11:15	Arrive Norman Manley International Airport. Car booked with J D Supercars for transport to office

*Can arrive later if check in online, but recommend arriving at least 90 minutes before departure

---

Figure 7.1.4 | Bethany's itinerary

Scheduling of appointments

The purpose of a business trip is usually to attend a meeting or other event. To ensure the trip is cost effective, many business people try to see several clients during one visit. Ideally appointments are made first and the travel arrangements are made around them. For example, Bethany Williams cannot travel on Tuesday and arrive in time to see Jasper Copley, so she will fly on Monday and stay overnight before the meeting.

Key facts about appointments for business travellers

- Business customs vary around the world, as do public holidays, vacations and the length of lunch hours, so check any differences that apply.
- Ask for confirmation of each appointment in writing (email is ideal).
- Record all of the key facts that the traveller needs: name of contact, address, telephone number and directions, if travelling by car.
- Do not make appointments too soon after long trips.

- Allow time between appointments in case they overrun or the distance between the locations is further than expected.
- List the documents needed for each appointment and place these in a folder that is labelled and numbered clearly.

Making hotel reservations

The choice of accommodation is important. A poor hotel with restricted check-in times or limited facilities in a noisy or remote location is unacceptable. For this reason, many organisations use well-known international hotel groups that cater for business customers, such as Hilton and InterContinental. However, these hotels can be expensive and may not be available in some areas.

Key facts about making hotel reservations

- Check that you know the budget (and grade of accommodation required – 3, 4 or 5 star), the dates of arrival/departure, type of room/facilities required and how the account will be settled.
- Use a map to minimise travel to and from meetings.
- Check the facilities available online, such as WiFi access, rapid check in and check out, coffee-making facilities or room service. Your manager might also appreciate a fitness centre.
- Executives usually require single occupancy, but they may prefer a king-sized room or a junior suite. Note that a double room has a double bed whereas a twin room has two separate beds.
- Check whether the room rate includes breakfast. This is unlikely in the US, but it may be part of the package in Europe and the UK.

Preparing travel folders

You will quickly accumulate paperwork for any trip – tickets, email confirmations, meeting documents, etc. Be well organised or you may lose something important.

Key facts about travel folders

- Start a new folder for each trip and label it with the traveller's name, the destinations and the date of departure and return.
- Put every relevant document in the folder, such as confirmatory emails, contact details, directions, e-tickets and invitations.
- When everything is finalised, put the papers into the order that they will be needed and throw away any draft documents.
- Photocopy important documents for the office file.
- Clip a copy of the itinerary to the inside cover before giving the folder to the person who will be travelling.

FIND OUT MORE

At www.bank-holidays.com you can check the public holidays anywhere for the current year. At www.executiveplanet.com you can check business etiquette abroad. Other useful sites include www.cyborlink.com and www.worldtravelguide.net/destinations.

DID YOU KNOW?

The headline rate for a hotel room is called the **rack rate**. Some organisations regularly use a particular hotel so that they can negotiate discounts well below this rate.

DID YOU KNOW?

Tell the hotel if the traveller will be arriving late to make sure they do not re-let the accommodation.

DID YOU KNOW?

It is better to keep personal documents handy, such as the passport, travel insurance and vaccination certificates, because the traveller may need to produce or refer to these at the airport. Include a photocopy of each in the travel folder in case the originals are lost or stolen.

TEST YOURSELF

1 You are booking hotel accommodation for two managers who are travelling to Belize. List FIVE facts that you need to know before you can investigate possible options.

Now check your answers against those on the accompanying CD.

Time zones

LEARNING OUTCOMES

By the time you have completed this section you should be able to:

• calculate time based on knowledge of time differences between two or more countries.

Figure 7.2.1 Times are different around the world

DID YOU KNOW?

Most people find it better to travel west rather than east because it is easier to cope with a longer day than a shorter one.

KEY TERMS

Greenwich Mean Time (GMT) is the standard reference against which time zones are calculated.

Time zones and their significance

Time zones affect people on long-haul flights because they can cause **jet lag**. This occurs when your body clock is out of step with the time in the place where you are, so you are awake when you should be sleeping and vice versa. The greater the difference in time between your point of departure and arrival, the more likely you are to suffer. So going from Port of Spain to San Francisco in summer (−3 hours) just means a slightly longer day, whereas going to London (+5 hours) means it will be bedtime before you are ready to go to sleep. If you travelled to Shanghai (+12 hours) then day and night would be reversed and it would take you several days to adjust.

The effects of jet lag can be minimised by avoiding alcohol during a flight, drinking plenty of water, having comfortable seating, and altering one's watch to the destination time at the start of the flight so that you start to adjust to the new time.

Jet lag and its effects must be taken into account when arranging business meetings on arrival. For example, if your manager has travelled through several time zones then they should be allowed at least 24 hours to adjust. You should also take note of the time difference before you accidentally phone with information in the middle of the night! If in doubt, send a text message instead.

Calculating time differences

You can visualise time zones by imagining the world as a large orange divided into segments. Each segment represents a different time zone. Travelling east means you go forwards in time, moving west means you go backwards in time.

Times are often stated as +/− **GMT (Greenwich Mean Time)**. Greenwich, in London, is home to the Royal Observatory, the location of the 0 degrees Prime Meridian Line. This effectively divides the world into west and east. West of this line means locations are minus GMT, east of the line means locations are plus GMT.

All territories in the Caribbean are west of London, so they are minus GMT. For example, Bridgetown is GMT −4 so this means that when it is 12 noon in London, it is 8am in Bridgetown. Kingston is GMT −5, so if you travel from Bridgetown to Kingston you will put your watch back one hour. This is why the journeys look different for Bethany's flights on page 112.

DID YOU KNOW?

Airline timetables always state **local times** at the airports of departure and arrival. Because destinations to the east are ahead in time, this makes eastward journeys look long and westward journeys look short.

FIND OUT MORE

If you ever visit London, you can go to Greenwich and stand on the Prime Meridian Line. You can also read more about it online at www.nmm.ac.uk/places/royal-observatory/meridian-line.

There are two other facts that you need to know about time zones.

- In summer, Daylight Saving Time (or Summer Time) means that clocks are put forward in many countries, including the US and UK. This changes the time difference by one hour between these countries and those that remain on Standard Time (including Caribbean territories).

- Obviously, you cannot keep going ahead in time as you travel east or you would go into the future! So, over the Pacific you cross the International Date Line. This means that you go backwards (or forwards) by a day, depending on your direction of travel. If you arrive on a different day to the one on which you left, this is shown on an airline schedule by an asterisk (*) and a note, for example: 'Arrives 1 day later'. You may even arrive two days later.

EXAM TIP

Make sure that you can add and subtract hours correctly to calculate times in different places.

FIND OUT MORE

Many online sites will calculate time differences for you. At www. happyzebra.com and www.timeanddate.com you can check out the world clock, time differences and travel distances across the world.

DID YOU KNOW?

UTC (Coordinated Universal Time) is the time standard used by computer servers and mobile phone networks that need a universal standard time. It is virtually the same as GMT.

Expression of time in 12-hour and 24-hour format

Many schedules are written using the 24-hour clock to avoid any confusion between am and pm. Because someone may ask you to look up a time using the 12-hour clock you must be able to convert times quickly and accurately. If you convert 17:00 hours to 7 pm there will be problems for everyone!

- Convert *to* the 24-hour clock by *adding 12* for any time after 12 noon.
- Convert *from* the 24-hour clock by *subtracting 12* for any time after 12 noon.

DID YOU KNOW?

Digital watches often show midnight as 00:00 hours. One minute past midnight is 00:01, and so on. If you are speaking, though, it is clearer to refer to midnight as 2400 hours (twenty-four hundred hours).

TEST YOURSELF

1 Copy out the table below and complete the columns. To help, the first one is done for you.

Destination	Time +/− GMT	Time in 12-hour clock when it is 12 noon in London	Time in 24-hour clock when it is 12:00 hours in London
Port-au-Prince	−5	7 am	07:00 hours
Istanbul	+3		
Tokyo	+9		
New Delhi	+5½		
Honolulu, Hawaii	−10		

Now check your answers against those on the accompanying CD.

Schedules and travel documents

LEARNING OUTCOMES

By the time you have completed this section you should be able to:

• interpret schedules

• explain the necessity for various travel documents.

DID YOU KNOW?

You should always look for a direct flight if you can, rather than one where a change is involved.

FIND OUT MORE

Check out the following schedules online.

• The Barbados bus service at www.transportboard. com/schedule.php. Work out when you can go from Speightsville to the airport (in Christ Church).

• The Trinidad–Tobago inter-island ferry service at www. patnt.com/ferry_schedule. shtml.

• Air Jamaica schedules at www.airjamaica.com. Find out how long it takes to travel from Kingston to New York.

Interpret schedules

Schedules show the departure and arrival times of most forms of transport. Today many are available online and this has two benefits.

• Whereas paper schedules go out of date, online schedules are continually updated.

• On many websites you enter the journey details and the system searches for the best option(s).

If you do refer to a printed (or online) schedule then make sure you:

• check the headings so that you know the content of each column

• check the meaning of any symbols and read any footnotes as these provide important additional information

• make sure you are referring to the correct day and date

• write down the options if there are several available, so that these are easy to refer to.

DID YOU KNOW?

If the outward and return journeys take a different length of time, this tells you that the places are not in the same time zone.

Different types of travel documents

A traveller usually needs tickets, a passport and money, but there are also some other documents that they may need to obtain. These are shown in Table 7.3.1.

Points to note about travel documents

Usually the holder must apply on a standard (or electronic) form and the travel document may take some time to issue. For that reason you should:

• allow adequate time before the trip to apply for any essential documents

• note the passport number and photocopy the identity page, which states the date and place of issue. If the passport is lost or stolen, notify the police and passport office. If it is lost abroad, contact your nearest embassy or consulate who can arrange for emergency travel documents to be issued

• keep a photocopy of all other permits and certificates

• note in the diary when the passport, any visas and other permits will expire.

Table 7.3.1	Different types of documents
Type of document	**Function**
Passport	A passport confirms the identity and citizenship of the holder. It is issued by the government and is valid for 10 years. It is important to note the expiry date as some countries insist on at least six months' validity on arrival. The passport must not become too full with entry or visa stamps – there should be at least two blank pages. To avoid problems business people may have two passports. This is also necessary for people who travel between certain politically opposed countries. For example, passports containing an Israeli stamp cannot be used in most Arab countries
Visa	Visas are needed to travel to certain countries and are issued by the embassy or consulate of the country concerned. There are many different types – some are for tourists or business visitors, others for those who want to work or study abroad. The country's website will give details of how to apply, the cost, the validity period and how long it takes to issue the visa. Most visas are stamped on a page in the passport. The expiry date is important because after this date the traveller cannot enter the country
Entry permit	This is similar to a visa but it is a printed document. It gives the holder the right to enter a particular country. Some countries (including the US) require residents who plan to leave the country for a long period to obtain a re-entry permit before they go. The proposed CARIPASS is a type of travel permit, designed to enable holders to pass through immigration quickly. The aim is to encourage travel between the 10 participating Caribbean states
Health certificate	Vaccination certificates are required by law in certain countries before entry. The World Health Organization recommends them or states that they are advisable in others. Information on the requirement for any country can be obtained from a doctor or medical centre, or the embassy or consulate of the country concerned
Tax clearance certificate	This document provides evidence that the holder does not owe any tax on the date the certificate is issued. It is required by certain countries before people (usually temporary workers) are allowed to leave, as well as for other purposes including contracting to do government business, applying for residency or a loan

FIND OUT MORE

Check out the CARIPASS at www.caripass.org. Find out how to apply for a US visa by looking on the website of your nearest US embassy.

DID YOU KNOW?

A visa gives you permission to travel to a country, but immigration officials still have the power to refuse entry on arrival.

Figure 7.3.1 Travel documents

TEST YOURSELF

1 Identify TWO documents you would need for a trip to the US. State the purpose of each one and the differences between them.

Now check your answers against those on the accompanying CD.

DID YOU KNOW?

The latest passports are **biometric**. In the US these are called e-passports. They are far harder to copy so they are more secure.

Monetary instruments and travel checklists

LEARNING OUTCOMES

By the time you have completed this section you should be able to:

• determine monetary instruments for use during travel.

Monetary instruments

Everyone needs money when they are travelling, and business people are no exception. In addition to day-to-day requirements, such as a cup of coffee or a tip to a taxi driver, business travellers may be expected to settle their own hotel and restaurant bills by using a company credit card. The main options are shown in Table 7.4.1.

Table 7.4.1	Monetary instruments
Monetary instrument	**Points to note**
Traveller's cheques	These are available from banks in a variety of currencies. Dollars and sterling are the most widely used because these are readily acceptable in most countries abroad. It is sensible to obtain cheques for a variety of denominations (for example $100, $50 and $20) so that the traveller never needs to cash more than is necessary. On receipt, the traveller should sign each cheque in front of the bank cashier. A separate note should be made of the number and value of each cheque in case of loss or theft. When the cheques are cashed the holder must produce their passport and sign the cheque again. **Advantages**: If any are lost or stolen a refund can be obtained, and this can be done almost immediately if there is a related bank nearby. Any unused cheques can be retained for future use, but only by the person to whom they were issued. **Disadvantages**: It is difficult to obtain currency on public holidays and weekends when the banks are closed.
Credit cards	Credit cards are a popular way of paying bills and obtaining currency abroad. The main ones are Mastercard and Visa. A business person may have a corporate card so that the bill is sent direct to the company. **Advantages**: Credit cards usually offer better rates of exchange than the local tourist rate. **Disadvantages**: The credit limit may be insufficient for complex or extended journeys or the card may not be accepted in some countries. For this reason many business travellers have two or more cards. Obtaining cash by using credit cards in ATMs is very expensive.
Debit cards	A debit card can be used to pay for goods and also to obtain cash in automatic teller machines (ATMs). **Advantages**: This is an easier way to obtain cash than using traveller's cheques. **Disadvantages**: In many countries ATMs may not exist. Banks charge a fee for debit card transactions abroad.
Letter of credit	This is a document, issued by a bank or other financial institution, which guarantees that a buyer can pay the supplier's bill. **Advantages**: The document protects the seller, who is assured of being paid. It also protects the buyer because the bank will not release the money until the goods have been received in good condition. **Disadvantages**: There will be a bank fee for issuing the document.

Bank draft	A bank draft is a cheque made out by the bank on its own account. It is used for large payments when the creditworthiness of the buyer is not known. The bank issues its own cheque to an account holder. When the cheque is cashed the bank transfers the money out of the account holder's account and into the bank's own account. **Advantages**: Because this guarantees payment it enables business to be done when the buyer and seller are strangers. **Disadvantages**: There is a charge for issuing the cheque.
Cash	Cash is often necessary for some purchases, such as a newspaper or taxi fare. In addition to using different types of currencies, some countries also have limits on the amount of currency that can be taken into or out of their country. The decision about which currency to purchase will depend upon the destination(s). The amount you obtain for your money will depend on the exchange rate between the two currencies you are selling and buying. Any unused notes can usually be changed back to the home currency when the traveller returns. **Advantages:** Cash is widely accepted for all transactions. **Disadvantages:** Cash can be lost or stolen.

Travel checklists

You now know that arranging travel can involve obtaining different types of information and carrying out several tasks. The only way that you can do these efficiently and promptly is to prepare a checklist of all the tasks you have to do, and cross these off methodically as you go. An example is shown in Table 7.4.2.

Table 7.4.2 A travel checklist

Checklist for Bethany Williams' trip to New York, 15 November	
Apply for/obtain US visa	✓
Confirm attendance at Design Seminar	✓
Arrange meeting with Peters and Lee, Manhattan	✓
Find flights, make reservations	✓
Book hotel room – single occupancy, 4 star, central location	✓
Arrange transfers from airport to hotel and return	✓
Obtain 200 US dollars	✓
Check all seminar tickets and programmes have been received	✓

Figure 7.4.1 What currency would you need for a trip to Paris?

DID YOU KNOW?

It is important that you refer to your checklist regularly and also put all of the deadline dates in your diary.

DID YOU KNOW?

It is often better to travel with an internationally accepted currency (such as US dollars, sterling or euros) that can be used in several countries.

DID YOU KNOW?

It is sensible to keep to a minimum the amount of cash that you carry when travelling in case of loss or theft.

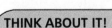

THINK ABOUT IT!

Can you suggest why obtaining a visa to go to the US is the very first entry in the checklist?

TEST YOURSELF

1 You are going on a trip abroad. Identify ONE advantage and ONE disadvantage of taking:

a traveller's cheques

b cash.

Now check your answers against those on the accompanying CD.

SECTION 1: Multiple-choice questions

1 Web check-in for a flight is ideal for business travellers because:

i They do not need a boarding card.

ii They can bypass the queues at the check-in desk.

iii They can take a laptop with them.

iv They can go direct to the gate if they only have hand luggage.

a i and ii only   **c** ii and iii only

b i and iii only   **d** ii and iv only

2 A trip from Barbados to Kingston appears to take 3 hours 35 minutes, but the return trip is shown as 5 hours 40 minutes. The main reason for this difference is:

a A faster plane is used for the outgoing trip.

b A different route is travelled both ways.

c Jamaica and Barbados are on different time zones.

d Strong headwinds slow down the plane on the return trip.

3 An essential hotel facility for many business people is:

a Separate meeting rooms.

b WiFi access in all rooms.

c A fitness centre.

d Car parking.

4 A tax clearance certificate:

a Clearly states how much tax you owe.

b Confirms you do not owe any tax.

c Clears you from paying any tax.

d Confirms you are due a tax refund.

5 Advantages of using a company credit card abroad include:

i The bill is sent direct to the company.

ii You can spend what you want.

iii It is useful for small items, like newspapers or taxi fares.

iv The traveller can settle their own hotel bill.

a i and iii only   **c** ii and iii only

b i and iv only   **d** iii and iv only

6 The cover of a travel folder should state:

a The name, the trip locations and the date.

b The name, the hotels booked and the date(s).

c The dates of travel and contents of the folder.

d The name, dates and times of travel.

7 Information in a passport includes:

i The holder's name.

ii The holder's date of birth.

iii The holder's nationality/citizenship.

iv The date of expiry.

a i, ii and iii only   **c** ii, iii and iv only

b i, iii and iv only   **d** All of the above

8 Your manager is visiting an art dealer and wants to buy a valuable painting for a client. The best way he can pay for this is:

a In cash.

b By credit card.

c By bank draft.

d By traveller's cheque.

9 Obtaining a visitor's visa for your manager means they have:

a Permission to travel to that country.

b Permission to enter a country.

c Permission to work in a country.

d Permission to live in a country.

10 Your manager is flying from Port of Spain to Bridgetown tomorrow. The flight takes 50 minutes and departs at 17:50. Using the 12-hour clock, at what time will you tell the taxi company that his flight is scheduled to land?

a 5.30 pm   **c** 7.50 pm

b 6.40 pm   **d** 8.40 pm

Further practice questions and examples can be found on the accompanying CD.

1 Identify TWO ways in which a business traveller may settle a bill for a hire car.

2 You are booking a taxi to meet an executive at the airport. List FIVE details you will need to give them.

3 Below are the LIAT and Sunstar Airlines flight schedules from Barbados to Guyana on 21 February. Which option would you choose for your manager? Give TWO reasons for your choice.

Flight		From/To	Time	
Sunstar Airlines	ST 49	Barbados, Grantley Adams Intl.	21 Feb	17:35
		Port of Spain, Piarco Intl.		18:35
Sunstar Airlines	ST 38	Port of Spain, Piarco Intl.	21 Feb	20:15
		Georgetown, Cheddi Jagan Intl.		21:25

Flight		From/To	Time	
LIAT	LI 781	Barbados (BGI)	21 Feb	08:00
		Guyana (GEO)	21 Feb	10:00

Flight schedules for Sunstar Airlines and LIAT

4 a Explain why jet lag occurs and suggest TWO ways that the effects of jet lag can be minimised.

  b Give TWO reasons why administrators need to take jet lag into account.

5 a Explain the purpose of an itinerary.

  b Describe FOUR types of information that you would normally include on this document.

6 Your manager is planning a trip to China. Identify FIVE items you would need to include on your travel checklist.

7 Identify FOUR types of document that would be included in a travel folder.

8 State FOUR checks you would make before booking an airline ticket.

9 State TWO reasons why it is important to establish the budget for a trip at the outset.

10 Identify THREE factors you would take into account when scheduling an appointment for an executive who is travelling to Madrid next month.

Further practice questions and examples can be found on the accompanying CD.

The role and functions of the human resource office

LEARNING OUTCOMES

By the time you have completed this section you should be able to:

• describe the functions of the human resource management office.

Figure 8.1.1 What factors keep you keen and motivated at work?

Carry out a needs analysis to establish a job exists

↓

Draw up a job description and a job specification

↓

Advertise the post

↓

Create a shortlist

↓

Interview and appoint the most suitable candidate

Figure 8.1.2 Steps in the recruitment process

Introduction to human resource management

The human resources of an organisation are its employees. If they are well trained and committed to the aims of the business it is far more likely to be successful.

HR is responsible for recruiting new employees, helping to keep staff motivated and monitoring staff turnover.

HR also ensures that the business complies with all its legal responsibilities on health and safety and employment protection.

The recruitment process

The steps in this process are shown in Figure 8.1.2.

What is a needs analysis?

A needs analysis helps to identify whether someone new is really needed. Replacing someone leaving may be unnecessary if business is slow, costs must be cut, tasks can be done by others or the vacancy may be a promotion opportunity for an existing worker.

DID YOU KNOW?

If a vacancy must be filled, the job should be reviewed to decide whether it has changed and new skills are required.

Job descriptions and job specifications

• The **job description** summarises the key facts relating to the job including the job title, the person responsible for the job holder, and the main duties and responsibilities.

• The **job specification** states the knowledge, skills and attributes of the person required, usually as essential and desirable requirements.

These documents provide the basis for the job advertisement. They tell job applicants what is expected of them and help to ensure that applicants with the right skills are chosen for interview.

Advertise the post

The job advertisement should state the main requirements of the job. It will:

• include a brief description of the business, its activities and location

• provide an indication of the salary

- state the qualifications and experience required by applicants
- state who to contact and any closing date.

The advertisement may be placed in the press, passed to a recruitment agency or posted on the company's website.

FIND OUT MORE

Check job advertisements in your regional press and online and decide which provide the best information for applicants.

Shortlisting

This means reducing the applications to a selected few for interview. This is necessary because businesses cannot interview every applicant but they want to select the best. They use certain criteria to ensure the process is fair, such as:

- **qualifications:** a minimum level and number are required, for example, at least five CSEC qualifications grade C and above including maths and English
- **specified skills,** for example, accurate typing, experience of Microsoft Word and Excel
- **specified abilities,** for example, ability to arrange meetings, knowledge of filing systems
- **personal characteristics,** for example, ability to organise and prioritise own work
- **personal attributes,** for example, discretion and tact
- **previous experience** in a similar job or industry.

Interview and appoint the best candidate

All interviewers should receive appropriate training, so that they ask 'open-ended' questions (not answerable with a 'yes' or 'no'), follow up unsatisfactory answers and query any gaps in employment history. All candidates must be asked the same questions and none should be discriminatory. Candidates should be told the terms and conditions of the job and asked if they have any questions. Candidates should be thanked for attending and told how and when they will learn the result.

Many organisations 'score' candidates on their performance against a set of criteria. If two candidates are equal then the person who would fit in better with existing staff is likely to be chosen. References should then be checked before an offer is made.

HR functions that relate to existing staff

HR activities relating to existing staff are shown in Figure 8.1.3.

Induction programmes

New staff should attend an **induction** programme when they first start work. This helps them to settle in more easily and become productive and efficient more quickly. Attendees are given basic

KEY TERMS

A **job description** states the key responsibilities and tasks involved in performing a job.

A **job specification** lists the skills and personal qualities needed to perform a particular job.

A **shortlist** is the list of top candidates who will be interviewed.

THINK ABOUT IT!

Look at the job description for the HR assistant on page 126. What knowledge, skills and attributes would be required to do that job?

DID YOU KNOW?

Some companies only offer junior roles to external applicants. More senior jobs are always offered first as promotion opportunities to existing staff.

DID YOU KNOW?

Usually all shortlisted candidates *must* have the essential requirements detailed in the job specification.

DID YOU KNOW?

A panel interview means a group of people interview the candidate. This usually occurs for a senior job.

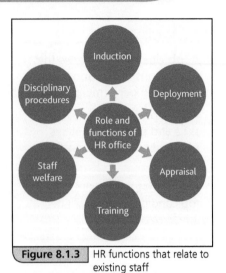

Figure 8.1.3 HR functions that relate to existing staff

KEY TERMS

Induction is a brief training programme to familiarise new staff with the organisation.

An **appraisal** is a confidential interview between an employee and line manager at which their work is reviewed.

health and safety information as well as information on staff facilities and methods of working. The programme usually includes an overview of the organisation, a tour of the premises and the opportunity to meet new colleagues.

Staff deployment

Deployment relates to staff job roles (see Unit 1, pages 12–15). The organisation should deploy staff to gain the maximum benefit from their employment. This means utilising people's skills and helping them to make the most of their abilities.

Staff may be redeployed if there is an organisational restructure. This can be a stressful time and HR should provide support by providing accurate and timely information and checking that the process is fair.

Appraisal

This is a confidential interview, usually between a manager and each member of staff. It is normally held once a year and covers:

- the work that the employee has done well during the year
- areas where the employee has performed less well
- a review of previous targets
- types of work (or jobs) that the employee would like to do in the future and the training that may be necessary.

Employees are expected to contribute positively to the discussion. A good manager will listen carefully, try to help with any concerns and link the employee's future ambitions to the overall aims of the organisation. A record is kept of the discussion and of actions agreed.

The benefits of appraisals are identified in Table 8.1.1.

Table 8.1.1 The benefits of appraisals

Benefits for the staff	Benefits for the organisation
Aspirations can be discussed, such as skills development or promotion aims	Training needs are identified across the organisation
Problems can be discussed and solutions agreed	Organisational goals can be linked to staff aims
Communication with their manager is improved	Evidence is provided for promotion (or dismissal)
It is motivational for staff to discuss aims in confidence with their manager	Performance-related pay and bonuses can be linked to targets each year
The appraisal may be linked to pay reviews	New skills and abilities may be discovered

DID YOU KNOW?

Some organisations appoint a **mentor** to look after someone new and give advice and support during the early weeks.

Training

Training courses take place both inside and outside the workplace. HR will notify staff about relevant courses and arrange attendance.

- **In-house courses** include induction, workshops and seminars to update staff or introduce new working methods. Areas covered include IT, health and safety, and team working. Attendance is free and may be compulsory for some staff.

- **External courses** are held at specialist centres or colleges. They may cover new software, first aid, telesales, customer service, teamwork and professional business courses. Employers may pay the fee or contribute towards it.

Staff welfare

By law employers must meet minimum standards of safety and provide a heathy and clean working environment. Sensible employers provide additional welfare benefits, knowing they will benefit from more satisfied employees who work harder and are less likely to seek employment elsewhere or engage in industrial action. Examples are used on page 135.

Employers must also ensure that no staff are subjected to harassment, bullying or discrimation.

Disciplinary procedures

These explain the action that the employer will take if employees break their contract of employment (see page 130), fail to comply with organisational rules (such as those on health and safety) or do not fulfil their responsibilities. The following are the main points to note.

- Having set procedures helps to ensure that all employees are treated equally and fairly. These procedures should be known by all employees.
- The response must always be appropriate for the offence. For example:
  - a verbal warning for a first or minor offence, such as being late
  - a written or final warning for a more serious or repeated offence, such as unauthorised absenteeism
  - dismissal for gross misconduct such as theft, drug-taking at work or fighting.
- Employees who attend a disciplinary interview should have the right to be accompanied by someone else and appeal against the decision.

The importance of HR and its relationship with other departments

HR supports existing employees by providing appropriate training, advice and assistance as needed. It will advise on pay rates and welfare facilities to attract and retain the best staff, and it will ensure the recruitment process is appropriate and effective. The business benefits because staff turnover is lower, staff are productive and motivated, and recruitment is cost effective. HR also ensures the organisation honours its legal responsibilities and that staff are treated fairly.

HR will liaise with other departments, such as sales and production, because HR will handle job vacancies. They will prepare advertisements and shortlists, advertise promotion opportunities and training courses, organise welfare and oversee the appraisal process and disciplinary issues for staff in all areas.

DID YOU KNOW?

Well-trained staff are more productive and efficient, and they are more motivated to do well and apply for promotion.

FIND OUT MORE

At the Googleplex (Google's HQ in California), staff can eat three free meals a day, have haircuts and massages at work and use the gym, swimming pool and games tables! The aim is to keep young workers committed and creative. See http://computer.howstuffworks.com/googleplex.htm.

DID YOU KNOW?

Many organisations have grievance procedures that tell employees what action to take if they have a serious complaint.

TEST YOURSELF

1 a Explain why disciplinary action may be taken against an employee.

 b Outline how an employer can safeguard against disciplining an employee unfairly or too harshly.

Now check your answers against those on the accompanying CD.

LEARNING OUTCOMES

By the time you have completed this section you should be able to:

- identify the duties and attributes of an assistant in the human resource office.

JASON MORGAN INC.
JOB DESCRIPTION
Department: Human resources
Job title: Human resource assistant
Hours of work: 9 am–5.30 pm, Monday to Friday
Accountable to: HR manager
Job summary: To provide support for the HR manager in record keeping, arranging interviews and staff welfare issues.

Work involved:
1 Maintaining a database of personnel records.
2 Preparing for interviews by recording applications, passing forms to managers, assisting with shortlisting procedures and notifying selected candidates of interview dates and times.
3 Attending to staff welfare issues.
4 Assisting with other functions of the HR management office as required.

| **Figure 8.2.1** | An example of a job description |

KEY TERMS

An **aptitude test** is a test of knowledge and skills and shows a candidate's suitability to work in a particular type of job.

DID YOU KNOW?

HR staff often need to work out staff absence and turnover figures, so the ability to do simple calculations is important.

The duties of a human resource assistant

All staff employed in the human resources department help with the recruitment process and deal with other aspects of the HR function, such as organising induction and other training programmes, keeping and updating staff records and attending to staff welfare issues. An example of a job description for this role is shown in Figure 8.2.1.

Personnel records

Personnel records may be kept on a manual system or on a computer database. It is easier to find and update electronic records, so this is normal practice in large organisations. The **individual staff record** will include the following information about each employee:

- their name and address, and their home and cellphone numbers
- date of birth, gender, nationality and emergency contact/next of kin details
- education and qualifications
- details of any known disability
- employment history with the company/service record (see page 130)
- terms and conditions of employment (pay, hours of work, holiday entitlement and benefits)
- details of any absences, training undertaken, disciplinary action or accidents connected with work.

See pages 130–131 for other types of records kept in HR.

Prepare for interviews

The task of the HR assistant may include:

- receiving application forms and keeping them safely
- notifying the shortlisted candidates and drawing up the interview schedule
- ensuring the interview room and waiting area is clean and tidy
- organising any **aptitude test** that may be needed
- greeting candidates and showing them to the interview room
- writing to named referees to ask them for a reference
- writing to candidates to advise whether they have been successful.

Attend to staff welfare

The role of the HR assistant may include handling requests for leave of absence (see page 131) and receiving and recording sick notes. Staff welfare issues must be handled sensitively as they may relate to medical, financial or other personal issues. The HR assistant must be able to provide prompt, accurate information, in confidence, to employees who need help or assistance.

Assist with the functions of the human resource management office

On a daily basis, assistance is likely to include answering the telephone, opening the mail, photocopying documents, maintaining the HR filing system and greeting visitors who call into HR. A comprehensive list of functions is given below.

Table 8.2.1	Human resource management functions
Advertising job vacancies, notifying staff of promotion opportunities
Receiving and recording job applications, arranging interviews and notifying candidates of the result
Sending a contract of employment and other information to new staff
Arranging staff training
Monitoring the working conditions of staff (for example, the temperature, ventilation and space per worker)
Checking health and safety, and keeping accident records
Recording sick leave and reasons for absence, and processing other leave applications
Carrying out company welfare policies, for example, long-service awards and company loans
Advising managers on the legal responsibilities of the company and its employees
Keeping records of grievances and disciplinary actions and their outcomes
Monitoring the terms and conditions of employment, including wage rates
Maintaining staff records
Liaising with trade unions that represent the workforce

Attributes

The attributes required by an HR assistant are as follows.

- **Confidentiality**, because discretion is paramount in this job. An HR assistant will know the personal details, medical history and earnings of staff in the organisation and must not discuss this information with other people either inside or outside the company.
- **Patience**, because other people may need information to be explained to them carefully and precisely.
- **Tact**, which means being diplomatic and not making thoughtless comments that could upset someone who is under stress or pressure. They may need to explain certain facts in such a way that it causes the least problems possible.

Figure 8.2.2 Confidentiality is important for anyone who works in HR

FIND OUT MORE

Look back at Unit 1, page 14, where you learned about other desirable attributes of administrators. Then decide which other attributes would be invaluable for someone who works in HR.

THINK ABOUT IT!

Marsha has applied for time off to go to the funeral of an elderly neighbour because they were very close. This has been refused because the neighbour was not a relative. Marsha would only be allowed to take time off if she is prepared to do so without pay. How would you tactfully explain this decision to her?

TEST YOURSELF

1 a List THREE duties regularly undertaken by an HR assistant.

   b Identify TWO important attributes required by an HR assistant and explain why these are necessary.

Now check your answers against those on the accompanying CD.

LEARNING OUTCOMES

By the time you have completed this section you should be able to:

• identify the benefits of legislation related to workers' welfare.

DID YOU KNOW?

A contract of employment (see page 130) is a legal document and both employer and employee must abide by its conditions.

DID YOU KNOW?

Children below the age of 13 cannot work at all. Those under 15 can only do light work, and activities up to the age of 18 are restricted.

KEY TERMS

Discrimination means treating someone differently or unfairly for a reason unconnected with the job, for example, because of their race, gender, ethnic origin or marital status.

Collective agreements are negotiated settlements secured for groups of workers, usually by a trade union.

Statutory provisions for employee protection

The word **statutory** means 'by law'. All organisations and individuals must comply, without exception, with laws that relate to them. Ignorance is no excuse for non-compliance, so HR must ensure that managers and staff are kept up to date with legislation that applies to them.

Today, all workers expect to receive equal treatment, to be paid a fair wage and to work in a safe environment. They expect to receive proper training to operate equipment and to be provided with protective clothing and equipment when necessary. They also have the right to join a trade union and not to be penalised for doing so. Equally, employers expect their staff to follow health and safety regulations and to treat other employees with respect.

ILO conventions

You first read about the International Labour Organization (ILO) on page 64. This organisation sets international labour standards, and its conventions are binding on all members, including all CARICOM territories that are signatories. ILO conventions on decent work are relevant to HR as they cover wages, holiday, maternity leave, health and safety, fair treatment and trade union rights. They also ban forced labour and restrict the use of child labour.

Discrimination and equal remuneration

Discrimination means treating someone differently or unfairly for a reason unconnected with the job. In Unit 3 (page 64) you learned that the law states that no worker should be discriminated against at work on the grounds of race, colour, sex, religion, political opinion, nationality or social origin. Discrimination is unlawful at any stage of the recruitment process, for example, when advertising, shortlisting or interviewing. All staff doing the same work, or work of 'equal value', must be paid at the same rate, have the same conditions and benefits, and be offered the same training and promotion opportunities.

Freedom of association and collective bargaining

These conventions guarantee that employers and workers can establish and join organisations of their choice, such as trade unions, and draw up their own rules. Workers cannot be dismissed or discriminated against because they join a trade union or participate in union activities. Trade unions can negotiate with employers on terms of employment and try to conclude **collective agreements** on behalf of their members.

The Factories Act

The aim of the Factories Act is primarily to ensure that anyone who works in a place where goods are manufactured, produced or adapted in any way will be protected. This is important because factories are potentially dangerous places with hazardous machinery and substances. The main provisions are shown in Table 8.3.1.

Table 8.3.1	Basic requirements under the Factories Act
Clean and hygienic workplace	
Safe, regularly maintained equipment	
Safe working practices, for example, safe storage of dangerous substances and chemicals, guards on hazardous moving equipment, non-slip flooring	
Provision of a first-aid box	
Adequate lighting and ventilation	
Fire safety precautions and adequate unlocked exit doors	
Appropriate training and the provision of protective clothing, for example, hard hats, goggles, safety boots (with reinforced toes), gloves, ear muffs, protective aprons and face masks	
Adequate working space per employee	
Provision of clean drinking water, washing facilities and separate sanitary conveniences for men and women	
The recording of all accidents and injuries that occur at work	

The Workmen's Compensation Act

The Workmen's Compensation Act enables workers who are injured or incapacitated at work, or who suffer an occupational disease, to claim financial compensation. In the case of death, this is paid to their next of kin. To protect themselves against large claims, all employers must take out insurance and they must abide by their legal obligations.

Occupational Safety and Health Act (OSHA)

The OSHA was introduced in the 1970s in the US to reduce the number of accidents and injuries occurring in workplaces. It has since been adapted and introduced in many countries. Under the OSHA, inspections or risk assessments are carried out so that hazardous conditions are identified. If these cannot be eliminated, precautions must be taken to warn and protect employees. With the advent of the OSHA, many companies in the Caribbean now have a department called HSE – Health, Safety and Environment.

DID YOU KNOW?

The title of laws relating to safety may vary from one Caribbean territory to another (for example, the Factories Act in Barbados and Jamaica and the Occupational Safety and Health Act in Trinidad and Tobago) but the aims are usually the same.

Figure 8.3.1 What benefits do employers gain by issuing protective clothing?

DID YOU KNOW?

The OSHA means that health and safety applies to all workplaces – such as offices, shops, schools and hospitals – and not just factories.

THINK ABOUT IT!

Employers gain several benefits from providing a safe workplace. There are fewer accidents, stoppages and disputes, and there is less chance of a major financial claim because of negligence. Now see if you can think of four benefits that employees gain.

TEST YOURSELF

1 a Identify THREE safety precautions that are taken in a factory workplace to protect employees.

  b Identify FOUR health provisions that are a legal requirement for all workers.

Now check your answers against those on the accompanying CD.

Records used in a human resource office

DID YOU KNOW?

HR may interview staff periodically to check that their records are up to date and accurate.

DID YOU KNOW?

A contract of employment is a legal document and both employer and employee must abide by its conditions.

EXAM TIP

Check that you can list at least four or five terms in a contract of employment.

DID YOU KNOW?

The terms and conditions of employment may be set out in the offer letter and this can act as the formal contract between you and your employer.

Human resource staff are responsible for maintaining several different types of staff records. You have already seen that these include individual personal records that are often held in a computer database.

Personnel records are very important because they contain vital information about employees. For that reason they must be accurate. It is also important that they are checked regularly to ensure they are correct and that the employee agrees with what is recorded.

Different types of personnel records

Contract of employment

This is a formal agreement about the job that states the terms and conditions that will apply. Once it is signed by both employer and employee it becomes legally binding and both parties have to abide by its terms. So, you cannot agree to start work at 8.30 am and arrive at 9 o'clock every morning! Similarly, if your employer agrees to pay you $1,500 a month you cannot be paid less than this.

Table 8.4.1	Terms in a contract of employment
Names of the employer and employee	
Date when employment began	
Job title or brief job description	
Hours of work and place of work	
Pay, and how often payments will be made	
Holiday entitlement	
Entitlement to sick leave and any entitlement to sick pay	
Pensions and pension schemes	
Notice required by employer and employee to terminate the contract	
Reference to disciplinary and grievance procedures and any trade union agreements that relate to the employee	

Service records

Once a new employee has started work, they commence their service with the company. Some organisations give long-service awards to employees who have been with the company for many years.

Service records are important because they include details of an employee's history with the company, including training courses attended, qualifications achieved, and promotions applied for and gained. Absences of leave will also be recorded. This entitlement to leave may increase, based on years of service, up to a fixed annual limit.

Types of leave

All employees will be allowed a set number of annual leave days for a vacation, often plus statutory and local holidays, normally with pay. Employees may also request to take time off for:

- sick leave
- maternity, paternity or adoption leave
- compassionate leave or time off because of a bereavement
- unpaid leave (for example, for an extended vacation)
- TOIL (time off in lieu) for working longer hours or doing unpaid overtime to help during a busy time
- study leave to gain a job-related qualification.

All vacation leave is recorded to ensure that no one takes more than their annual entitlement. If sick pay is paid for a certain number of days per year this is also checked against the annual sick leave taken.

Personal history/records

On page 126 you learned that each member of staff will have an individual record that is usually held on the computer database. In addition, a manual file may be kept that includes any documents that apply to the person, for example:

- the application form or letter of application that they submitted and/or their CV
- references they provided and interview records
- applications for leave of absence
- training records
- medical certificates
- completed appraisal forms
- any disciplinary or grievance records.

Appraisal forms

Appraisals are normally carried out by a person's supervisor or manager but copies of the blank forms will be held in HR and the completed form may be held in the personal file.

This is important because it will summarise the actions that the employee has agreed to take before the next appraisal, such as to develop specific skills or attend a particular training course. These will form the basis for discussion when the next appraisal interview is held.

Job description and job specification

These were discussed on pages 56 and 122. Turn back to those pages now to check that you remember the content of each.

DID YOU KNOW?

Many organisations have a qualifying period before an employee is confirmed in a permanent job and/or before they will be eligible for sick pay.

DID YOU KNOW?

A departmental leave schedule is normally essential. This allocates vacation time fairly but ensures that key tasks are always covered.

EXAM TIP

Remember that all staff records are strictly confidential. Stress this in any answer you give.

Figure 8.4.1 What aspects of an employee's performance do you think should be assessed?

TEST YOURSELF

1 a You have just started work in an HR office. List FOUR types of records you may be asked to maintain.

  b Explain why leave records are important and why they must always be kept up to date.

Now check your answers against those on the accompanying CD.

THINK ABOUT IT!

An employee regularly promises to develop her word-processing skills, but always finds an excuse not to attend a course when it is offered to her. What action do you think the employer should take and why?

Factors that contribute to employee turnover

LEARNING OUTCOMES

By the time you have completed this section you should be able to:

- describe the factors that contribute to employee turnover in an organisation.

KEY TERMS

Employee turnover is the rate at which people enter and leave an organisation. However, it is normally thought of in relation to the length of time people stay in a job before they leave to go elsewhere.

DID YOU KNOW?

The longer people work for a business the more likely they are to stay there. So, the greatest turnover is likely to be in recent recruits.

Figure 8.5.1 Which is worse – too much work or not enough?

Employee turnover is the rate at which staff enter and leave an organisation. If it is high – meaning many staff leave quickly – this can cause problems and also give a bad impression of the business.

More about employee turnover

HR staff can calculate the rate of employee turnover in their organisation. The simplest measure is to look at the number of leavers over one year and work out their percentage against the total labour force. So, if a business has 200 workers, and 20 people leave during the year, the turnover figure would be 10% ($20 \div 200 \times 100$).

A high labour turnover creates several problems. The recruitment process is expensive, so having to hire new people frequently will increases these costs. It also costs money to train new staff and familiarise them with the way the business operates. This is wasted if they leave soon after joining. It is also disruptive for other employees, who may have to do extra work until the leavers are replaced. If this happens often, then either the recruitment process is not finding the best people for the job, or there are other factors that are causing people to leave.

Factors that contribute to employee turnover

Organisations should try to find out what is causing a high employee turnover. It is pointless advertising for staff, interviewing candidates and appointing people if they leave shortly afterwards. The factors that affect this can be divided into two types: internal and external factors.

Internal factors that contribute to employee turnover

The internal factors are those that exist *within* the organisation. The external factors exist *outside* the organisation and the business can do little to change to these. They are both explained in Table 8.5.1.

THINK ABOUT IT!

As you read through Table 8.5.1, think about the possible changes that an organisation could make to internal factors to reduce the rate of labour turnover.

DID YOU KNOW?

The first sign that staff are unhappy or dissatisfied may be an increase in unauthorised absenteeism.

Table 8.5.1	Internal and external factors that contribute to labour turnover
Internal factors	**Reason**
Working conditions	These are all the aspects relating to the job except pay, such as facilities at work, holiday entitlement, physical environment (temperature, ventilation and space per worker), noise levels, mechanisation, health and safety aspects and other 'perks' such as laptop computers, smartphones and company cars for sales staff. If the pace of work is too fast then workers will become stressed and feel ill. Staff may leave if working conditions are better somewhere else
Low salary	All organisations should know the pay rates offered by their competitors for similar jobs. Offering a salary at or above the average rate will attract staff. A rate below this level may only attract workers if unemployment is high
Lack of job satisfaction	Most people need to be stimulated and interested in their work. Boring work is tedious, so is having little to do. Feeling unappreciated and receiving no support is also demotivating. These factors contribute to an employee deciding to leave
Lack of training opportunities	Training is an important part of staff development. People want to be eligible for promotion, and this is difficult without learning new skills
Redundancy	This is when the business does not have enough work for employees to do, or is relocating or closing down and has to dismiss staff. The organisation must follow an agreed procedure to make sure that all dismissals are fair
External factors	**Reason**
State of **the economy**	The economy affects the demand for goods and labour. If it is growing then demand will be high and wages will increase. The business must keep pace with these increases in order to attract good staff. If the economy is declining then demand will fall. Unemployment will increase, and that reduces wages, but the business will have to make staff redundant if there is not enough work for them to do
Better opportunities	Local firms may offer better conditions and pay rates, more high-tech, specialised or interesting jobs. Opportunities may exist overseas and pay rates may be higher
Competition for job placement	If many applications are received for each job then the business can choose which candidate it wants, even if wages are relatively low. If few applications are received, because competition for labour is high, the business may struggle to find anyone suitable at the wage it can afford to pay

KEY TERMS

The economy is the financial situation of a country as a result of all the items that are produced and consumed there.

TEST YOURSELF

1 Staff turnover is considered to be too high in the sales department. Make FIVE recommendations to the sales manager that may help to reduce this.

Now check your answers against those on the accompanying CD.

SECTION 1: Multiple-choice questions

1 The confidential session at which an employee's strengths and weaknesses are discussed is called:

a An interview.   **c** Needs analysis.

b Staff welfare.   **d** An appraisal.

2 A serious offence at work, such as taking drugs or stealing, would result in:

a Transfer to another department.

b Dismissal.

c A verbal warning.

d A written warning.

3 Internal factors that can contribute to employees leaving the organisation include:

i Critical supervisors who provide little help or support.

ii Long working hours.

iii Another business opening and offering better wages.

iv Boring and tedious work.

a i, ii and iii only   **c** ii, iii and iv only

b i, ii and iv only   **d** All of the above

4 The document that lists the tasks that a successful candidate will carry out is called:

a The job description.

b The job specification.

c The application form.

d The contract of employment.

5 The HR department will liaise with other departments on:

i Advertising vacancies in their department.

ii Shortlisting applicants and preparing an interview schedule.

iii Pay rates offered to new staff.

iv Vacation leave records for staff in their department.

a i, ii and iii only   **c** ii, iii and iv only

b i, iii and iv only   **d** All of the above

6 Staff are made redundant when:

a There is high unemployment.

b The company cannot afford to pay high wages.

c There is no work for them to do.

d They have broken their contract of employment.

7 Safety provisions included in the Factories Act are:

i Non-slip floors.

ii Protective clothing.

iii Good lighting and ventilation.

iv Interesting work.

a i, ii and iii only   **c** ii, iii and iv only

b i, iii and iv only   **d** All of the above

8 When staff are being recruited, the normal procedure is as follows.

a Needs analysis, job description/ specification, advertise, shortlist

b Job description/specification, advertise, needs analysis, shortlist

c Shortlist, advertise, job description/ specification, needs analysis

d Needs analysis, advertise, job description/ specification, shortlist

9 Marcia is pregnant and will not be working for the next few months. This is an example of:

a Adoption leave.   **c** Unauthorised leave.

b Unpaid leave.   **d** Maternity leave.

10 The benefits of holding an induction programme include:

i New staff become productive more quickly.

ii Staff can find their way around the building more easily.

iii Staff settle in more quickly.

iv Staff understand the organisation and the work that it does.

a i, ii and iii only   **c** ii, iii and iv only

b i, iii and iv only   **d** All of the above

Further practice questions and examples can be found on the accompanying CD.

1 List FIVE items of information that you would find on a person's individual staff record, apart from their personal details and contact information.

2 Explain what is meant by a 'collective agreement'.

3 Identify FOUR types of records routinely maintained by HR staff.

4 Give THREE benefits to an employer of providing a safe environment and welfare provisions for staff.

5 List TWO examples of in-house training courses for staff and say why each may be necessary.

6 Identify TWO types of confidential information dealt with by HR staff and give ONE example of an occasion when an HR assistant may have to be patient or tactful.

7 List THREE benefits of introducing an appraisal system:
   a for the organisation
   b for the employee.

8 List FOUR items of information found in a contract of employment.

9 Explain the purpose of a needs analysis.

10 Read the following list of staff welfare provisions and identify FIVE that you would recommend to a new business to attract talented new employees. You should also research the facilities offered by Google at the Googleplex (its HQ in California) to attract young workers and help to keep them committed and creative at http://computer.howstuffworks.com/googleplex.htm.

Staff welfare examples

- a staff bonus scheme, linked to profits, so staff benefit if the company does well
- a pension scheme to which the employer also contributes
- long-service awards to reward staff loyalty
- sick leave and sick pay
- good working conditions and facilities including rest rooms, cloakrooms, kitchen facilities and/or a canteen, recreational equipment
- flexible working opportunities
- medical check-ups and professional help with specialist problems such as drug or alcohol dependency
- support with personal problems such as confidential counselling, compassionate leave, an advance of salary or access to a benevolent fund.

Further practice questions and examples can be found on the accompanying CD.

9.1 The role and function of the accounts office

LEARNING OUTCOMES

By the time you have finished this section you should be able to:

- describe the role and functions of the accounts office.

DID YOU KNOW?

Most businesses do not pay for goods immediately when they buy them. Instead they are allowed a credit period (about a month) to settle their account.

KEY TERMS

Credit refers to any situation where money is allowed to be owed.

A **credit period** is the length of time a customer is allowed before they must pay the amount owing.

Credit control means monitoring the amount of money owed by individual customers and chasing up overdue payments.

DID YOU KNOW?

Some businesses offer a discount for prompt or early payment.

Introduction to accounts and financial services

All business organisations deal with money. This involves three main activities – receiving money, paying out money and keeping accurate records of these events.

In this unit you will learn about the activities undertaken by an accounts office and the documents that are prepared there.

Tasks carried out in the accounts office

The accounts office processes payments in and out of the business and prepares financial documents to record these transactions. This means undertaking several tasks.

Preparation of payroll

The payroll lists the money paid to all staff as wages for a week or month. The accounts office must ensure that each individual's pay is calculated correctly and payments are always made on time, for example, at the end of each month (see also page 140).

Credit control

When you buy something you are expected to pay immediately. However, most trading between businesses is carried out on a **credit** basis. So, when your school buys books or paper it is allowed time to pay, usually a month. This is known as the **credit period**.

The seller requests payment by sending **an invoice**, which states the credit terms, such as 28 days. At the end of each month a **statement of account** (see page 142) is issued, summarising all of the transactions with the customer during that month. The seller checks that the payment is received. If not, the buyer is contacted and asked for payment. This procedure is known as **credit control**.

Normally organisations have a set procedure for obtaining payment, beginning with a polite reminder. This may end with legal proceedings if the customer still does not pay. The supplier will not allow the customer to buy any further items until the debt is paid.

Credit control is important because businesses must obtain money for goods sold otherwise they cannot make a profit. If they do not obtain payment promptly they could run short of cash to pay their own bills and be unable to buy new stock or pay staff salaries.

The accounts office must identify all overdue payments and take appropriate action. Some businesses use a computer accounts package that automatically signals when payments are overdue.

Collection of accounts

Sending an invoice is the first step in collecting money owed, as you will see on page 173.

Treatment of debit and credit notes

These documents are used to correct mistakes made on an invoice. If too *little* is charged then a **debit note** is issued for the additional amount. This may happen if:

• the customer was undercharged for the goods
• too many, or better, goods were sent and kept
• an item was omitted from the invoice.

If too *much* is charged then a **credit note** is sent. This may happen if:

• the customer was overcharged
• some goods were returned to the supplier
• fewer items were delivered than stated on the invoice.

Any discount terms on the credit note *must* be identical to those shown on the original invoice.

Preparation of an audit

When accounts are **audited**, they are checked to ensure everything is being done properly. Auditors are employed by accountants or specialist financial companies that are independent of the business being audited. The auditors may check all of the petty cash records (see page 150) or follow a purchasing process through from the receipt of the invoice to payment, as shown on the bank statement.

Auditors can arrive unannounced, but they normally give a few days' notice. Accounts office staff must make sure that:

• all finance documents are filed correctly and are easily accessible
• all documents are completed correctly and are up to date.

These tasks must be maintained on a daily basis so that little extra preparation is needed for an audit.

Working with different types of bank account

Banks offer a wide range of services to business and private customers (see page 145). Accounts staff must know which bank accounts are used by the business, how to deposit money received and how to make payments by cheque from an account.

see page 145

see page 150

page 173

THINK ABOUT IT!

If you had a business, what checks would you carry out before you allowed a new business customer to have credit facilities, and why?

KEY TERMS

A **debit note** states the extra amount owed to correct a shortfall on an invoice.

A **credit note** states the amount that can be deducted to correct an overcharge on an invoice.

An **audit** is an independent check of a business's financial affairs.

Figure 9.1.1 What type of documents do auditors check?

TEST YOURSELF

1 a Define the term 'credit control'.
  b State TWO reasons why credit control is important.

Now check your answers against those on the accompanying CD.

EXAM TIP

If you must define a term, just state clearly what it means.

LEARNING OUTCOMES

By the time you have completed this section you should be able to:

* identify the duties and attributes of a clerk in the accounts office.

| Figure 9.2.1 | People who work expect to be paid |

KEY TERMS

Gross pay is the total amount of money a person earns including overtime and bonuses.

Deductions are the amounts of money subtracted from the gross pay figure.

Net pay is the amount of money the employee takes home after deductions.

FIND OUT MORE

Find out the name of the government agency in your territory that collects income tax and other statutory deductions. Then search their website to find out how income tax is calculated and what deductions there are.

Duties of an accounts office clerk

Preparing the payroll

At their interview employees are usually offered a specific salary. This is their basic pay. They may also receive extra money for overtime working or bonuses. This makes up their **gross pay**. Unfortunately this is not the amount they receive, because there are usually **deductions** to be made, for example:

* income tax and National Insurance (pays for health services)
* pension contributions
* union subscription
* charitable donations (this is an optional deduction).

The amount that the employee then receives is their **net pay**. The payroll list includes this information for each employee (see page 140).

Writing cheques

One of the main functions of the accounts office is to make payments to people and businesses who are owed money by the organisation. One way of doing this is to provide a cheque. You will learn more about cheques on pages 142–143.

Reconciling accounts

Reconciling accounts means checking that all of the information on a financial transaction is correct on all the relevant documents. An example is checking the **bank statement** to make sure that all of the entries are correct. See page 149.

Making ledger entries

Ledgers are books that are used to record financial information. The two main types used by businesses are sales and purchase ledgers.

* **The sales ledger** is a record of sales. For each item, the entry should include the date, name of the customer, types and price of products sold, and payment and date received. Any returned goods should also be recorded.

* **The purchase ledger** is a record of all purchases made by the business. As with the sales ledger, full details are recorded including payments made.

Preparing statements of account

Suppliers send a **statement of account** to all customers at the end of each month. This summarises all transactions that have occurred during that month including invoice totals, payments made, amounts of debit and credit notes that have been issued. Rather than send payment for each invoice individually, it is accepted practice that customers wait for the statement of account before making a payment.

The information for a statement of account comes from invoices, debit notes and credit notes issued, together with records of payments received from the customer.

Writing up the cash book

A cash book is a formal record of all receipts and payments of a business. The information is obtained from cash receipts, chequebook stubs, records of payments made into the bank and bank statements.

The receipts are regularly totalled and the payment amounts are subtracted to give a balance. It is essential that entries are made in the cash book promptly and totalled accurately (see page 149).

Preparing final accounts

Final accounts summarise the financial information about a business over the year. There are three main documents: the **trading account**, the **profit and loss account** and the **balance sheet**.

- A **trading account** shows the **gross profit** after the **cost of sales** has been subtracted from the total amount of money received from customers (the total sales figure).
- The **profit and loss account** produces the **net profit** figure. It is found by subtracting the total of all payments made (including purchases and staff wages) from the total sales figure.
- The **balance sheet** has two sets of figures. One shows all the business's **assets**, such as buildings, equipment, stock and cash, and the value of each. The other list shows all the **liabilities**. These are amounts the business owes, such as bank overdrafts and money owed to suppliers. It is called a balance sheet because the total of each list of figures is the same. In other words they *balance*.

The figures in all of the final accounts are summaries of individual documents produced by the accounts office.

Attributes of an accounts office clerk

People who work in an accounts office should have the following attributes.

- **Integrity**. They can be trusted to handle sums of money, particularly cash.
- **Confidentiality**. They can be trusted not to disclose sensitive information such as special discounts given to customers, or employees' salaries.
- **Reliability**. They can be depended upon to deal with all tasks thoroughly and accurately.

TEST YOURSELF

1 Explain the purpose of a statement of account.

Now check your answer against the one on the accompanying CD.

DID YOU KNOW?

Making an entry into a ledger is sometimes called **posting** the information.

DID YOU KNOW?

Although this is called a *cash* book, it also includes other receipts such as cheques.

DID YOU KNOW?

The cost of sales for a retail business is the amount spent on stock.

Figure 9.2.2 | Making a profit is essential to business survival

EXAM TIP

Always remember that assets are good to have, liabilities are not.

Documents in the accounts office

LEARNING OUTCOMES

By the time you have finished this section you should be able to:

- prepare simple documents in the accounts office.

THINK ABOUT IT!

If you were producing G Sobers' payslip from the information given in the payroll list and his time card, what figures would you enter in spaces A to I below? You can check your answer on page 143.

Preparing simple documents

You must be able to prepare simple documents that are used in an accounts office. Examples are shown in this section. It is very important that you understand all of the headings and the key information that is included under each one.

Payroll documents

You need to be able to complete:

- a payroll list – a list of payments made to employees that shows how each employee's pay is calculated
- a time card – which itemises the hours worked at different pay rates, and the total earned
- a payslip – which shows the gross pay, all deductions and the net pay that the employee receives.

Name	Gross pay ($)	Income tax ($)	National Insurance ($)	Pension ($)	Union subscription ($)	Total deductions ($)	Net pay ($)
B Lara	505	50	15	10	2	77	428
G Sobers	642	70	15	10	2	97	545
C Lloyd	390	20	15	10	2	47	343

Figure 9.3.1 An extract from a payroll list

BUSINESS MACHINES LTD – PAYSLIP	
Name/Works number	G Sobers/621
Period	7 to 14 April 2012
Tax code	140M
NI number	YA 83 35 45 C
PAY DUE	
Basic pay	A
Overtime	B
Total – gross pay	C
DEDUCTIONS	
Income tax	D
National Insurance	E
Pension contribution	F
Union subscription	G
Total deductions	H
Net pay	I

Figure 9.3.3 A pay advice slip

TIME CARD				
Employee no.: 621	Department: Production	Week commencing: 27/5/2012		Name: G Sobers
	Standard time Hours	Overtime Hours	Payment	
			Standard @ $12	Overtime @ $18
Monday	8		96	
Tuesday	8	2	96	36
Wednesday	8		96	
Thursday	8	3	96	54
Friday	8		96	
Saturday		4		72
		TOTAL	480	162
			GROSS PAY	642

Figure 9.3.2 A time card

Debit and credit notes

The layouts of these documents are very similar. Key items of information that you may be expected to enter are:

- the date
- the name and address of the customer
- the quantity of items
- a description of the items
- the price per item
- the total amount – this is the quantity multiplied by the price.

DID YOU KNOW?

Deductions from gross pay are made up of statutory/compulsory and voluntary items. The main statutory items are income tax and National Insurance. Voluntary items could include pension contributions, charity donations and union subscriptions.

DEBIT NOTE
Novelty Sales Company
16 Town Street
Port of Spain
TRINIDAD

| Tel: 932 8541 | Email: accounts@novelties.com.tt |
| Fax: 932 5814 | Website: www.novelties.com.tt |

To: Bits and Pieces	Invoice no.: 12/690
20 Country Road	Debit note no.: 34
Port of Spain	Date: 6 March 2012
TRINIDAD	

Quantity	Description	Price	Amount
2 packs	Postcards – Caribbean selection (missing from original invoice)	$10.00	$20.00
		TOTAL	$20.00

Figure 9.3.4 | A debit note

THINK ABOUT IT!

Examples of a debit note and credit note are shown in Figures 9.3.4 and 9.3.5. Check these carefully and make sure you understand all of the entries and why they have been made.

CREDIT NOTE
Novelty Sales Company
16 Town Street
Port of Spain
TRINIDAD

| Tel: 932 8541 | Email: accounts@novelties.com.tt |
| Fax: 932 5814 | Website: www.novelties.com.tt |

To: Bits and Pieces	Invoice no.: 12/650
20 Country Road	Credit note no.: 163
Port of Spain	Date: 20 March 2012
TRINIDAD	

Quantity	Description	Unit price	Amount
3	Boxes of 6" Caribbean Views coffee mugs (boxes damaged and mugs broken)	$6.00	$ 18.00
		TOTAL	$ 18.00

Figure 9.3.5 | A credit note

Statements of account

These summarise the transactions between a supplier and customer over a month. Key information that you must be able to enter and describe is as follows.

- **The balance owing** – this is the amount carried forward as unpaid from last month's statement.
- **The debit column** – this shows the amounts the customer is being charged this month, either because an invoice or a debit note has been issued.
- **The credit column** – this shows the amounts that the supplier is deducting from the account, either because the customer has made a payment or because a credit note was issued.
- **The balance column** – this shows a running balance, because it is recalculated after every individual debit or credit has been added.
- **The amount due** – this is the final balance when all of the calculations have been completed.

> **THINK ABOUT IT!**
>
> Figure 9.3.6 is an example of a statement of account. Check each balance figure carefully to make sure you understand how it has been calculated.

> **EXAM TIP**
>
> If you are asked to insert figures and make calculations in any documents, read the headings carefully so that you understand what you are being asked to do.

STATEMENT OF ACCOUNT
Novelty Sales Company
16 Town Street
Port of Spain
TRINIDAD

Tel: 932 8541   Email: accounts@novelties.com.tt
Fax: 932 5814   Website: www.novelties.com.tt

To: Bits and Pieces
20 Country Road
Port of Spain   Date: 31 March 2012
TRINIDAD

Date	Details	Debit ($)	Credit ($)	Balance ($)
1 March	Balance owing			800.52
4 March	Invoice 10013	2823.52		3624.04
4 March	Cheque		800.52	2823.52
10 March	Debit note 34	20.00		2843.52
20 March	Credit note 163		18.00	2825.52
		AMOUNT DUE		2825.52

Figure 9.3.6   A statement of account

Cheques

Cheques are a common method of making payments. An example is shown in Figure 9.3.7. The key information you may be asked to add is:

- the date
- the name of the person being paid (called the **payee**)
- the amount being paid. This is written in figures in the rectangular box and in words and figures after 'The Sum Of'. Make sure there are no blank spaces so no one could add anything before or after your writing. Note that any cents may be written as a fraction or written in words.

The cheque is then signed by the **drawer** – the person who is making the payment.

The cheque may also be crossed so that it has to be paid into a bank account. This means drawing two horizontal lines down the centre and writing the words 'Not Negotiable' or 'A/C payee only' sideways between them (see also page 147).

DID YOU KNOW?

The business receiving the cheque will pay it into the bank. It must then wait for the money to be transferred or 'cleared' before payment is received into its account.

KEY TERMS

The payee is the person to whom the cheque is made out and who is receiving payment.

The drawer is the person who wrote the cheque and is drawing money out of their account to pay it.

EXAM TIP

Look carefully to see whether you should sign the cheque. Also verify whether the cheque should be crossed.

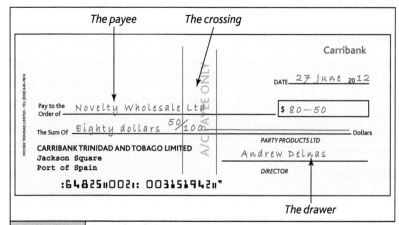

The payee   The crossing

Carribank

DATE 27 June 2012

Pay to the Order of — Novelty Wholesale Ltd

The Sum Of Eighty dollars 50/100 — Dollars

$ 80—50

CARRIBANK TRINIDAD AND TOBAGO LIMITED
Jackson Square
Port of Spain

PARTY PRODUCTS LTD
Andrew Delnas
DIRECTOR

:64825ıı002ı: 003ı5ı942ıı"

A/C PAYEE ONLY

The drawer

Figure 9.3.7 | A completed cheque

THINK ABOUT IT!

Look at the completed cheque in Figure 9.3.7. What do you think would happen if the wrong year was entered? You will find the answer on page 147.

TEST YOURSELF

1 Copy the layout of the statement of account on page 142 to produce a statement to Bits and Pieces, from the Novelty Sales Company, for the 30 April 2012. As this will follow on from the March statement, this will provide your balance owing figure. Transactions in April were as follows: on 16 April Bits and Pieces sent a cheque for $2,000. They bought goods on invoice 10032, dated 6 April, value $350.50, but two items were damaged. These were returned and a credit note, number 172, was issued on 25 April, value $70. Bits and Pieces also bought further goods listed on invoice 10045 on 17 April, value $280.25.

Now check your answers against those on the accompanying CD.

EXAM TIP

Remember that on a statement of account all items are entered in date order and a running balance is calculated.

The answer for G Sobers' payslip is as follows.

A=$480, B=$162, C=$642, D=$70, E=$15, F=$10, G=$2, H=$97, I=$545

Resources used in the accounts office, and types of financial institutions

LEARNING OUTCOMES

By the time you have finished this section you should be able to:

- identify hardware and software resources used in the accounts office
- identify types of financial institutions and their services.

DID YOU KNOW?

Having a printed record means it is much easier to check that all entries have been made correctly.

KEY TERMS

Cash flow is concerned with predicting the amount of money flowing in and out of a business's bank account. This means that the total in the account can be calculated for any given time.

FIND OUT MORE

Visit the FirstCaribbean Bank website, www. firstcaribbeanbank.com and investigate the following types of account: personal banking, savings accounts, foreign currency accounts, credit card accounts, loans.

Hardware resources

Calculators

Simple calculators process numbers, work out percentages and have a small memory and a display panel. Some incorporate a printer so a paper record can be produced. Many used in an accounts office will also carry out more complicated calculations such as **cash flow** and compound interest.

Adding machines

These were an early mechanical form of calculator and may still be used in some offices.

DID YOU KNOW?

The first type of calculator was an **abacus**. It consisted of a wooden frame with wires across and beads threaded on the wires. Abacuses are still used in China and Japan.

Computers

Most accounts offices now use computers to carry out the majority of tasks, such as:

- keeping a record of sales and purchase transactions
- producing invoices, debit and credit notes and statements of account
- producing debtor reports (reports of customers who owe money)
- producing a payroll and payslips
- storing the names and contact details of customers and suppliers.

Printers, scanners and copiers

These machines produce and copy documents (see page 9).

Software resources

Accounting packages

In most accounts offices, the computers undertake accounting tasks by using a special accounts software package. This may be customised to suit the needs of the business. A typical package would enable the accounts staff to store and produce:

- **sales information** – data on customers, current and past orders, payments, outstanding debts
- **purchase information** – data on suppliers, orders placed, payments due and those made
- **month-end reports** – including trial trading accounts, profit and loss accounts and balance sheets.

Spreadsheets

A spreadsheet is a computer application program that enables you to create a worksheet containing columns and rows in a grid formation. The numbers entered into the cells can be used in many ways, from simple addition or subtraction to more complex 'what if' calculations. For example, if projected profits are invested for the next 12 months, *what* would happen *if* bank interest rates increased by 2 per cent. Spreadsheets can also be used to forecast **cash flow**.

Financial institutions and their services

The financial institutions that you need to understand are summarised in Table 9.4.1.

Figure 9.4.1 FirstCaribbean Bank, a commercial bank

Table 9.4.1 Financial institutions

Type of financial institution	Services
Central bank	All Caribbean territories have a central bank that controls their overall financial policy. The main functions of the bank are to keep inflation down, to encourage commercial banks to lend money to promote the economy, to act as the government banker and to issue currency
Commercial banks	These are the high street banks that you see every day, such as Scotiabank. They deal with businesses and private persons by setting up bank accounts for them, accepting deposits and issuing loans. They provide account holders with regular bank statements that can be checked (reconciled) against the person's or business's records for accuracy (see pages 148–149)
Investment companies	These are businesses that invest in other businesses
Credit unions	These are financial institutions that are owned and run by their members. Members save money with the union. Credit unions will also lend money to persons, for example, to buy a house
Insurance companies	Insurance companies enable people to protect themselves against misfortune, such as fire or flood. Policyholders pay a regular premium so that they will be recompensed if the insured event occurs. Some types of insurance are required by law, such as car insurance. Many large companies offer a wide range of policies to cover business and domestic property, vehicles, house contents and to protect against redundancy
Bureau de change/cambios	These businesses specialise in buying and selling foreign currency. They make their money by selling at one price and buying at a higher price and/or charging commission on each transaction

FIND OUT MORE

Check out the City of Bridgetown Credit Union (www.cobcreditunion.com) to find out about services offered by credit unions. Then check Scotiabank (www.scotiabank.com) to see the services available.

EXAM TIP

Remember to think about the use of each resource specifically in an accounts office.

TEST YOURSELF

1 Identify THREE hardware resources used in an accounts office and explain ONE use for each item.

Now check your answers against those on the accompanying CD.

Making and receiving payments

LEARNING OUTCOMES

By the time you have finished this section you should be able to:

- outline the procedures for making different types of payment
- interpret the information on cheques.

Advantages and disadvantages of cash and cheque payments

Table 9.5.1
Cash – advantages A quick way of settling a debt Recipient knows payment received
Cash – disadvantages Stolen cash impossible to trace A receipt is essential to prove that payment was made
Cheques – advantages Safe to send by post if crossed Bank record is proof of payment Two signatures by senior staff helps protect against fraud
Cheques – disadvantages Must be taken to bank May 'bounce' (be returned unpaid) if drawer has insufficient funds in account

DID YOU KNOW?

In many countries, governments are suspicious of large cash transactions because of money laundering. There are regulations to prevent businesses accepting large cash payments from unknown persons.

Types of payments

There are several different ways in which payments can be made and received in business.

Cash and cheques

There are advantages and disadvantages in both of these methods. These are shown in Table 9.5.1.

Credit cards

Credit cards are frequently used to pay for purchases. They work as follows.

- The credit card account holder is issued with a credit card and allowed credit to a fixed level each month.
- The card is used to make purchases.
- The company that issued the card pays the retailer the amount involved minus a small percentage.
- The credit card company keeps a record of all the payments made and sends a statement once a month to the account holder.
- If the account holder pays off the total in full, no interest is charged. If only part is paid off, the card holder pays interest on the balance owed.

Money orders and postal orders

These are both supplied by post offices.

- **Postal orders** are for small, fixed amounts, and are paid for and posted by the sender to a named person or business. They are mainly used by people who do not have a business bank account.
- **Money orders** are for larger amounts and are paid for by the sender. The recipient must take the order to the post office to receive the money. If the payment is a large sum from overseas, this is usually paid through the Central Bank.

Electronic transfers and credit transfers

These are both methods of transferring money between bank accounts without the need for cash, cheques, postal or money orders. The sender simply instructs their bank to transfer an amount of money to the receiver's bank and provides ID or a password to prove that the transaction is genuine.

Standing order

This is a special form of electronic transfer. An example would be where a business pays its insurance premium by fixed instalments on a particular day every month. It could instruct its bank to make this payment every month until told to stop. The advantage is that it saves the business having to make a separate transfer every month.

Bank draft

This is a cheque made out by a bank on its own account. Payment is therefore guaranteed by the bank. This means drafts are widely accepted for large payments and for overseas transactions. The customer pays the amount to the bank, plus a fee for the service. The bank then issues the draft in order for payment to be made.

Letter of credit

A letter of credit is produced by a customer's bank guaranteeing to a supplier (often from overseas) that the amount of money owed will be paid providing that the goods are supplied as specified. It reassures a supplier that they will get their money.

Types of cheque

There are several types of cheque. The characteristics of each, and how they are used, are shown in Table 9.5.2.

DID YOU KNOW?

Most stale-dated cheques are written at the start of the year, when people accidentally write the old year instead of the new one on the cheque. This means that the cheque looks as if it was written a year ago and it will be refused by the bank.

DID YOU KNOW?

A **debit card** can also be used to make payments. These cards are issued by banks to persons who hold current accounts. When they are used to make a payment, the money is immediately transferred from the purchaser's account to the seller's account.

Figure 9.5.1 Can you explain the difference between a credit card and a debit card?

Table 9.5.2 Types of cheques and their characteristics

Type of cheque	Characteristics	How they are used
Open cheque	Does not have two vertical parallel lines printed/drawn on it	Can be paid into the receiver's bank account or exchanged for cash at the bank on which it is drawn
Certified/ manager's cheque	Signed by the manager or other designated senior staff member at the bank branch	Used to pay a recipient who may be concerned about the creditworthiness of the buyer. Payment is guaranteed by the bank
Counter cheque	Made out at the counter of the payer's bank. Similar to a bank draft	Can be cashed by the receiver at any bank
Crossed cheque	Two parallel vertical lines are drawn on the cheque. Normally, 'not negotiable' or 'A/C payee' is written between the lines	Can only be paid into the bank account of the named receiver. Cannot be paid into anyone else's account
Endorsement	Written on the back of an uncrossed (open) cheque	Instruction to the bank about who should be paid the proceeds of an open cheque
Post-dated cheques/ stale-dated cheques	Post-dated means the date written on the cheque is for some time in the future. Stale-dated means that the date on the cheque is more than six months ago	Post-dated cheques will not be accepted by the bank. The same applies to stale-dated cheques. Normally businesses have up to six months to present cheques to their bank from the date written on the cheque

TEST YOURSELF

1 List TWO advantages and TWO disadvantages of a business accepting large cash payments from its customers.

Now check your answers against those on the accompanying CD.

Bank statements and reconciliation

LEARNING OUTCOMES

By the time you have finished this section you should be able to:

- identify and interpret entries on a bank statement
- reconcile bank and cash book balances.

Entries on a bank statement

Bank statements are normally sent to account holders every month, listing all of the transactions that have taken place. Study the example in Figure 9.6.1. Then check that you understand each explanation in Table 9.6.1.

Other features associated with bank statements

- **Outstanding cheques**. These are cheques sent to pay for something but not yet received, processed or banked by the payee, so the money has not been deducted from the drawer's bank account.

Table 9.6.1   Types of entry on a bank statement

Item	Type of entry	Explanation
A	Opening balance	Closing balance from last month carried forward
B	Deposits (credits)	Money going into the account, including cheques and cash
C	Money withdrawn (debits)	Money withdrawn, such as in cash and from cheques written
D	Direct debit	An electronic transfer payment. Mrs Williams has authorised the electricity company to withdraw money from her account on agreed dates. They must notify her if the amount changes
E	Standing order	Mrs Williams has authorised her bank to make a fixed payment on certain date(s) to an organisation. To change or stop these, she must notify the bank
F	Service charge	Bank charge for administering the account
G	Interest	Bank interest paid on a credit balance

ISLAND BANK
Manchester Road Branch
Black River
JAMAICA   TEL. 696 5126
Current Account Statement
1 March to 31 March 2012

Account Holder   Account number 65142
Mrs Jennie Williams
1 Hope St
Black River
JAMAICA

TRANSACTIONS

Date	Description	Details	Money out (debits) $	Money in (credits) $	Balance $	
1 March	Opening balance				1625.30	A
5 March	Cheque	Income tax refund		50.00	1675.30	B
9 March	Withdrawal	Cash machine	100.00		1575.30	C
10 March	Direct debit	JPS (Electricity)	47.00		1528.30	D
14 March	Standing order	Salvation Army donation	10.00		1518.30	E
20 March	Cheque	26946	620.00		898.30	C
23 March	Service charge	For February 2012	12.00		886.30	F
29 March	Interest	For February 2012		6.25	892.55	G
31 March	Automated credit	Salary – Education Department		1275.00	2167.55	B
31 March	Closing balance				2167.55	A

Figure 9.6.1   A bank statement

- **Outstanding deposits**. The cheque or cash has not yet been credited to the account because the deposits still have to be processed by the bank.
- **Insufficient funds**. The drawer does not have enough money in their account to cover the cheque. This is stamped 'NSF' and returned to the payee. It never appears on the bank statement.

Procedures for reconciling bank and cash book balances

The **cash book** is used to check how much money is flowing in and out of the business. For that reason, all payments made and received are recorded as soon as they happen. This enables the business to identify how much money should be in the bank at any time.

Reconciliation means comparing the two sets of information (the cash book and bank statement) to identify and explain any differences. It involves a two-step procedure:

- reconciling bank statements with cash book balances
- reconciling cash book balances with bank statements.

Reconciling bank statements with cash book balances

First, tick off items that appear in both the cash book and the bank statement. Next, look for items on the bank statement that are not ticked because they are not in the cash book. For example, if the bank has just added bank charges these will not be recorded in the cash book.

Reconciling cash book balances with bank statements

Now look in the cash book for items that are not in the bank statement. For example, the cash book may list a cheque received two days ago that has not yet been taken to the bank. This can be added to the bank account record to give a true balance.

Bank reconciliation statements

These are prepared in order to balance the cash book and the bank statement. The statement in Figure 9.6.2 shows differences found by the accounts clerk at Northern Stationery Trading.

- A $25 cheque from Cyan Stationery, paid into the bank yesterday, is in the cash book but not on the bank statement.
- A credit transfer of $150 received from J Smith is only on the bank statement.
- Bank interest charges of $85 are also only on the bank statement.
- A cheque paid to Trinidad Trading for $100 has not been cashed and it is only entered in the cash book.

The bank reconciliation statement is now produced (Figure 9.6.2).

FIND OUT MORE

Study the bank statement in Figure 9.6.1 and note the entries and column headings. Check the calculations to make sure you understand how each entry in the 'Balance' column has been reached.

DID YOU KNOW?

Insufficient funds is sometimes called 'NSF' – Not Sufficient Funds.

KEY TERMS

Reconciliation means comparing two sets of information that should be identical to discover whether there are any differences.

DID YOU KNOW?

Staff errors can mean there is a difference between cash book entries and bank statements. An example would be wrongly recording the amount of a cheque.

NORTHERN STATIONERY TRADING
Bank Reconciliation Statement

Date: 31 October 2012
Closing balance - Bank Statement
$670.00

Add item(s) not credited

Cheque from Cyan Stationery	+$25.00
Credit transfer from J Smith	+$150.00
Subtotal	**$845.00**
Less	
Cheque not presented –	
Cheque for Trinidad Trading	−$100.00
Bank charges	−$85.00
Corrected cash book balance	**$660.00**

Figure 9.6.2 A bank reconciliation statement

TEST YOURSELF

1 Write a clear explanation of EACH of the following terms for a new accounts clerk: direct debit, standing order, payee, drawer, deposits.

Now check your answers against those on the accompanying CD.

LEARNING OUTCOMES

By the time you have finished this section you should be able to:

- explain the procedures for the payment and control of petty cash using the imprest system.

DID YOU KNOW?

The word 'petty' means 'small'. So the term **petty cash** refers to small amounts of cash.

DID YOU KNOW?

The amount of money kept in the petty-cash float will vary from one organisation to another. A small firm may only keep $100, but a large one may allocate far more.

KEY TERMS

A **cash disbursement sheet** is a way of recording all petty-cash transactions and allocating them to different budget headings. The term 'disbursement' simply means 'money paid out'.

DID YOU KNOW?

Some businesses use a **petty-cash book** in place of a cash disbursement sheet. However, the purpose is the same.

The need for petty cash

In this unit you have learned that businesses have various options for making and receiving payments to/from other businesses. The main ones are cheques, electronic transfer of funds and cash.

Cash is not a suitable form of payment for high-value transactions because of the security risk – it could be stolen and is usually untraceable. However, there are some situations where cash is needed for small transactions, such as:

- taxi fares
- magazines for reception
- milk for coffee
- window cleaning
- special packaging for fragile items being posted.

The petty-cash clerk

Usually a petty-cash clerk is in charge of petty cash to ensure that:

- expenditure from petty cash is only for authorised payments
- all expenditure is recorded accurately
- there are no discrepancies between recorded expenditure and the amount actually paid out
- security procedures for keeping petty cash are followed correctly
- the **cash disbursement sheet**, or petty-cash book, balances at the end of the week or month.

The voucher system

To make sure that only correct amounts are paid out, petty-cash vouchers are used to record the money spent. All vouchers are numbered and are issued in *numerical* order.

- The vouchers are usually issued *before* the money is spent.
- Junior staff must obtain authorisation from a supervisor *before* spending any money on behalf of the organisation or claiming any money from petty cash. When authorisation is given the supervisor countersigns the petty-cash voucher (as shown in Figure 9.7.1).
- Senior members of staff may spend money first and then present the petty-cash voucher together with the receipt for reimbursement.
- An official receipt should be attached to the voucher as proof of the amount spent.
- Vouchers for multiple items must be checked to ensure the addition is correct.
- Completed vouchers are filed in numerical or date order.

Petty-cash voucher	Number
	135
	Date :
	24/3/2012
Type of purchase(s)	Amount ($)
Magazines for reception	10.00
Total	10.00
Approved by *Jerome Allayne*	
Received by *Zara Talma*	

Figure 9.7.1   A petty-cash voucher

THINK ABOUT IT!

Why do you think it is important that petty cash is kept in a lockable tin and is the responsibility of one person? Where do you think the tin should be kept?

Balancing petty cash using the cash disbursement sheet

Each item of expenditure is entered on the cash disbursement sheet. At the end of a fixed period, such as a week or a month, the petty-cash clerk will total all of the entries, balance these and restore the **imprest**. This means that the amount held in petty cash will be brought back up to the full, fixed amount allocated for the petty cash float.

Summarising expenses

When expenditure on petty cash is recorded, it is usually divided into different categories so that a check can be kept on the amount being spent on items such as travel, stationery, postage, etc. Usually there is a miscellaneous heading (for example 'office expenses') where items can be recorded that do not fit in any of the other categories.

The individual totals for each category, at the end of the period, will equal the total expenditure of petty cash. When the petty-cash clerk claims back this amount to restore the imprest, the total amount spent over that period is then recorded in the main cash book.

KEY TERMS

The **imprest** is a fund for small items of expenditure that is always restored to its agreed amount at the end of the period.

DID YOU KNOW?

As a quick check, the total of the vouchers issued, deducted from the amount of the float, should always equal the amount of money left in the petty-cash tin.

THINK ABOUT IT!

Page 153 shows a cash disbursement sheet for a petty-cash system. Study this carefully and then do question 10. The balance brought forward (b/f) is the amount of money unspent from the last period. This is carried forward at the end of the current period. Check that you understand all of the entries and could quickly summarise to your supervisor the expenses for the period.

TEST YOURSELF

1 List FOUR of the duties of a petty-cash clerk. Then explain why security is also an important part of this person's job.

Now check your answers against those on the accompanying CD.

SECTION 1: Multiple-choice questions

1 Checking that customers pay their bills on time is called:

  a Order control.   **c** Cash control.

  b Financial control.   **d** Credit control.

2 Deductions from gross pay to produce the net pay figure usually include:

  i Income tax.

  ii National Insurance.

  iii Cost of travel to work.

  iv Union subscription.

  a i, ii and iv only   **c** ii, iii and iv only

  b i, iii and iv only   **d** All of the above

3 The document you receive that states the pay you have received is:

  a A time card.   **c** A payslip.

  b A payroll.   **d** A payment note.

4 Which items are included in a statement of account?

  i All invoices sent that month.

  ii All credit notes sent that month.

  iii All debit notes sent that month.

  iv All payments received that month.

  a i and iv only   **c** i, ii and iv only

  b ii and iii only   **d** All of the above

5 What is the main reason for crossing a cheque?

  a To make sure the right person receives it.

  b To make sure it is paid into the right person's account.

  c To make sure it is easy to read.

  d To make sure it is not stale-dated.

6 Financial institutions that offer savings accounts to customers are:

  i Central banks.

  ii Commercial banks.

  iii Credit unions.

  iv Investment companies.

  a i and ii only   **c** ii and iv only

  b ii and iii only   **d** iii and iv only

> **EXAM TIP**
>
> Read each question at least twice to make sure that you know exactly what you are being asked to do.

7 A new client who has to make a very large payment should be asked to do this by:

  a Money order.   **c** Cheque.

  b Credit card.   **d** Bank draft.

8 The documents that you need in order to carry out a bank reconciliation exercise are:

  i The chequebook.

  ii The cash book.

  iii The credit card statement.

  iv The bank statement.

  a i and ii only   **c** All of the above

  b ii and iv only   **d** None of the above

9 The major benefit of using a spreadsheet is:

  a To manipulate figures in a worksheet easily.

  b To incorporate graphics into the document.

  c To prepare invoices and final accounts.

  d To record business transactions.

10 To reclaim money from petty cash you need to:

  i Obtain permission for the purchase.

  ii Complete a petty-cash voucher.

  iii Pay for the item in cash.

  iv Obtain a receipt from the shop.

  a i, ii and iii only   **c** i, ii and iv only

  b ii, iii and iv only   **d** All of the above

> Further practice questions and examples can be found on the accompanying CD.

1 List THREE items of information that would be entered onto a payslip.

2 State TWO actions that a business can take if a customer does not pay their bill when it is due.

3 Identify TWO steps that an accounts clerk should take to prepare for an audit.

4 Identify TWO differences between a bank statement and a statement of account.

5 Explain THREE functions of an accounts office.

6 Give TWO reasons why a cheque sent to a customer may not appear on the next bank statement.

7 Explain the difference between a credit card and a debit card.

8 Part of a consignment of goods to a customer is damaged in transit and returned. The customer says he will not therefore pay the invoice that has been sent. Explain how the accounts office will resolve this situation.

9 Explain THREE services offered by commercial banks to their customers.

10 The cash disbursement sheet below has an imprest of $200. The balance brought forward (b/f) is the amount of money unspent from the last period. This is carried forward at the end of the current period.

Study the entries carefully and then calculate the amount that was spent on petty cash (xxxx) and which was therefore reclaimed to restore the imprest on 27 March.

Received $	Date	Details	Voucher no.	Total payment $	Office expenses	Books and stationery	Travel	Postage
152.00	20 March	Balance b/f						
48.00	20 March	Cash received						
	20 March	Stamps	131	18.00				18.00
	21 March	Flowers	132	10.00	10.00			
	22 March	Taxi fare	133	20.00			20.00	
	23 March	Stationery	134	15.50		15.50		
	24 March	Magazines	135	10.00	10.00			
	24 March	Parcel	136	8.00		8.00		
	24 March	Window cleaner	137	22.00	22.00			
		TOTAL		XXXX	42.00	23.50	20.00	18.00
		Balance c/f		96.50				
96.50	27 March	Balance b/f						
XXXX	27 March	Cash received						

EXAM TIP

Remember to double-check your total by checking that the total of the payments column DOWN is the same as the total of the summary expenses ACROSS.

Further practice questions and examples can be found on the accompanying CD.

10.1 The role and functions of the procurement office

LEARNING OUTCOMES

By the time you have completed this section you should be able to:

- describe the functions of the procurement and inventory management office.

KEY TERMS

Procurement simply means buying goods.

Inventory means stock, including raw materials, finished goods and even stationery.

Introduction to procurement

Procurement and **inventory** management is concerned with how businesses buy goods. Purchasing is a major expenditure for most businesses so strict procedures are followed to ensure that money is spent wisely.

Stock, or inventory control, is important because running out of stock of a particular item could lose customers. However, holding too much stock takes up space and risks items becoming obsolete. You will learn about all of these aspects in this unit.

Functions of the procurement and inventory management office

Determine the items to purchase

There are four main types of purchase that are made by business organisations. These are summarised in Table 10.1.1.

Table 10.1.1 Types of purchase

Type of purchase and purpose	Examples
Raw materials and components used in manufacturing	Timber for a chair manufacturer Empty cans for a soft-drinks manufacturer
Goods to be resold to customers at a higher price than the price paid – to make a profit	Groceries for a grocery store Clothes for a dress shop
Consumables – disposable items regularly needed to run the business	Cleaning materials, photocopier paper and other stationery
Capital items – essential equipment and buildings used to run the business	Vans for delivering products to customers Computers for office staff to process information

Liaise with other departments

All departments liaise with purchasing. Table 10.1.2 summarises this.

Table 10.1.2 Liaison between purchasing and other departments

Name of department	Examples of links with purchasing
Sales and marketing	Forecasts of future sales will determine the amount of raw materials and components (or resale goods) that are required. Sales and marketing will need furniture, equipment and consumables, and perhaps cash registers. They may also need to book advertising space or pay for the printing of leaflets or posters

Operations/ Production	This department will need production machinery and materials, as well as personal protective safety equipment for workers
Accounts	Computers, including software, will be a requirement, as well as paper and other consumables. This department must be informed when goods are delivered, and payment will only be approved if the goods are as ordered and undamaged
Despatch and transport	This department will need transport vehicles, fuel for these vehicles, and packaging materials
Human resource management	Again, office furniture and equipment will be required, as well as consumable items

Manage inventory

You will learn how the amount of inventory is managed and controlled later in this unit. At this point you should note that when stock is being used on a regular basis then periodically it has to be reordered. In some businesses purchasing controls the main stores, so that they can easily see when goods need to be reordered.

Terminology and abbreviations used in purchasing documents and literature

There are several terms that are used to define the nature of the contract between the business that is selling the goods and the business purchasing them. These mainly relate to whether the buyer or the seller is responsible for certain payments.

Table 10.1.3	Purchasing terms and meanings
Terminology/ abbreviation	**Meaning**
Free on board (FOB)	The seller pays all of the charges involved in delivering and loading the goods at the port of departure, after which the buyer is responsible
Cost, insurance and freight (CIF)	This also applies to sea transport, but the seller is responsible for all of the costs (including insurance and transportation costs) of moving the goods to the port of arrival
Errors and omissions excepted (E&OE)	Found on invoices, price lists and some advertising material. It means that the information may contain errors or may be subject to future changes so it cannot be legally relied on
Cash on delivery (COD)	Whoever delivers the goods to the customer collects payment and sends this money back to the seller. If payment is not made, the goods are returned to the seller, who is therefore protected against non-payment
Excluding works (ex works)	The buyer is responsible for all of the transport costs from the seller's premises
Discounts	Sellers often offer a percentage discount on the official price. Reasons for this include: • buying a large quantity (called 'bulk purchase') • prompt payment within a specified period • loyalty discounts for regular customers

THINK ABOUT IT!

Think about an organisation that you know well, perhaps your school. Write down three items of capital equipment that it has bought and three consumable items it will buy from time to time.

EXAM TIP

Make sure you know what abbreviations stand for – such as COD. Check that you can easily calculate simple discounts, for example, $250 less 5 per cent.

TEST YOURSELF

1 Suggest TWO reasons why the following departments in a jeans factory might liaise with purchasing:

a the sales and marketing department

b the accounts department

c the production department.

Now check your answers against those on the accompanying CD.

LEARNING OUTCOMES

By the time you have completed this section you should be able to:

- identify the duties and attributes of a clerk in the purchasing department.

KEY TERMS

Purchase orders are produced by the purchasing department and sent to suppliers. They are often produced as a result of a purchase requisition.

The **unit** is the volume in which the goods can be bought, such as 100 envelopes or a ream of paper.

Duties of a purchasing clerk

Preparing and processing purchase requisitions

Purchase requisitions are used *within* a business, whereas **purchase orders** go outside the business from customer to supplier. The requisition asks that an order is placed for certain goods. In Figure 10.2.1, the production department has sent a requisition to purchasing for 200 spools of white cotton thread. The purchasing clerk then makes out a purchase order to send to the suppliers.

DID YOU KNOW?

A person who is authorised to sign documents such as purchase requisitions and cheques is known as a **designated signatory**.

Filing of purchasing records

Copies of all requisitions and purchase orders are filed for future reference and in case there is a problem later, such as:

- the wrong type/number was sent
- a query about the amount of money requested on the invoice
- the goods are lost in transit.

Purchase requisitions may be filed first alphabetically according to the originating department and then in date order (chronologically) within that file.

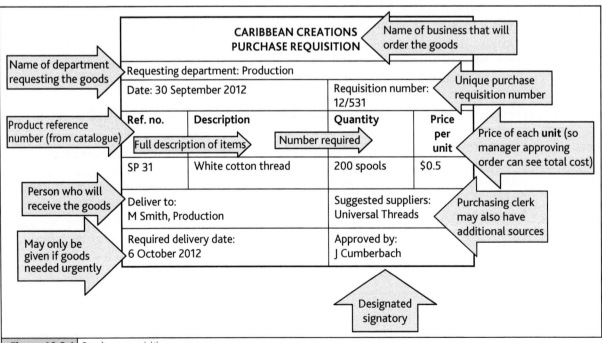

Figure 10.2.1 Purchase requisition

Maintaining stock records

Some types of stock are used every day, such as raw materials for production. The number held in stock must be constantly updated because at a certain level the item must be reordered. Each time stock is used it must be recorded promptly on the stock record and subtracted from the opening stock to obtain the current balance (see page 162).

Maintaining a database of suppliers

The purchasing department often has to find suppliers to provide items requested. For that reason it is useful to have a database of suppliers for reference. This will consist of suppliers that have been reliable in the past, sold quality items and offered good value for money.

Verifying orders received

All goods received must be checked for damage, and any discrepancies resolved before the supplier is paid. Normally, goods received are accompanied by a delivery note listing details of the items supplied. The recipient signs the note and lists any damage. This is then passed to the purchasing department, which checks the delivery note against the order and contacts the supplier if there are any problems.

Attributes of a purchasing clerk

Integrity and honesty

'Honesty' means telling the truth. 'Integrity' means being consistently honest all of the time, having strong principles and being true to these even in difficult situations. It is particularly important to be honest if you have made a mistake. People may not like it but at least they will respect you for being honest and will value your integrity. Both attributes are essential for people who are responsible for ordering goods on behalf of a business and have access to stock and order forms.

Initiative

Taking the initiative means solving problems without having to ask for help. This can save other people time. For example:

- If an established supplier goes out of business, the purchasing clerk can try to find an alternative source.
- If a supplier rings up complaining that they have not been paid, the clerk should check that the paperwork is correct and the goods have been received before contacting the accounts department.

Detail orientation

Purchasing clerks must be thorough and methodical when completing purchase orders. This means concentrating and checking that all details are correct – especially figures and calculations. Otherwise problems can occur, such as a delivery for many more items than you intended, which may prove costly for your employer.

DID YOU KNOW?

Many businesses in the Caribbean give a **Merit Award** to proven suppliers. This enables them to use a single supplier without having to obtain competing quotations.

Figure 10.2.2 Why is it necessary to check that goods are not damaged on delivery?

THINK ABOUT IT!

Your friend in purchasing brags about being able to pilfer paper and printer cartridges from the stock room. When you protest he laughs and says that the company is rich enough to afford it. He now plans to alter a large computer order to include one for himself. What would you do and why?

TEST YOURSELF

1 List THREE attributes that a purchasing clerk needs to possess. For each attribute, give ONE reason why it is important.

Now check your answers against those on the accompanying CD.

Purchasing procedures and influencing factors

LEARNING OUTCOMES

By the time you have completed this section you should be able to:

- outline procedures for purchasing goods and acquiring services.

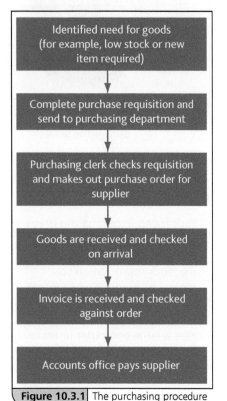

Identified need for goods (for example, low stock or new item required)
Complete purchase requisition and send to purchasing department
Purchasing clerk checks requisition and makes out purchase order for supplier
Goods are received and checked on arrival
Invoice is received and checked against order
Accounts office pays supplier

Figure 10.3.1 The purchasing procedure

DID YOU KNOW?

Unscrupulous businesses may offer the purchasing officer personal bribes or gifts to make a sale. Most organisations have a policy that bans this practice.

Factors influencing purchasing procedures

The normal purchasing procedure is shown in Figure 10.3.1. Sometimes this has to change because of an unexpected development.

Urgency

After placing the order it often takes several days to receive the goods. If they are needed urgently this requires a different approach.

- A trusted supplier can be phoned and a price and fast delivery agreed. Confirmation is sent by fax or email.
- A new supplier may want payment before releasing the goods and may issue a pro forma invoice (see page 173) or request a bank draft for a large order (see page 147).
- There may be an extra charge for express delivery.

Cost

Purchasing clerks normally want to obtain the goods for the lowest price, but other factors could influence this decision, such as:

- urgency (see above)
- quality – the cheapest goods available may be poor quality
- reliability of the supplier
- after-sales service – especially important for expensive equipment or vehicles (for example, what warranties are there and what support is available? Are engineers on call seven days a week?)
- what discounts are available (see pages 172–173).

Incentives

Incentives are initiatives offered by the supplier to persuade potential purchasers to buy their product(s). Some examples are:

- offering a discount on the catalogue-listed price
- adding extra free items to the order (for example, printer cartridges)
- extending the payment period
- offering an extended warranty on items such as computers.

Availability

If a particular item is difficult to find then this may mean that the price of it increases. Unless a substitute can be found, the purchasing department may have to agree to the extra cost.

Procedures for purchasing

Catalogues and price lists

Suppliers often produce a catalogue containing a list of products with illustrations and detailed information. There is a product code for each item and usually a separate price list. This enables the company to reissue the price list quickly if prices change, and it saves them the expense of producing another catalogue. Purchasing clerks must check that the price list they are using is the latest version.

Tenders and enquiries

These procedures are normally used when a large number of items are required (say photocopier paper over a year) or an expensive purchase or service is needed, such as refurbishing a large office suite.

- **A tender** is a formal written offer to supply goods or services for a fixed price. The purchaser publishes details of the items required, often in a journal or newspaper, and invites suppliers to submit offers to provide these at a quoted price. When the tenders are received they are normally kept in sealed envelopes until the specified closing date. Usually, the supplier who quotes the lowest price gets the order. Tenders are often used by government departments to demonstrate that they are spending public money wisely.
- **An enquiry** is made when a purchaser asks other businesses for a quotation for goods or services. Again, purchasers specify what they require and ask for a price. Normally three quotations are sought and the lowest price is usually accepted.

Quotations

The supplier submits a quotation in response to a tender or enquiry. It shows a price for supplying the goods and may include other information, such as the delivery date.

Order placement

Placing an order with the supplier creates a legally binding contract as the customer must now pay for the goods after delivery. Most orders are submitted on a standard form, but if an order is complex or for an expensive item, a special contract may be issued.

e-commerce

Today purchasers can check catalogues and prices online, request quotations, place orders, make payments electronically and track deliveries. As communication is faster, a range of suppliers can be found via a good search engine and electronic payments are prompt and secure. The main danger is placing an order with an unknown supplier who delivers late or not at all.

Shipment and delivery

Purchasing clerks must know when delivery will take place and the terms of the shipment (see page 155). Important issues to check are:

- who is responsible for delivery. Usually it is the seller, but there may be an additional charge
- what customs duties and taxes are payable on imported goods before the goods are released
- who is responsible for insuring the goods against theft or damage in transit.

(see page 155)

FIND OUT MORE

Buyers often queue for hours to obtain new Apple products on the first day they are released, otherwise they may have to wait for weeks for new stock to arrive. If you wanted a new Apple device immediately, what options would you have and at what cost? Search online to get some ideas.

DID YOU KNOW?

Many companies place an online catalogue on their website for customers to view.

THINK ABOUT IT!

You want a new cellphone and have obtained prices for the same handset from three suppliers. What reasons could you have for not wanting to buy the cheapest one?

DID YOU KNOW?

If an order is for a large quantity, the supplier may quote to deliver the goods in separate batches.

TEST YOURSELF

1 Suggest TWO advantages of using e-commerce to buy goods rather than the traditional purchasing process, and ONE disadvantage.

Now check your answers against those on the accompanying CD.

Purchasing documents and inventory management

LEARNING OUTCOMES

By the time you have completed this section you should be able to:

- prepare documents used in the purchase of goods and services

- explain the importance of inventory management.

FIND OUT MORE

Look back at the example of a **purchase requisition** on page 156 to refresh your memory.

KEY TERMS

A **purchase requisition** is sent by a department to the purchasing department. Its purpose is to ask for goods to be ordered from an outside supplier.

DID YOU KNOW?

A centralised purchasing department can gain better discounts by placing orders for the whole organisation.

EXAM TIP

Always double-check the entries you make in a form.

Purchase requisition forms

These documents are only used internally. They are sent by a department to the purchasing clerk as a request to buy goods.

Checking the requisition

The purchasing clerk checks each requisition carefully before making out the purchase order. This may involve contacting the supplier or referring to the catalogue and latest price list. If other requisitions have been received for the same goods these can ordered at the same time, as a discount may be available for a bulk purchase.

Table 10.4.1 Purchase requisition checks

✓	The description of the goods is sufficient to uniquely identify them
✓	The description and reference number match
✓	The price is correct
✓	The supplier can deliver by the date requested
✓	There are no better/cheaper suppliers than those suggested
✓	The form has been signed by an authorised person

Purchase order forms

The purchase order is sent to an external supplier requesting the supply of certain goods. It follows the receipt of an internal purchase requisition. An example is shown in Figure 10.4.1.

CARIBBEAN CREATIONS
George Street
Kingston 5
JAMAICA

Tel: 00-1-876-283793   Email: purchasing@ccreations.com.jm

PURCHASE ORDER NO.......1629........

To: Universal Threads Ltd Unit 12 Jasper Commercial Complex Kingston 4	Requisition number(s): 8324DK
	Date: 1 October 2012

Ref no.	Quantity	Description	Price per unit	Total price
SP31 SP42	200 100	Reels of white cotton thread 7" blue metal zips	$0.50 $1.00	$100 $100
			TOTAL	$200

Deliver to: M Smith, Production	Date of delivery: 6 October 2012
Signed: Jolene Marshall	Designation: Purchasing manager

Figure 10.4.1 Purchase order

A purchase order is similar to a purchase requisition. Purchase orders also have the following features.

- There is space for the supplier's name and address.
- The purchase requisition number is copied from the original so that the order can be traced back if there is a query.
- The total price column is the unit price multiplied by the quantity.
- If there are multiple items on the order, the total price is inserted at the bottom of the 'Total price' column.
- The form must be signed by an authorised person.

The importance of inventory management

Prevention of pilferage

'Pilferage' means theft. It can be minimised by:

- recruiting people who have good references
- having a clear disciplinary policy (see page 125). Normally, anyone caught stealing would be instantly dismissed
- having secure storage places for valuable or desirable items with access limited to named keyholders
- having regular stock reconciliations so pilferage is soon discovered.

Inventory control

This means finding a balance between holding too little stock and keeping too much. If stock runs out, production may have to stop and customers could be disappointed. If there is too much stock, items could go out of date or take up too much storage space.

The key tasks of controlling inventory are:

- recording all stock entering and leaving the store (see Figure 10.5.1) to ensure that the quantity of each item in stock is known
- carrying out **stock reconciliations** to check the accuracy of recorded stock levels
- setting maximum and minimum levels of stock for each item
- reordering stock when the minimum level is reached and ensuring that the amount held never exceeds the maximum level.

Signalling of market trends

This relates to stock levels of finished goods. If these fall quickly because demand is high, output must be increased. If they are static, then production may be reduced or stopped for that product.

Availability of capital

Capital is money used to buy buildings, equipment and stock. Businesses try to keep stock levels low to avoid using up too much capital which could be used for other purposes such as upgrading machines or computer systems.

Storage space

Sufficient storage space is needed for the maximum amount of stock required. This costs money in terms of buildings, lighting and air conditioning so it is more economical to keep storage space to a minimum.

DID YOU KNOW?

Orders for very expensive items can usually be signed only by a senior manager or the chief executive officer.

Figure 10.4.2 Why do retailers hold a sale?

KEY TERMS

Stock reconciliations are carried out by manually counting the number of each item in stock.

The **reorder level** is the level at which more stock is ordered.

DID YOU KNOW?

JIT stands for 'just in time'. This is a way of reducing the amount of stock held for production. Instead, trusted suppliers deliver quickly on demand.

TEST YOURSELF

1 Give THREE reasons why businesses must monitor stock levels.

Now check your answers against those on the accompanying CD.

LEARNING OUTCOMES

By the time you have completed this section you should be able to:

• maintain stock records (manual and electronic).

EXAM TIP

Check that you know the difference between a stock requisition and a purchase requisition.

THINK ABOUT IT!

Check the calculations on the stock control card and make sure that you understand them. Remember that card layouts vary – some have separate columns for items received and issued.

EXAM TIP

Before you make any entries, always read the headings carefully in any form that you have to complete.

DID YOU KNOW?

A store that sells perishable goods will use FIFO as items must be sold quickly.

Maintaining stock records

Stock requisitions

This internal document is completed when a department wants items from the stores. The form contains details of the item, quantity, department name and the signature of an authorised person.

Stock record cards

Businesses monitor stock levels so that they know when to reorder. A typical stock control card is shown in Figure 10.5.1.

STOCK CONTROL CARD Item: Sticky Notes		Unit: Packs of 12		Maximum: 40 packs Minimum: 10 packs		
Date	Received	Issued	Dept	Req no		Balance
3 Dec						18 packs
7 Dec		8 packs	Sales	3023		10 packs
16 Dec	30 packs					40 packs
17 Dec		2 packs	Production	3180		38 packs

Figure 10.5.1 A stock control card

Storage of office supplies

Office supplies, such as photocopier paper and pens, are normally kept in a lockable store or cupboard, preferably on slatted shelves so that air can circulate freely. This helps to prevent damage if humidity is high. The storage area should be away from direct light, which also causes the deterioration of many items. In addition:

• access should be limited to minimise theft

• new stock should be stored at the bottom (or back) so that the oldest items are used first. This takes effort but it is important

• items should be stacked with descriptive labels facing outwards, and heavy items should be placed low down so that they cannot fall from a height and hurt someone

• fast-moving items should be easily accessible

• potentially dangerous items must be stored carefully. For example, drawing pins should be in boxes and flammable liquids should be kept on the floor so that any spillages can be cleaned up quickly.

Reporting on stock levels

Periodically, the value of items in stock must be calculated. There are three ways of doing this.

• **FIFO**: **f**irst **i**n, **f**irst **o**ut (stock bought first is sold first).

• **LIFO**: **l**ast **i**n, **f**irst **o**ut (stock bought last is sold first).

• **AVCO**: **a**verage **c**ost (the average price paid for stock is used to calculate the value).

A worked example

Caribbean Creations buys special white fabric at the following prices:

- 10 rolls at $20 on 15 January
- 10 rolls at $25 on 17 February.

On 8 March 15 rolls are used. On 20 March 10 rolls are purchased at $30. What is the value of the stock at the end of March?

THINK ABOUT IT!

Work through each example by *date* and not by column. Remember that the balance column always shows the current situation and includes previous purchases.

CARIBBEAN CREATIONS – PURCHASING DEPARTMENT
RECORD OF TRANSACTIONS
January–March   **FIFO METHOD**

Date	Receipts	Issues	Balance	Stock value
15 January	10 @ $20		10 @ $20	$200
17 February	10 @ $25		10 @ $20 + 10 @ $25	$200 + $250 = $450
8 March		10 @ $20 5 @ $25	5 @ $25	$125
20 March	10 @ $30		5 @ $25 + 10 @ $30	$125 + $300 = **$425**

Stock issued comprises **10** rolls from January and **5** rolls from February.

CARIBBEAN CREATIONS – PURCHASING DEPARTMENT
RECORD OF TRANSACTIONS
January–March   **LIFO METHOD**

Date	Receipts	Issues	Balance	Total value
15 January	10 @ $20		10 @ $20	$200
17 February	10 @ $25		10 @ $20 + 10 @ $25	$200 + $250 = $450
8 March		5 @ $20 10 @ $25	5 @ $20	$100
20 March	10 @ $30		5 @ $20 + 10 @ £30	$100 + $300 = **$400**

Stock issued comprises **5** rolls from January and **10** rolls from February.

CARIBBEAN CREATIONS – PURCHASING DEPARTMENT
RECORD OF TRANSACTIONS
January–March   **AVCO METHOD**

Date	Receipts	Issues	Balance	Total value	Average value per item
15 January	10 @ $20		10	$200	$200/10 = $20
17 February	10 @ $25		10 @ $20 + 10 @ $25	$200 + $250 = $450	$450/20 = $22.50
8 March		15 @ $22.50	5 @ $22.50	$112.5	$22.50
20 March	10 @ $30		5 @$22.50 + 10 @ $30	$112.5 + $300 = **$412.5**	$412.50/15 = $27.50

Average value is recalculated after every purchase:
Total cost of goods in stock
Number of items in stock

Figure 10.5.2 FIFO, LIFO and AVCO calculations

EXAM TIP

Show all of your workings for calculations so that if you make a simple error you can still gain marks for knowing the principles involved.

DID YOU KNOW?

An EPOS system will process sales and simultaneously adjust stock levels in the warehouse. You can read about these on page 163.

TEST YOURSELF

1 Between April and June, Caribbean Creations bought and used blue fabric as follows. On 3 April 5 rolls were purchased at $20; on 3 May 20 rolls were purchased at $25; and on 1 June 15 rolls were used. On 17 June 10 rolls were purchased at $40. Copy out the forms in Figure 10.5.2 and calculate the stock value on 30 June using:

a FIFO

b LIFO

c AVCO.

Now check your answers against those on the accompanying CD.

SECTION 1: Multiple-choice questions

1 A car manufacturer buys tyres to fit to the vehicles that it is producing. This is an example of purchasing:

  a Capital equipment.

  b Goods for immediate resale.

  c Consumables.

  d Components for the product.

2 Discount for bulk purchase means:

  a Payment within a specified period.

  b Reducing the price by a percentage for buying a large quantity.

  c Always buying from the same supplier.

  d Not charging for delivery.

3 Purchase requisitions contain the following information.

  i The name of the department requesting the goods.

  ii A description of the goods.

  iii The telephone number of the supplier.

  iv The method of transport required.

  a i and ii only   c i and iv only

  b i and iii only   d ii and iii only

4 The term 'stock reconciliation' means:

  a Theft of stock items.

  b Delivering stock items to a department.

  c Physically counting the items of stock in a store.

  d Tidying up the storage area.

5 The purchasing process may sometimes have to be varied because:

  a The delivery van broke down.

  b Goods are needed immediately.

  c The purchasing clerk is on holiday.

  d There is more money to spend on stock.

6 Catalogues and price lists are supplied separately because:

  a It is cheaper to print them that way.

  b Prices can change more frequently than product items.

  c Someone might want several price lists.

  d Catalogues are much heavier than price lists.

7 The advantages of using e-commerce are:

  i Everyone likes to use the internet at work.

  ii Information can be communicated more quickly than by ordinary mail.

  iii Goods are always cheaper online.

  iv It is easier to search for alternative suppliers.

  a i and ii only   c ii and iii only

  b i and iii only   d ii and iv only

8 A stock requisition form is:

  a A request for the purchasing department to place an external order.

  b A request for a stock reconciliation to be carried out.

  c An internal document asking for goods from stores.

  d An order sent to an external supplier.

9 Pilferage can be kept to a minimum by:

  i Not storing things of value.

  ii Only recruiting staff who have good references.

  iii Having a police car parked outside the factory.

  iv Sacking people who are caught stealing.

  a i and ii only   c ii and iii only

  b i and iii only   d ii and iv only

10 One problem of having large amounts of stock of a particular item is:

  a The purchasing department has nothing to do.

  b The storeman will be annoyed.

  c Capital that could be used for other things is tied up.

  d Some items may be stolen.

Further practice questions and examples can be found on the accompanying CD.

1 State TWO reasons why the finance department may liaise with purchasing.

2 Explain the meaning of the term E&OE.

3 Explain the main purpose of a purchase requisition.

4 Define FOB, CIF and ex works.

5 Describe TWO duties of a purchasing clerk.

6 a Your supervisor has asked you to order 10 boxes of A4 photocopy paper ref 179D at $8.00 and 4 blue A4 lever arch files ref 203C at $6.00 each, as requested on purchase requisition 230/19. Send the order to Paper Products Ltd, Harbour Road, Kingston for delivery to your stores in seven days' time. The next purchase order number is 20813.

   Copy out the purchase order form shown in Figure 10.4.1 and complete it using today's date, but do not sign it.

   b If your company received 5 per cent discount, what would the new total price of the order be?

7 Your brother runs his own grocery store but struggles to keep his stock records up to date. He has heard that an EPOS system can provide a perpetual inventory, where the stock list constantly updates, so that stock levels can be viewed at any time. He is not sure what is meant by EPOS but knows you are studying Office Administration and has asked for your advice. Read the information shown below and then summarise FOUR important benefits that he would gain by introducing this type of system. Remember to relate your answer to the needs of a grocery store.

Use of software, electronic devices and bar-code scanners

Computers and EPOS (electronic point of sales) systems have made inventory control easier in several ways.

- Computerised stock control packages enable new and issued stock to be entered easily, and balances are adjusted automatically.
- The system can be used to analyse sales trends.
- Low stock is automatically flagged for reorder.
- Purchase requisitions and orders can be sent electronically.
- Stock valuations (using FIFO, LIFO or AVCO) can be done automatically.
- EPOS systems call up the price(s) from the database, produce an itemised bill and also adjust stock levels automatically to show a perpetual inventory. (This means that the stock list constantly updates, so the balance of each item can be viewed at any time.) Additional hardware, such as bar-code scanners, can also be attached to cash registers.

8 List the steps in the purchasing procedure.

9 Identify THREE types of purchases made by a business.

10 Suggest THREE stock control measures that a business could implement to prevent pilferage.

Further practice questions and examples can be found on the accompanying CD.

11 Sales, marketing and customer service

11.1 The sales office and the duties of a sales clerk

LEARNING OUTCOMES

By the time you have completed this section you should be able to:

- explain the functions of staff involved in sales
- identify the duties of a clerk in the sales office.

DID YOU KNOW?

Sales revenue is vital if the business is going to make a profit and continue trading.

Figure 11.1.1 Why are sales office staff vital for the success of a business?

DID YOU KNOW?

Keeping a list of customer email addresses enables newsletters to be sent out regularly by email.

DID YOU KNOW?

Sales representatives who work for production companies may need to liaise with the production department about delivery dates for special items.

Introduction to sales, marketing and customer service

Sales, marketing and customer service are important areas for all businesses. It is pointless having superb products or services if no one buys them. All businesses must look after their customers, particularly if they have a query or problem. This unit covers all of these areas as well as the duties of clerks and the documents they produce.

Functions of the sales office

Maintenance of sales records

Sales records are kept to help to increase future sales but they must be kept up to date. Details are shown in Table 11.1.1.

Table 11.1.1 Sales records and their purpose

Sales record	Purpose
Customer database with customer names, contact details and previous purchase record	Easy to contact customers, reward loyalty, send out promotional material to retain interest
List of credit sales with any large amounts still owed highlighted	To prevent large unpaid debts by refusing further credit until the customer has settled their account
A list of stock lines with weekly/monthly sales against each one	Identifies popular lines that need restocking and slow-moving items that may need discounting
A list of sales analysed by store/branch, sales person or sales representative	Enables comparisons to be made, encourages competition, tactics for success can be shared
Reports from representatives about calls they have made and the outcome	Provide useful information on customers – what they like/dislike and want in the future
List of recent enquiries with caller's name and address	For sending future mailshots or catalogues to promote goods

Stock control

Sales staff should know what items are stocked, what items are on order and when these will arrive. If demand is high for a product then stocks need to be increased. For this reason, many stores have EPOS (electronic point of sale) systems (see page 165).

Liaising with other departments

Sales will liaise with several departments, as shown in Table 11.1.2.

Table 11.1.2	Sales and departmental liaison
Departments	**Reason for liaison**
Operations	Staff in the sales department must know production schedules and agree delivery dates of orders with the production department. Sales must know about any production problems that might affect customers
Finance	Finance may need to check a customer's credit rating before sales are agreed. Finance will be involved when there are problems with customer payments
Purchasing	Sales trends should influence the purchase of raw materials and goods for resale. Purchasing should know about any promotional events
HR	HR will help recruit new staff and temporary sales people during busy seasons
Marketing	Marketing must liaise with sales over promotions and adverts so that sales staff can expect and handle enquiries
Customer services	Customer services must pass on customer feedback that could affect future sales

Customer follow up

Customer feedback can help a business to improve and increase sales. For that reason, after a sale has been made it is important to find out whether the customer was satisfied with the service and/or their purchase. There are various ways of obtaining this information.

- 'Customer happy calls' are short follow-up telephone calls to check the customer has no worries or needs that have not been met.
- Customer comment cards can be placed in a retail store or on restaurant tables, asking customers for their views and suggestions.
- Questionnaires can be given to customers – such as those placed in hotel rooms before guests depart – asking for feedback on the service they have received.

The duties of a clerk in the sales office

The sales clerk is responsible for maintaining sales records, answering the telephone and assisting callers, and liaising with other departments. They also have the following responsibilities.

Prepare sales documents

These include quotations to respond to customer enquiries, and invoices (or a pro forma invoice) sent to request payment.

File sales records

These may be filed alphabetically by customer or geographically if sales cover several territories. A large business may allocate a customer reference number to each sales record and use this as the major indexing unit of the file.

Maintain mailing lists

Mailing lists must be up to date. People move house, change their name, etc., and some may ask to be taken off a mailing list. Equally, new customers should be added to the list.

DID YOU KNOW?

Harley Davidson, the motorcycle manufacturers, expects its managers to ride with customers at least 10 to 15 days a year to find out what they really think!

DID YOU KNOW?

All sales staff must be able to deal with customers in a confident and friendly manner.

DID YOU KNOW?

A way of enticing customers to provide their personal information is by offering to send mailshots containing special offers.

TEST YOURSELF

1 Your friend is applying for a job as a sales clerk in a large office. Outline FOUR duties that she may have to undertake in this role.

Now check your answers against those on the accompanying CD.

LEARNING OUTCOMES

By the time you have completed this section you should be able to:

- explain the functions of staff involved in marketing
- identify the duties of a clerk in the marketing office.

KEY TERMS

A **logo** is a graphic or symbol that represents the business name or products.

Digicel

| Figure 11.2.1 | An example of a company logo |

DID YOU KNOW?

A company website communicates with consumers, so its style and content is usually the responsibility of the marketing department.

FIND OUT MORE

Check your local newspaper or stores for promotional events. Then consider how each one will promote the business to its target customers.

Functions of the marketing office

The marketing office undertakes the activities that tell potential customers that the business exists, reminds existing customers about the brand and promotes new products or services.

Organise promotional activities

Promotional activities create awareness of the business, brand or product. They must be appropriate for the business and the target customer. So, the activities for a new cellphone would not suit a grocery store. Examples include trade shows, exhibitions, roadshows, window displays, lunch meetings, entertainment evenings, competitions, sponsorship of a sports team and giveaways (such as pens or balloons that have the company **logo** on them).

Design marketing strategies

The marketing strategy identifies activities that will raise awareness and boost sales such as:

- market research to find out consumer opinions
- comparing product prices and features with those offered by competitors
- launching new products or adapting/developing existing ones
- selling in new territories or online
- promotional activities and advertising
- public relations, such as giving talks and radio interviews, and sending out press releases
- offering discounts or incentives to sales people or customers
- starting a loyalty programme to reward regular customers.

Budgeting

The marketing budget must be used wisely. Different activities must be costed and decisions made about which should provide the best returns. Afterwards, the effectiveness of advertisements and promotions should be assessed so that only those with a positive effect on sales or brand recognition are repeated.

Advertising

Adverts may be placed in the local press, in magazines and journals, in the cinema, and on radio and television. Posters and billboards are other options. Any advert must appeal to the **target market** and be placed where they will see it – which is why magazines like *Essence* feature beauty products.

Publishing

This includes the production of newsletters, catalogues, price lists, house magazines (produced by the organisation for its employees), brochures, posters, leaflets and mailshots. Large organisations may have the resources to produce many items in-house, but small businesses would use the services of a specialist printer.

Liaise with internal and external advertising entities

The content of advertisements must be decided, agreed and approved. Photographs of products may be required plus technical advice on product details.

- **Internal contacts** include staff in other departments, such as production and sales, who can provide technical information or products for displays.
- **External contacts** include a specialist advertising agency, photographers, graphic designers, staff at the local newspaper, printers and website designers.

Duties of a marketing clerk

Assist in preparing advertising material

The marketing clerk may draft basic adverts for the local press, but complex or expensive advertisements will be created by specialists. The clerk should obtain any technical information needed and check that all of the details are accurate and approved by a manager before the publication deadline.

Assist with promotional activities

These include organising publicity events, issuing invitations, creating window displays and attending trade fairs, exhibitions or social events.

Maintain mailing lists and records

Sales and marketing must liaise to ensure that mailing lists and records are up to date (see page 167).

Assist in preparing press releases

Press releases are statements featuring the business. They are issued to the press – usually a local newspaper – to gain free publicity when they are published. How to write these and an example was included in 2.5 on page 34. Turn back to this page now to refresh your memory.

Organise travel

Marketing and sales staff may travel extensively to promote company products by visiting potential purchasers or attending overseas trade fairs and exhibitions. The marketing clerk may be responsible for making travel arrangements (see Unit 7).

TEST YOURSELF

1 Suggest FOUR promotional activities that would benefit a new children's toy store.

Now check your answers against those on the accompanying CD.

DID YOU KNOW?

Marketing has been called 'looking at the company through the customer's eyes'.

DID YOU KNOW?

One way of checking which methods best raise awareness is to ask new customers: 'Where did you hear about us?'

KEY TERMS

The **target market** is the main group of buyers that the company aims to attract.

THINK ABOUT IT!

Spot how your favourite adverts follow the AIDA principle – Attract **Attention**, Raise **Interest**, Create **Desire**, Encourage **Action**. Adverts promoting an event also include the four Ws – **Who** they are, **What** is happening, **Where** it is and **When** it is. Find some to see if they do.

DID YOU KNOW?

Businesses advertising on search engines are listed at the top or side of your screen with your search results. They pay the search engines a fee whenever someone clicks through to their site. This is called 'pay per click' advertising.

KEY TERMS

An **embargo** on a press release prevents the article being published before a given date.

The customer services department and the duties of customer services clerks

LEARNING OUTCOMES

By the time you have completed this section you should be able to:

• explain the functions of staff involved in customer services

• identify the duties of a clerk in the customer services department.

KEY TERMS

Customer satisfaction is a measure of how customers feel after the purchase and whether the product or service met their needs and expectations.

DID YOU KNOW?

Some businesses say they aim to **delight** their customers by exceeding their expectations.

Functions of the customer services department

Customer services must ensure that customers are satisfied with the product or service and any queries or complaints are handled promptly and effectively. Staff must have good product knowledge, be able to give explanations clearly and know how to help customers with a problem.

Ensure customer satisfaction

Customers will only make repeat purchases or recommend a business to others if they are satisfied with their experience. This means that they receive goods promptly and undamaged, and the product meets or exceeds their expectations. Services should be carried out professionally and be value for money. Wise businesses know that they must provide a consistent and reliable service to guarantee **customer satisfaction**.

Handle customer complaints

Customers may complain for many reasons – a product is late, damaged, faulty or poor quality, a service was performed badly or not at all, charges were higher than expected or items have not been received. Dealing with complaints is difficult unless you know what to do. There are two skills involved. The first relates to the way the complaint is dealt with, the second concerns the way the person is handled. Guidelines are shown in Table 11.3.1.

Advise customers on product offerings

Customer services staff need to have a good knowledge of the products and/or services available and prices. Because they

Table 11.3.1	Checklist for dealing with complaints	
Stay calm and positive yourself throughout the conversation, listen carefully and do not interrupt		✓
Do not take the complaint personally. Think of it as a problem that you may be able to solve		✓
Look (or sound) sympathetic and interested so the customer knows you want to help, and make notes if the matter is detailed or complicated		✓
Apologise on behalf of your employer for the problem. This is *not* the same as admitting responsibility		✓
Do not make judgements about a customer, and never say that your employer is at fault		✓
Carefully question the customer to find out what action they want you to take. Some may simply want to tell you what happened or ask you to pass on the information to your supervisor		✓
If you can solve their problem then do so, but never promise anything that is outside your area of responsibility		✓
Get help immediately if a visiting customer threatens you or if you are losing control of the situation		✓

cannot always memorise these, they need to know where to find the information, such as in a catalogue, brochure or database. Customer services staff in a company selling expensive items or services, such as electronic equipment or insurance, should be able to give detailed information and advice based on their own knowledge and training.

Answer questions and queries

Customers expect to receive accurate and up-to-date information about a product, service or even the organisation itself. Customer services staff should always know the basic facts, for example:

- the business address, phone number, website address, opening hours
- the people who can answer certain types of queries or problems
- the products/services that are supplied and those that are not
- the literature or printed information available for callers
- the organisation's rules for dealing with problems.

Liaise between the customer and company

Customer services is the main liaison point between customers and the business. Telephone callers often have to choose between 'sales' or 'customer services' when they make a call.

Duties of a clerk in the customer services department

Interface with customers

Customer services staff often deal with enquiries, complaints and problems that relate to other departments. They are the 'interface' because they deal with customers *on behalf of* these areas. They may need to ask a caller to wait while they check out a situation with a colleague in another department, or agree to call someone back when they have obtained the information that is needed.

Liaise with customers

Customer services staff liaise with customers over a particular requirement, such as a delivery date or product refund. This means establishing what the customer wants and then seeing whether these needs can be met. Customer services staff must enjoy dealing with people and want to help them. They should also be able to explain, courteously, why this may not be possible.

Inform customers about promotions and offers

Customer services staff must be aware of current promotions and offers being made by their organisation so that they bring these to the notice of customers.

Answer customers' queries

Customer services staff need the knowledge and expertise to answer routine questions asked by customers. They should also know how to find the answers to more difficult queries that they may receive.

DID YOU KNOW?

Many companies now include on their website the email address of their customer services department.

Figure 11.3.1 | What do customer services clerks do?

DID YOU KNOW?

Being able to give a customer a special offer can often convert a problem into a positive experience.

DID YOU KNOW?

The FAQs pages on websites are designed to answer most of the usual questions that customers ask.

TEST YOURSELF

1 Suggest THREE reasons why a clerk in the customer services department may liaise with a customer.

Now check your answers against those on the accompanying CD.

Sales and marketing documents and discounts

LEARNING OUTCOMES

By the time you have completed this section you should be able to:

- prepare documents used in sales and marketing
- distinguish between different types of discounts.

DID YOU KNOW?

All quotations have a time limit or validity period. This is to protect the supplier in case prices increase.

TRADE DISCOUNT CALCULATIONS

Discounts reduce the amount charged on the invoice. They are deducted from the selling price before any taxes are added. Trade discount means that Charles Gray would not pay $5,000. The calculation would be:

Goods	5,000.00
Less trade discount 10%	−500.00
Goods (net value)	4,500.00
Plus VAT @ 17.5%	787.50
TOTAL DUE	5,287.50

EXAM TIP

Make sure that you can calculate discounts, and remember to show your working.

Preparation of sales and marketing documents

There are three documents that are prepared by sales and marketing clerks. These are:

- **quotations**, which are offers to provide goods or services at a certain price
- **invoices**, which demand payment from a customer who has received goods or services
- **pro forma invoices**, which may be sent before any goods are despatched (see below).

Quotations

A standard quotation will include a description of the goods (or services) to be provided, the quotation number and date, the payment terms that would apply and the total amount. The document is normally produced on headed paper, addressed to the potential customer and signed by a manager. An example is shown below.

A–Z Office Supplies Ltd
The Quay
Bridgetown
BARBADOS
Tel: (246) 273 2938
Website: www.azofficesupplies.com
QUOTATION

Quotation No: ML39108   Date: 14 March 2012
Charles Gray
Grays Court
Town Street
BRIDGETOWN

Product code	Description	Qty	Unit price	Amount
MT120	Office task chairs	6	$150	$900
MD208	Executive chairs	2	$350	$700
ML2083	Fire-resistant 4-drawer filing cabinet with digital lock	2	$1700	$3400
			TOTAL	$5000

Remarks
Prices: All prices are in US dollars and subject to VAT @ 17.5%
Validity: Prices valid for 60 days from the date of this quotation
Trade discount: 5%   Terms: 2.5%/10 days
Delivery within 7 days of receipt of order
Carriage paid

Signed   *Justine Browne*

Figure 11.4.1 | Example quotation

Invoices

A supplier sends an invoice after the goods have been delivered. This asks for payment and contains the following information:

- standard information. This includes the names and addresses of the seller and the buyer and other contact details
- information taken from the quotation. This includes the reference numbers, product codes, descriptions and prices
- the calculations. This shows the money owing after any discounts are applied
- the payment terms. For example, 2.5%/10 means the buyer will get 2.5 per cent cash discount if the bill is settled within 10 days.

Pro forma invoice

The layout of a pro forma invoice is similar to a normal invoice – except that it says 'Pro forma Invoice' at the top. It includes the type of goods, their quantity and/or weight, their value and any transportation charges. The main difference is that the customer will not have received the goods when they get the pro forma invoice, and usually a final invoice still has to be issued for payment.

The pro forma invoice confirms that a seller will provide certain goods at a stated price, so is proof of value to customs. It may also be sent out with goods on approval or consignment.

Discounts

A seller might offer a discount to a purchaser as an inducement to buy. The main types of discount are summarised below.

Table 11.4.1	Types of discounts
Trade discount	Offered to traders in the same business, for example, a paint store dealing with a professional decorator
Cash discount	Offered for prompt payment
Special discount	Offered as a reward to a regular customer or for a limited period to clear excess stock
Quantity discount	Offered for bulk orders
Goods on consignment	Commission or discounts may be given to a consignee who sells goods on behalf of a consignor who leaves goods on approval. For example, a photographer leaves pictures for sale in retail outlets at no charge. Each store gets a percentage of the selling price and can return any unsold items

DID YOU KNOW?

Invoices have the letters E&OE at the bottom which stands for 'Errors and omissions excepted.' It means if there are any mistakes or items omitted, the supplier can send another invoice to charge the extra amount still owing.

DID YOU KNOW?

Sometimes a pro forma invoice may be sent to a new buyer as a notice that an advance payment is required.

DID YOU KNOW?

Tax rates are different across Caribbean territories. For example, in Trinidad and Tobago it is 15 per cent. It can be changed by the government and only applies to businesses that sell more than a specified value of goods a year.

CASH DISCOUNT CALCULATIONS

If a cash discount is included, this is deducted before VAT is calculated, so the tax due is reduced. For Charles Gray's purchase the calculation would be:

Goods (net after cash discount deducted)	4,500.00
Less 2.5% cash discount	112.50
	4,387.50
Plus VAT @ 17.5%	767.81
TOTAL DUE	5,155.31

TEST YOURSELF

1 List FIVE items that are included on an invoice.

Now check your answers against those on the accompanying CD.

SECTION 1: Multiple-choice questions

1 The marketing budget is used to:

  a Pay for advertising and promotions.

  b Pay the marketing staff salaries.

  c Buy stationery for the marketing department.

  d Buy goods that will be resold to customers.

2 A pro forma invoice may be sent when:

  i   Goods are sent on approval.

  ii The value of goods needs to be evident for customs.

  iii A new customer must pay before the goods are despatched.

  iv To confirm an agreed transaction between buyer and seller.

  a i, ii and iii only　　c ii, iii and iv only

  b i, ii and iv only　　d All of the above

3 A seller offers 3 per cent cash discount if $1,000 of goods are paid for within 10 days. If the buyer ignores this offer, the additional price he will pay for the goods is:

  a $3　　　　　　　　c $30

  b $10　　　　　　　d $100

4 Samuel increases his order from 2,000 to 5,000 pairs of socks and gets an extra discount. This means he has benefitted from:

  a A trade discount.　　c A special discount.

  b A bulk discount.　　d A cash discount.

5 You work in customer services and receive a complaint from a customer who says the price he was charged is more than stated in his price list. When you check, you find the price list was updated recently and the new price has been applied. The best thing to do is:

  a Tell the customer he is wrong.

  b Immediately offer the customer an extra discount.

  c Tell the customer to return the goods.

  d Apologise and explain that his price list is, unfortunately, out of date.

6 Tasks carried out by a sales clerk include:

  i   Updating customer records.

  ii Liaising with other departments.

  iii Making customer follow-up calls.

  iv Preparing press releases.

  a i, ii and iii only　　c ii, iii and iv only

  b i, ii and iv only　　d All of the above

7 An example of a promotional activity is:

  i   Liaising with customers.

  ii Updating a mailing list.

  iii Holding a discount sale.

  iv Having a stand at a trade exhibition.

  a i and ii only　　　c ii and iii only

  b i and iii only　　　d iii and iv only

8 Sales may liaise with operations about:

  a The price that customers are charged for goods.

  b Proposed delivery dates.

  c Advertising materials.

  d The content of the website.

9 A customer mailing list is used to:

  i   Tell customers about special offers.

  ii Tell customers about discount sales.

  iii Invite customers to promotional events.

  iv Invite customers to complain.

  a i, ii and iii only　　c ii, iii and iv only

  b i, iii and iv only　　d All of the above

10 Snips hairdressing salon buys shampoos and conditioners from an industry supplier and is rewarded with a 10 per cent discount. This is an example of:

  a Cash discount.　　　c Trade discount.

  b Budgeting.　　　　d Special discount.

Further practice questions and examples can be found on the accompanying CD.

SECTION 2: Short answer questions

1 List THREE marketing strategies that a clothes store may have.

2 Give THREE reasons why sales staff should make customer follow-up calls.

3 Define the term 'target market'. Explain how this would differ for a Disney or Pixar film and a smartphone.

4 Identify TWO other departments that a customer services clerk might liaise with about a customer complaint.

5 You are writing an advertisement to tell people about your school's Gala Fête. List FOUR facts that you must remember to include.

6 Give TWO reasons why a marketing clerk might need to arrange travel for colleagues.

7 a Study the example invoice in below and identify:
   i   the invoice number
   ii the date of the invoice
   iii the amount of trade discount
   iv the tax payable in Antigua.

   b Explain why the letters E&OE are included on an invoice.

8 Define the term 'validity' on a quotation and say why this is necessary.

9 Give TWO reasons why a customer might be given a special discount.

10 Identify FOUR items that would be included on a customer sales record.

Artworld Ltd
Harbourside
Free Town
Antigua
Tel: (268) 480 3827

INVOICE
To:
Blue Horizon Restaurant
Church Walk
St John's
Antigua

Your order no.	Customer account no.	Date	Invoice no.
05/703	1234	05/02/2012	16702/06

Item code	Quantity	Description	Item price $	Net value $
PP1003	Set of 3	Caribbean seascape prints	60.00	180.00
		Less 10% trade discount		18.00
			SUBTOTAL	162.00
			VAT @ 15.0%	24.30
			TOTAL DUE	186.30
E&OE				

EXAM TIP

You must be able to recognise the main items on an invoice such as the items ordered, the price of each and the total amount requested.

Further practice questions and examples can be found on the accompanying CD.

12 Operations, despatch and transport services

12.1 The functions of the operations office

LEARNING OUTCOMES

By the time you have completed this section you should be able to:

• explain the functions of the operations office.

KEY TERMS

Coordination means ensuring that different aspects of a factory work together effectively. For example, stores must deliver materials to manufacturing when they are needed.

Figure 12.1.1 Why are safety goggles and hard hats important in some factories?

DID YOU KNOW?

Check page 129 to remind yourself about the Factories Act and OSHA. These are both laws that help to protect workers.

Introduction to operations, despatch and transport

The term 'operations' relates to all of the activities involved in manufacturing goods to sell to customers. This means ensuring that machinery, people and materials are organised so that goods are produced and despatched efficiently and on time. These tasks are carried out by operations, despatch and transport clerks. This unit summarises their main activities.

The functions of the operations office

Coordinating activities related to production

The use of materials, machines and labour must be planned so that goods are completed on time to meet customers' requirements. When these factors are **coordinated**, work proceeds smoothly. For example, operations must check that enough materials are in stock before a product is made.

Protecting workers and the environment

Employers have a duty to protect their workers by reducing the likelihood of accidents occurring. This means providing equipment and materials that are safe to use, ensuring safe methods of work, and giving staff proper training.

The factory office must ensure that all workers are trained to operate their machines safely, and are provided with the correct safety equipment. The office can help to protect the environment by minimising the waste of materials and power and ensuring that unavoidable scrap material (including paper) is recycled whenever possible.

Maintaining factory records

The documents used by the factory are described on pages 178–179. Records used in manufacturing include inspection reports, efficiency figures and maintenance schedules, which must be completed accurately and filed carefully so they can be retrieved easily.

DID YOU KNOW?

Aeroplane manufacturers keep a record of every component used, and who fitted it, so that if there are any future problems the history can be traced.

Quality control

Sometimes problems occur that cause products to be faulty, such as poor quality raw materials, machine faults or mistakes by operators. **Quality control** is a process of inspecting or testing products during the production process to identify problems. All faulty products are removed and details of the problem are noted. The control aspect of the procedure means finding the reason for the problem and putting it right. The factory office must check the inspection records and pass this information promptly to someone who can correct the problem.

Costing of finished products

Costing a product means calculating how much it costs to make. This information is important because the sales department uses it to decide how much to charge a customer. The selling price should cover these costs and include a contribution to profits.

The cost of manufacturing a product is made up of two parts.

- **Direct costs** are those that can be directly linked to a product. For example, the quantity of materials used and the number of hours of labour used (such as denim cloth and the cutter's wages in a jeans factory). Because these costs vary depending upon the number of items produced, they are known as **variable costs**.
- **Indirect costs** (also known as **overheads**). These are expenses incurred by the factory that cannot be directly linked to a product, such as electricity for air conditioning, and clerical salaries. The accounts office will state how to allocate these costs between different products. Indirect costs are **fixed costs** because they are not linked to the number of items produced and sold.

Liaising with other departments

Table 12.1.1 shows the links between operations and other departments.

Table 12.1.1	Links between the operations office and other departments
Department	**Nature of liaison activity**
Production	Listing order requirements, production schedule, product costing, scheduling, production reports and other items listed on pages 178–179
Sales and marketing	Receiving orders from customers, including the type of product required, quantity and delivery date
Purchasing	Requesting production materials – type, quantity and date
Despatch/transport	Informing when products will be delivered for despatch and transport
Finance	Assistance in costing of products – particularly how to allocate overheads
Human resource management (HRM)	Assistance with selection of staff

KEY TERMS

Quality control means checking for any faults that occur, recording the reason for the problem and taking action to correct it. Checks are made during production as well as at final inspection.

Direct costs are monies spent in direct proportion to the number of items produced and sold.

Variable costs fluctuate depending upon the number of items produced.

Indirect costs arise no matter how many items are produced.

Overheads is another name for indirect costs.

Fixed costs are not linked to the number of items produced and sold.

EXAM TIP

Make sure that you can list and describe the main functions of the operations office, and say why any particular area relies on another department.

TEST YOURSELF

1 a Explain what is meant by 'costing' a product.
  b Suggest ONE variable (direct) cost in a jellybean factory and explain why this is 'variable'.

Now check your answers against those on the accompanying CD.

LEARNING OUTCOMES

By the time you have completed this section you should be able to:

• explain the duties of a clerk in the operations office.

KEY TERMS

Shifts are periods of the day when different groups of workers do the same job in relay. Work takes place in shifts when an operation runs continuously and needs to be staffed for 24 hours a day.

DID YOU KNOW?

Shift work also takes place in hospitals, police stations and other organisations that need to operate 24 hours a day, seven days a week.

Figure 12.2.1 Why do some factories operate shift working?

Duties of a clerk in the operations office

Preparation of a shift roster

Some factories work continuously over 24 hours, five or seven days a week. This means that staff have to work in **shifts**. For a particular machine, the planned **shift roster** could be as follows:

Monday 15 September:

6 am–2 pm – F Alsop   2 pm–10 pm – P Ellis   10 pm–6 am (Tues) – M Daly

To make sure that the factory runs smoothly, the schedule should ensure that every workstation is always covered by a fully trained operative.

Preparation of daily production reports

Senior managers in a factory need to know how well production is going, so the production office clerk produces a daily report summarising performance. This could include:

• number of items produced against a planned target
• percentage rejects
• machine breakdown time
• amount of materials used.

Preparation of documents used in production

An operations clerk will complete several different documents. These are discussed below.

Completion of forms used in the factory office

Job cards

These are issued by the operations office and passed to production. They contain authorisation and instructions about how the product must be made. An example is shown in Figure 12.2.2.

Mr T T-shirts Job Card	
Date 15 December 2012	Job Number 3261
Job description White T-shirts	
Material used 400 metres white cotton cloth ($260) 50 spools of white cotton thread ($20)	
Quantity 200	Description Style D, size large
Equipment One cutting machine 3 standard sewing machines	Labour One cutter for 2 hours Three sewing machinists for a total of 100 hours
Pay rates Cutter $10 per hour Sewers $7 per hour	Authorised by F Bloggs
Inspected and passed by A White	

Figure 12.2.2 A completed job card

Job cost cards

These cards list all of the planned costs associated with manufacturing a product. One important use is to help to determine the selling price. You already know about **fixed** and **variable** costs (see page 177). The variable costs can be calculated by using the information on the job card. So, from the job card above, the variable cost would be:

Materials (cloth plus cotton)	=	$280
Cutter 2 hours @ $10	=	$20
Sewing machinists 100 hours @ $7	=	$700
Total variable cost	=	$1,000

The allocation of fixed costs (lighting, power, etc.) is decided by the accounts department. A simple method is to add a percentage to the total variable cost. If the figure was 40 per cent, the calculation would be:

Overhead cost $= \$1,000 \times \dfrac{40}{100} = \$400$ fixed costs

The total cost of manufacturing the shirts is $1,000 + $400 = $1,400

Cost analysis

This means identifying the costs of producing a number of products. It helps management to decide the most profitable items to manufacture and/or where savings could be made. An example is shown in Figure 12.2.3. This information is taken from the individual job cost cards produced for each product or batch of products.

Planning master

This chart details all jobs planned for a certain time/day. It shows which jobs will be done on each machine and by each operator. It identifies production unit efficiency by answering questions such as:

- Are any machines not being used at certain times?
- Are there any possible delays in planned delivery times?
- Are there any delays because of shortages of materials?

Cost cards

These are an extension of the job cost cards showing the actual costs of production against the planned figures. This information may identify problems with the original estimates or show inefficiencies in production, such as too much material being used or wasted.

Time cards

A basic time card is used when hourly-paid employees 'clock in' for work. When they insert their card into a machine on arrival and departure it is stamped with the time. The cards are used to check attendance and to calculate wages, particularly when overtime is worked. Modern systems use plastic cards (similar to credit cards) that workers swipe in a card reader.

Another type of time card is used when an employee records the amount of time spent on different production tasks. This is often the best way of calculating the costs of production if tasks are complicated and unpredictable.

DID YOU KNOW?

The difference between the cost of making a product and its selling price is known as the **markup**.

Cost item	T-shirts	Blouses
Materials	$280	$600
Labour	$720	$900
Total direct cost	$1,000	$1,500
Overheads a (40% of direct cost)	$400	$600
Total cost of manufacture	$1,400	$2,100
Number of items produced	200	200
Unit cost	$7	$10.50

Figure 12.2.3 An extract from a cost analysis card

THINK ABOUT IT!

The figures in Figure 12.2.3 compare the cost of making T-shirts and blouses. You should see that blouses are more expensive to make, with both the material and labour costing more than for T-shirts.

TEST YOURSELF

1 List FOUR items of information that are entered onto a job card.

Now check your answers against those on the accompanying CD.

Functions and clerical duties of the despatch and transport offices

By the time you have completed this section you should be able to:

- explain the functions of the despatch and transport offices
- explain the duties of clerks in the despatch and transport offices.

DID YOU KNOW?

A business that sends goods to another business is known as the **consignor**. The firm that receives them is the **consignee**.

DID YOU KNOW?

A special licence is needed to export crocodile eggs.

DID YOU KNOW?

Specialist shipping agents will carry out all of the tasks involved in shipping goods overseas, including completing the documents required.

KEY TERMS

A **courier** specialises in transporting goods. They may use different types of carriers including lorries, aircraft and sea transport.

Functions of the despatch office and duties of the despatch office clerk

Complete and maintain documents for despatched goods

The despatch office receives goods from production and prepares them for delivery to the transport office. It is responsible for packing and labelling these goods as well as completing the necessary paperwork. The clerk must ensure that everything is correct by referring to the customer's original order and checking that:

- the product is correct in terms of size, colour and description
- the quantity is correct
- the goods have been inspected and passed by quality control, and have not been damaged since then.

The clerk must record this information and complete documents for transporting and delivering the goods. These vary depending upon the type of goods and the destination. Normal goods for despatch locally require less paperwork than exotic items being sent abroad.

The despatch office must know all legal requirements, such as licences required. Internal forms must be revised when necessary, and copies of completed forms filed for future reference.

Maintain a database of couriers and keep records about their use

Goods can be transported using the firm's own vehicle(s) or an external **courier**. A business with its own transport has more control over how the vehicles are used and the service standards, but breakdowns or driver absences can cause serious problems. It may be more cost effective to use a specialist company, particularly when goods are being exported. The despatch clerk should therefore keep a database record that includes:

- the names of different local couriers, the services they offer and the area they cover (local, regional or international)
- the type(s) of goods they handle
- the notice they need to collect and deliver goods
- their reliability in the past – such as whether collection and delivery was prompt and whether any goods were damaged in transit. Couriers that cause problems should be removed from the list
- their charges for transport and delivery.

Work in collaboration with the sales office

The sales office receives the customer's order (see Unit 11) and notes specific requirements, such as the delivery address and dates/times when deliveries can be made. The sales department and despatch office must liaise to ensure deliveries are efficient and customer requirements are met.

Adhere to statutory requirements

The despatch office must know the legal requirements relating to goods being sent and ensure that the company complies with these. The goods may include:

- items that require export and/or import licences
- dangerous chemicals that need special packaging and labelling
- heavy packages that need to be lifted mechanically.

On page 182 you will see the forms that must be completed.

Coordinate the delivery of goods

Often transporting goods from consignor to consignee involves two or more transport systems, such as a van to the airport, air freight to another island, contractor's vehicle to final destination. Coordinating these different methods means that goods move smoothly and rapidly from one form of transport to the next. All of the appropriate forms must be completed accurately so that there are no delays.

Functions of the transport office and duties of the transport office clerk

Maintain transportation records, including destination sheets

The transport clerk keeps a record of all deliveries planned and made. This is needed to answer customer queries and if there is a problem, such as damage discovered after unpacking or part of the order is missing. For each delivery, the records will include the type of goods, the customer's name and address, the expected delivery date and time, and the type of transport and name of driver.

Liaise with customers

The transport clerk will answer customer queries and also liaise with customers:

- if there is going to be an unavoidable delay with a delivery, for example, because of bad weather
- if it would suit the delivery schedule to deliver goods earlier than requested
- if there is a query about the delivery address.

Schedule maintenance of vehicles

Many manufacturers specify that vehicles should be serviced at least once a year, and this may be a condition of the warranty. Although this means taking vehicles off the road for a short period, it results in fewer breakdowns. Therefore, servicing and maintenance plans are incorporated into the vehicle planning schedule, which is often displayed on a wall planner.

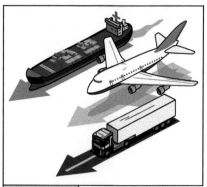

Figure 12.3.1 What type(s) of transport are used for large, heavy items?

FIND OUT MORE

Check out the couriers and shipping agents in your area by looking online and in Yellow Pages. Look at the services they offer and how these differ between companies.

DID YOU KNOW?

Wise businesses know that the delivery service is an important part of customer service. So they use clean, modern vehicles, they train drivers to be polite and helpful, and they provide them with a smart uniform.

DID YOU KNOW?

The American space shuttle Columbia set a record by taking only 88 days to be serviced in between flights.

TEST YOURSELF

1 List TWO duties of a clerk in the despatch office and TWO duties of a clerk in the transport office.

Now check your answers against those on the accompanying CD.

Documents used in operations, despatch and transport offices

LEARNING OUTCOMES

By the time you have completed this section you should be able to:

- prepare documents used in operations, despatch and transport offices.

Completing different documents

There are several documents that may be required for a delivery, and these need to be completed accurately by the clerk involved with the task. Table 12.4.1 lists these.

THINK ABOUT IT!

Study Table 12.4.1 and make sure you understand the purpose of each form. Then read the guidance below about how to complete a blank form in the exam.

Table 12.4.1 Transport documents

Document title	Purpose	Information contained
Delivery schedules	To provide the delivery driver with information about the deliveries they have to make	Times and locations of a delivery schedule, and the route to take to minimise doubling back at any point
Destination sheets	These show the deliveries planned by all of the company vehicles on a particular day	Details of the vehicles being used. Registration numbers, description of goods being delivered, names of drivers and assistants
Delivery notes	To be signed by someone at the receiving company as proof of delivery	Name and address of consignee, list of items delivered
Bills of lading	Used in a similar way to delivery notes when goods are transported by sea	Similar to the delivery note, but they include the name of the company that operates the ship
Customs forms	Used by customs to decide if any duty must be paid	Consignor's and consignee's names and addresses. Description and a valuation of the goods
Insurance certificates	Goods being transported need to be insured against loss or damage	Names and addresses of consignor and consignee. Name of insurance company. Value of goods
Airway bills	Similar to delivery notes and bills of lading. These are issued by the airline and act as a receipt for items that are sent by air freight	Names and addresses of consignor and consignee. List of goods to be carried. Signature of person receiving the goods
Manifest	List of all goods being carried on a ship or aeroplane	Summary of all items on individual bills of lading or airway bills
Export licences	Needed for certain types of goods that the government wants to control, for example, works of art	Name of exporting business and consignee. Details of goods
Import licences	The government may wish to restrict the import of certain types of goods, such as weapons	As above

Advice note	A note sent to the customer stating when goods are expected to be delivered. This gives them time to plan to receive the delivery	Similar to a delivery note but with a delivery date included
Certificate of origin	Shows which country goods being imported came from and enables customs to decide whether any duties or taxes are payable	Details of goods, consignor and consignee plus the name of the country of origin
Freight note	A document produced by the carrier stating the cost of transporting the goods	List of goods transported, name and address of payee and amount charged

DID YOU KNOW?

Countries sometimes ban the import of some types of goods from certain other countries for political reasons.

DID YOU KNOW?

A delivery schedule enables the driver to load the van with goods in the sequence that they will be delivered.

TEST YOURSELF

1 Copy the blank delivery note in Figure 12.4.2. Then complete it using the following information:

Delivery note is number 12/157 and the date of the delivery note is 4 June 2012

The customer's address is Fab Gear, 15 George Street, Kingston, Jamaica and their order number is 12/197

The items ordered are five white T-shirts (medium), code T10, and 10 blue blouses (small), code B5.

Enter your own signature and name in the two spaces at the bottom and date it 5 June 2012.

COMFY CLOTHING
Charles Street
Kingston
Jamaica
Tel: 462 6587
Email: comfyclothing@jamaican.net
DELIVERY NOTE

Delivery note no.: ....   Date ....

To: ....
....
....   Your order no.: ....

Code	Quantity	Description

Customer's signature ....   Date ....

PRINT NAME ....

Figure 12.4.2 Delivery note

Now check your answers against those on the accompanying CD.

Figure 12.4.1 Some goods need a special licence before they can be imported or exported

EXAM TIP

Think about the purpose of the document before you start to complete it. Then check the empty spaces and match these against the items on the list you are given. Fill in the items that you are sure about first.

SECTION 1: Multiple-choice questions

1 An important function of the operations office is to:

  a Coordinate the activities related to production.

  b Make sure that the workers wear overalls.

  c Contact customers each morning.

  d Check that the window cleaner is paid promptly.

2 Quality control means:

  a Checking that there are enough materials in the store.

  b Making sure that products are produced at the least cost possible.

  c Making sure that finished products have no faults.

  d Selling off rejected products at a lower price.

3 The operations office has to liaise with sales and marketing in relation to the following.

  i The type of van used for delivery.

  ii The number of products in an order.

  iii The delivery date required.

  iv The number of faulty goods allowed in an order.

  a ii and iii only   **c** i and iv only

  b ii and iv only   **d** All of the above

4 Some operations offices need to schedule shift working because:

  a The weather forecast is poor.

  b Production has to run continuously over 24 hours.

  c The operators like plenty of overtime.

  d A sudden, urgent order might arrive from the sales office.

5 Items on the daily production report produced by operations may include:

  i How many cans are dispensed by the drinks machine.

  ii The number of items produced.

  iii The temperature in the rest room.

  iv The time lost due to machine breakdown.

  a i and ii only   **c** ii and iv only

  b ii and iii only   **d** iii and iv only

6 The following are examples of overhead costs.

  i Materials used.

  ii Air conditioning.

  iii Lighting.

  iv Overtime by a production worker.

  a i and ii only   **c** i and iv only

  b i and iii only   **d** ii and iii only

7 The consignor is:

  a The person who takes the mail to the post office each day.

  b The person who packs the products ready for despatch.

  c The driver of the delivery lorry.

  d The business that sends products to another business.

8 Information on a database of couriers could include:

  i The delivery area they cover.

  ii The type of loads they can carry.

  iii Their reliability for delivering on time.

  iv The amount of money they charge.

  a i, ii and iii only   **c** ii, iii and iv only

  b i, iii and iv only   **d** All of the above

9 An example of a direct cost for a book publisher is:

  a The cost of the machinery.

  b The electricity used to work the machinery.

  c The cost of paper.

  d The wages of the van drivers.

10 A delivery schedule given to a delivery driver will probably include:

  i The names and addresses of the consignees.

  ii The sequence of deliveries using the most efficient route.

   iii The name of the driver and which vehicle is to be used.

   iv The dates of the most recent deliveries to each of the customers.

  a i, ii and iii only   **c** i, ii and iv only

  b ii, iii and iv only   **d** All of the above

Further practice questions and examples can be found on the accompanying CD.

SECTION 2: Short answer questions

1 Explain the importance of calculating the manufacturing cost of all finished products in a factory.

2 Explain the purposes of job cards and cost cards.

3 Give TWO reasons why the careful scheduling of shift work is important.

4 State the purpose of a planning master.

5 The cost of labour and materials for a job are $200 and $300. If overheads are calculated as 40 per cent of direct costs, calculate the total cost of this particular job.

6 Briefly describe the purposes of the two types of time card that could be used by a production operator.

7 Identify TWO items of information that the despatch office will need from the sales and marketing office to ensure it meets the customer's requirements.

8 State TWO benefits for the despatch office of keeping a database of couriers.

9 Identify THREE items of information contained on a destination sheet.

10 Explain the purpose of each of the following documents.

  a Export licences

  b Advice notes

Further practice questions and examples can be found on the accompanying CD.

Index

Note: Key terms are in **bold** type.

Index